English for Engineers and Technologists

Volumes 1 and 2 (Combined Edition)

Course Authors
Department of Humanities and Social Sciences
Anna University

Course consultants for the first edition
English Department
Thames Valley University
formerly, Ealing College of Higher Education,
United Kingdom

The book, first published in 1990 as two volumes, is the outcome of an English language teaching project undertaken by the Department of Humanities and Social Sciences, Anna University, Chennai, as part of a collaborative programme between the governments of India and the UK.

Acknowledgements

The publishers are grateful to the following for the use of the following texts either in original or in adaptation in the book:

Hari Srinivas: hsrinivas@gdcr.org for the adapted text, 'An Introduction to Rainwater Harvesting'; rediff.com India Limited for the adapted text, 'BPOs are Now Moving to Villages'; The India Today website for the extract 'Getting a Visa'; bbcworld.com for the adapted text, 'Oil and Alternative Sources'; BBC News for the adapted text of 'US and India Seal Nuclear Accord'; V K Shashikumar, The Christian Science Monitor for 'Leaks at India's Nuclear-Power Plants'; http://telosnet.com/wind/The Case for Wind Power for the adapted text, 'The Case for Wind Power'; Frontline for 'Solar-powered Car sets New World Record', 'Interactive Publishing' for the extracts 'Dream Machines', 'In the Middle of a Chain Reaction', 'Seaweed Power', 'Going with the Wind' and 'Wavepower from the West'; Ashok Jhunjhunwala for the extract from 'Can Information Technology Help Transform India?'; info@techsers.com (copyright Techsers and/or its affiliates) for the adapted text, 'eLearning'; http://www.narin.com/Attila for 'Myths of Artificial Intelligence' created by Attila Narin from Judea Pearl, *Heuristics*, Reading, Massachusetts: Addison Wesley, 1984); www.bytesforall.org for the extract 'Call it e-Philanthropy' by Lakshmi Chaudhry; http://www.roadpeace.org/ articles/World First Death.html for 'Road Safety'; Alastair Sarre for the extract 'Looking down the Track at Very Fast Trains'; the Department of Genetica e Morphologia and Department of Nutrition, University of Brazil for 'Cassava Leaves as a Source of Protein'; The Telegraph for 'Excellence in Adversity' by Ashok Mitra; Rachel Carson for 'Silent Spring'; The Hindu for the article, 'Goodbye Pictures, Hello Pixels' by Anand Parthasarathy; E R Schumacher for 'Small is Beautiful'; www.funehumor.com for 'The English Language'; Henry Dreyfuss for an extract from the Symbol Sourcebook; Parade for 'Will Newspapers Survive?'; Frontline for the extract from 'Presenting Traditions'; Philip Agre for 'Building an Internet Culture'; Indian Express for the extract from Cleaning the Heights; www.thegrist.com for 'Climate Change in Short'; The State of India's Environment for 'Dams and their Adverse Environmental Effects'; www.theecologist.co.uk for 'Bags of Rubbish'; The Hindu for the blackbuck news report; Granada for the extract from 'Encounters with Animals' by Gerard Durrell; Span for the tile-making article; A and M for 'Personal versus Professional Relationships'; Customers Run your Company, they Pay the Bills! for 'The Deadly Sins of Customer Service'. The publishers would like to thank Ms Shruti Ravindran for the photographs on pages 87, 137 and 152.

Every attempt has been made to contact holders of copyright. The publishers would be glad to have source and copyright information for the following extracts in order that due acknowledgement is made in future editions of this volume: 'Silver is Gold', 'Smart Materials', 'Oil and the World Economy', 'OPEC Agrees to Boost Oil Production', the extract from 'Can Information Technology Help Transform India?' by Ashok Jhunjhunwala; 'Traditional Printing Methods'; parts of the article on Salim Ali; 'Animals at Night'; 'The Dry Cell Battery'; 'Virtual Reality', 'Training in Industrial Organisations'.

Orient Blackswan Private Limited
Registered office
3-6-752 Himayatnagar, Hyderabad 500 029 (A.P), India
Email: centraloffice@orientblackswan.com

Other offices
Bangalore/Bhopal/Bhubaneshwar/Chennai/Ernakulam/Guwahati/
Hyderabad/Jaipur/Kolkata/Lucknow/Mumbai/New Delhi/Patna

© Anna University, Chennai 1990, 2002, 2006
First published by Orient Longman Private Limited 1990
Reprinted 1991, 1992, 1993, 1994 (twice), 1995, 1996 (twice), 1997, 1998 (twice), 1999 (twice), 2000
New Edition 2002
Reprint 2002(six), 2003(Twice), 2004, 2005(Twice)
This Edition 2006
Reprint 2006(Twice), 2007(Twice), 2008
First Orient Blackswan Impression 2008
Reprinted 2009
ISBN 13: 978-81-250-3019-5

Design and Typeset by Salil Divakar Sakhalkar for Sixth Sense Corporate Communications, Bangalore
Printed by SS Colour Impression Private Limited, Chennai 600 106
Published by Orient Blackswan Private Ltd, 160 Anna Salai, Chennai 600 002
Email: chennai@orientblackswan.com

Foreword

It is a matter of great pride that the Department of Humanities and Social Sciences, Anna University, is continually adapting and modifying its teaching methodology and materials to suit the language needs of the students of engineering and technology. In a globalised world where success in work depends to a great extent on one's communication skills, this textbook provides able support in the form of materials and tasks that will help students of engineering and technology develop their communication skills. The textbook, *English for Engineers and Technologists,* was the outcome of a unique project jointly undertaken by the Department of Humanities and Social Sciences and the Overseas Development Administration of the United Kingdom and the British Council Division, Chennai. The objective of the project was to develop suitable course materials for students of engineering and technology who found the earlier, conventional General English course, which was primarily literature-based, irrelevant to their needs.

The counterpart institution in the United Kingdom, which collaborated in this project, was the Ealing College of Higher Education, now known as Thames Valley University, London. Professor Rod Ellis helped in the formulation of the project, and Ms Pauline Barr, Ms Susan Axbey and Mr Richard Hornsey, experts from Thames Valley University, visited Anna University as consultants on the project, planned and monitored the progress of the work. Mr Robert Bellarmine, the then English Studies Officer, British Council Division in South India, was instrumental in coordinating the work of the project teams at Ealing College and Anna University. The project coordinator in Anna University was Dr V R Narayanaswami, the then Head of the Department of Humanities and Social Sciences, Anna University. The materials were produced by a team of staff members led by Professor T K Subramaniam, Professor of English in the Department. I compliment all the members of the Department on their excellent work.

When this book was first published in two volumes in 1990, it proved to be a veritable turning point, both in terms of materials and methodology, in the teaching of English for science and technology, As a part of their effort to change teaching materials according to the changing requirments of students, the textbook was revised and the second edition was brought out in 2002. The present edition of the textbook, which is a single volume, is most suitable for use in the affiliated colleges which have adopted the non-semester pattern from this year.

This edition of the textbook retains the best features of its earlier editions even while making changes that are necessary to make it suitable for the present generation of students. I am confident that the book will help in developing the relevant skills of all engineering and technology students in the best possible way.

Anna University
Chennai

Dr D VISWANATHAN
Vice-Chancellor

Preface to the third edition (2006)

English for Engineers and Technologists completes its sixteenth year of publication with this new edition. The book, formerly in two volumes, now appears in a combined single volume edition, making it a clearer fit for use in classrooms where students of engineering and technology can practise the effective use of international English. The present version of the textbook is the crystallisation of our experiments and experiences in the English classroom with students possessing varying levels of communicative competence.

The principle of *freshness* has guided the planning of the edition. In its new large size and re-styled design, the book has a more 'relaxed' magazine-style look, and is generously illustrated. Students today look for study material that has very high interest value and can be rapidly assimilated. Keeping this in mind, new texts have been included, and the exercises arranged in formats which make for easy comprehension and interactive work. Exercises and tasks have been further varied so that students work with a range of texts which include diagrams, tables, charts and pictograms.

As in earlier editions, *relevance* to the context in which learners live and work has been an important criterion, as has been the effort to relate all work to future careers, and career skills.

In our continuing endeavour to facilitate the easy learning of English for students of engineering and technology through the production of suitable teaching materials, the Vice-Chancellor, Dr D. Viswanathan, has been very supportive and encouraging. We would like to place on record our gratitude to him.

2006   Staff of the Department of Humanities and Social Sciences
                         Anna University, India

Excerpts from the Preface to the second edition (2002)

This new edition of English for Engineers and Technologists has been prepared in response to suggestions for improvement from learners and practising teachers across the country as well as overseas. In planning it, the authors and editors have drawn on continuous feedback from the classroom, action research projects around the volumes which included error analysis, revised materials and their trailing, surveys conducted to list topics which had new as well as enduring relevance, and seminars.

The skills approach has been strengthened by regularising the difficulty level across texts and tasks. In response to suggestions from teachers, there is now a greater emphasis on accuracy work (grammar, vocabulary, genres of writing and mechanics such as spelling and pronunciation). It is hoped that the new layout and illustrations will contribute to enhancing both learners' and teachers' engagement with the book.

2002   Staff of the Department of Humanities and Social Sciences
                         Anna University, India.

Preface to the first edition (1990)

An English language teaching project, funded by the British Overseas Development Administration and managed by the British Council Division, Chennai, is in progress at Anna University, Chennai. This book was prepared by the staff of the Division of Humanities and Social Sciences as part of the project for use by the first-year students of degree courses in engineering and technology.

This book marks a departure from the conventional textbook such as an anthology of prose selections. It also presupposes a shift in the philosophy of English language teaching which has been in practice until now. With the conventional textbook, the English class was mostly teacher-centred. The method of teaching was mainly lecture-oriented. The new materials are task-based and skills-oriented. They demand an actual use of the English language by students in the classrooms and encourage interaction among them.

We acknowledge with gratitude the permission granted by the authors concerned to use their material in the preparation of the reading texts in this book. In this context, we would particularly like to thank *The Hindu* on whose published material we have drawn liberally.

We are grateful to the British Overseas Development Administration and the British Council Division, Chennai, for their generous financial and administrative support of the project. We particularly wish to thank the course consultants, the staff of the English Department, School of Language Studies, Ealing College of Higher Education, London, for their valuable guidance and help in the preparation of this book.

We are indebted to our Vice-Chancellor Dr V.C. Kulandaiswamy for his sustained encouragement and support at every stage of the project.

1990   Staff of the Department of Humanities and Social Sciences
        Anna University, India

A Teachers' Book and a CD with listening texts are available for the teachers' use. The Teachers' Book provides guidance in methodology, lesson plans, transcripts of the listening texts and an answer-key for accuracy-based answers. Please email the Marketing Department, Orient Longman at chegeneral@orient longman.com

Introduction

The course materials presented in this book are meant for use by first-year students of degree courses in engineering and technology. They are organised around eight topic areas, namely, Resources, Energy, Computers, Transport, Technology, Communications, Environment and Industry. The topics have been chosen taking into account the needs and interests of students.

The exploitation of each of these topics is done in such a way that interest and motivation are maintained and a balanced programme of carefully graded activities is offered. Each topic comprises three units, (except communication which has two units) each of which provides work for four contact sessions.

The teaching of mixed groups of students with a wide range of abilities in English always presents a considerable challenge to English departments in our universities and colleges. The design of these materials offers a way of answering this challenge by providing special guidance and support for weaker students. Each unit consists of a main section (Parts 1 and 2) to be tackled by all students. The support materials in the form of Preparation and Follow-up sections are designed to help students who need help to cope with the main section.

The work in these materials is task-based and skills-oriented. A range of language functions of particular relevance to engineering and technology is exemplified in the texts for reading and listening, and practised in oral and written work. These materials require students to work in a communicative way, practising the use of English for different purposes, with encouragement and some guidance from the teacher.

These materials are flexible enough to be handled in a way different from that outlined above in diverse situations, depending on the constraints of the number of periods allotted per week in the time-table for the study of English, and their duration. **This is possible because the materials have been designed primarily to help develop the linguistic skills of students and not to test their memory of the contents. It is important that those in charge of the conduct of examinations bear this in mind in the design of papers.**

Note to the Teacher

As teachers will have realised from the Introduction, these materials require a teaching methodology which is quite different from the traditional 'lecture method'. At Anna University, we ourselves were using the lecture method until 1990. It is now accepted by most academics that the lecture method does not give students scope to practise language skills in the classroom. The focus has now shifted to guiding the learning process through a series of carefully designed activities or tasks.

We found the activities approach well received by our students. In fact, one might characterise the professional activities of engineers and technologists as the solution of problems. Therefore (this is entirely appropriate and justifiable) in this method, teachers use a problem-solving, task-based approach in the English classroom.

In this approach, all the four skills involved in learning a language, namely reading, listening, speaking and writing are developed through various tasks. By working through the activities, students, both fluent and less fluent, should be able to improve their effectiveness in using English in real life situations especially for their chosen profession.

How to handle the main sections (Parts 1 and 2)

1. Reading tasks should be done by the students themselves, working in pairs or groups, or individually. Teachers should resist any temptation to explain the whole text whilst the students read. Instead they should encourage the students to rely on their own resources and monitor their progress. When they have finished, the right answers can be arrived at by discussion among students or at times the teacher too can check the answers with the whole class.

2. The present edition has an accompanying CD which has a collection of listening tasks. These give students practice in taking notes. Alternatively, teachers can also present a talk using an informal lecture style. They should not read aloud from the 'Teacher's notes', but must prepare well in advance and present the information in the form of an informal lecture. This will require some skill, and even a little rehearsal on a teacher's part. But it allows for the listening material to be presented in a manner suited to the ability of the students.

If the class has students who need help, speaking more slowly with less complex grammar and with some repetition will help. With other students, mini-lectures can be made more challenging. Whatever they do, teachers should not read aloud from a prepared script! It is important to be natural and to remember that spoken language is often less formal and often contains slips, false starts and hesitations, and these are likely to be present in mini-lectures.

3. Role-play, discussions and oral pair-work exercises should be made lively by the teacher encouraging each student to participate in the given task. She must not worry about the noise level in the classroom; indeed, this may indicate the degree of participation and involvement by the students in the task.

4. Writing tasks must be closely monitored. The teacher should move among the students correcting their language. He should not wait for all of them to complete the whole task. Those who are slow should be closely monitored and more help can be given to them. Although teachers will naturally want to correct students' written work, they should not attempt to mark all the work themselves. Instead, students should be encouraged to criticise, edit and correct their own work. In this way teachers can help them become mature, independent writers. Staff in other faculties will be grateful for such efforts.
Commenting on written work will provide teachers with an opportunity to deal differently with students of differing abilities. The less able student can perhaps be encouraged to produce work which has good ideas. Although accuracy of grammar and spelling are ultimately very important, correcting these mistakes too rigorously in the early stages will discourage students. In any case, making mistakes is an important part of any learning process. When dealing with a more fluent student, on the other hand, the teacher may want to point out even small mistakes so that he is encouraged to improve himself, and not to sit back, unaware of the errors.

5. Language focus exercises should be done without the need for long explanations from the teacher. As far as possible, grammatical labels should not be used. Students need to be able to use English for their own purposes, and detailed grammatical analysis may not help them achieve this goal. Instead, language focus activities should be used to develop students' awareness of the language and how it works. English teachers working with engineering and technology students are often apprehensive about dealing with anything related to engineering or technology in their classes, since their students are likely to know more than the teacher. However, with a communicative methodology, this can be seen as a strength. Students are only too pleased to explain technical points to their English teacher, and other students will soon speak up if the information is incorrect. These explanations provide samples of genuine communication and thus give excellent opportunities for students to practise oral communication. We have found that our students expect us to be experts only in *English*, not in other subjects as well. The experience of other teachers is likely to be similar. A spirit of cooperation is thus created in the classroom, and this will benefit everyone.

Working with students who need help

Ideally, such students should be taught the Preparation and Follow-up materials in a separate special class. They should be able to follow the main materials in their regular class. In such special classes, particular attention should be paid to psychological aspects. The teacher should explain very carefully, in the mother-tongue if necessary, what the purpose of these 'extra' lessons is. They must be made to understand that these lessons are designed to increase their rate of learning so that they are not held back in their studies by their difficulty with English. Also, a lot of encouragement must be given to them whenever they attempt to complete a task, whether or not they make mistakes. Fluency must sometimes be encouraged in preference to accuracy. The teacher should always use simple language. It is encouraging if the teacher holds back on answers so that the students feel compelled to use English to explain things, thus getting more practice.

Stretching abler students

Since this textbook aims at the development of the basic skills (LSRW) involved in language learning, those students who have already an excellent command of English may feel that these materials do not provide sufficient challenge. Such students' help may be effectively utilised by making them 'adopt' students who need help and helping them complete their tasks. This will encourage both the strong and the help-needing students. Also tasks can be further stretched so that the creative ability of other students may be seen at work. For example, they may be asked to collect supplementary materials connected with the topic from different sources including the library. They can play a leading role in tasks such as discussion, oral practice and role-play, guiding the slow learner on the right lines so that at a later stage the special group may face these tasks independently with confidence and without external help.

It is never easy for teachers to change their methodology. By extended practice, it becomes a habit, and to deviate from that requires a lot of effort and conscious labour. We have tried using a communicative learner-centred approach and found that we enjoy it. We want to encourage other teachers to try this methodology and we hope they too will enjoy it.

Note to the Student

These materials, on different topics, have been prepared with you, the student, very much in mind. Students who have already used this book have found the topics interesting and useful. We hope you will also find them so. We believe that you can learn better if you are encouraged to join in discussions to solve problems and to express your ideas freely. These materials provide many opportunities for you to take part in classroom activities of various kinds. The teachers will only guide and monitor you. You will often be asked to work with other students in pairs or in groups. In this way you can learn to speak English fluently and with confidence.

We have designed the main parts of each unit to enable you to read more efficiently. Practice in note-taking will help you with work in your other subjects too. Discussions and role-play will improve your fluency levels, and language focus exercises will deepen your understanding of how the English language works. All of these will help you to write better English in the writing tasks.

If you have difficulty in understanding English, you will find the Preparation and Follow-up sections in each unit very useful. The Preparation enables you to follow Parts 1 and 2 better. The Follow-up lesson helps you consolidate your learning from Parts 1 and 2.

Do not worry too much about grammar, but try to make your meaning as clear as you can. Do not hesitate to ask other students or your teacher for help. If you do the various activities with genuine interest, you will definitely benefit from this course.

Whatever your level, this textbook encourages you to improve and refine your own English. If you are proficient in English, you can help other students, encouraging them to participate in classroom activities and helping them learn with you.

course overview

Theme resources

▶ Unit 1: Water

preparation
oral fluency using specific words in context
language focus (vocabulary) preparing for the reading text
reading scanning text following guidelines
writing describing objects

part 1
reading (An Introduction to Rainwater Harvesting) skimming text
oral fluency (Rainwater Harvesting Techniques)
role-play (promoting a product, buying and selling)
reading scanning for detail
oral fluency role-play (buying and selling)

part 2
listening (The Water We Need) completing notes
oral fluency (Saving Water) discussion

follow-up
language focus spelling, grammar
oral fluency describing the features and uses of something; the passive voice
writing sequencing

▶ Unit 2: Gold and Silver

preparation
oral practice discussion on people, gold and silver
language focus (vocabulary) adjectives related to jewellery;
pre-reading: matching words and meanings
language focus (vocabulary) suffixes with -al, -ic, -ical etc
writing descriptions with adjectives

part 1
reading (The Importance of Gold) gapped reading
language focus active to passive
listening (The Uses of Gold) note-taking
reading (Extraction of Gold) scanning for specific information;
post-reading task completing a flow-chart
writing (Industrial Uses of Gold) paragraph-writing using notes from earlier task

part 2
listening descriptive words and phrases
reading (Silver is Gold) skimming for gist; reference words
and what they refer to; pair-work: explaining meanings of
words in the reading text
language focus (Worth a Fortune) supplying appropriate vocabulary
oral fluency group discussion followed by reporting
reading (Smart Materials) comprehension

follow-up
language focus prefixes with –un, -im etc
reading comprehension and channel conversion (text to flow-chart)
writing sequencing sentences in logical order to make a paragraph

Theme resources

▶ **Unit 3: Human Resources**

preparation
vocabulary words related to professions
oral fluency word stress
language focus (grammar) present and continuous tenses
oral fluency discussion in pairs (What are Human Resources?);
interpreting bar-charts

part 1
oral fluency issues related to energy
reading comprehension (pair-work)
reading (BPOs are now Moving to Villages) channel conversion (text to bar-chart)

part 2
reading (The Continuing Spell of Srinivasa Ramanujan)
scanning based on pre-reading questions;
guessing meaning from context; comprehension
writing biographical/autobiographical sketch based on listening task

follow-up
language focus prepositions and adverbs; tenses
reading (Getting a Visa) making notes
oral fluency role-play (interviewing and being interviewed)

Theme energy

▶ **Unit 1: Oil**

preparation
reading comprehension
oral fluency asking and answering questions
reading (Oil and Alternative Sources) comprehension
language focus (vocabulary) prefixes with multi- and under-;
key words from reading text

part 1
reading (Solar Energy) scanning by checking answers
to pre-reading questions; comprehension: true/false
Language Focus (Solar Heaters) grammar

part 2
language focus (Prospecting For Oil) sequencing in logical order
oral fluency (A World without Oil) discussion
writing: predicting future conditions

follow-up
language focus (grammar) comparisons

Theme energy

▶ unit 2: Nuclear Power

preparation
oral fluency: discussion on theme (pair-work)
language focus (vocabulary): words from the reading text; identifying appropriate vocabulary; comprehending discourse features

part 1
reading (US and India Seal Nuclear Accord): predicting content of reading text from pre-reading questions and opening sentences of paragraphs; assigning headings based on paragraph topic
listening and oral fluency (Two Kinds of Nuclear Reactor): guided note-taking

part 2
reading (Dangers and Disasters): note-making; skimming to suggest headings
language focus (Safety in Nuclear Plants): identifying discourse features
oral fluency: asking and answering text-related questions (pair-work)
reading (Leaks at India's Nuclear Power Plants): skimming for gist, for information
writing paragraph based on notes made earlier

follow-up
writing: making comprehension, expressing a point of view

▶ unit 3: Alternative Sources

preparation
language focus (vocabulary): selecting appropriate words; antonyms
oral fluency: stating opinions
language focus (grammar): suffixes

part 1
language focus (vocabulary) (Alternative Energy Sources)
selecting appropriate words and phrases
oral fluency: responding to statements (pair-work)
reading (Two Alternative Energy Devices): channel conversion to table
writing (A Device for Rural India): completing a chart as a basis for extended writing

part 2
oral fluency (Energy for Cooking): discussion (pair-work)
reading: skimming, matching titles with text
oral fluency (Renewable Sources of Energy): role play: interviewing decision-makers
writing (Energy for India): discussional writing

follow-up
listening and reading: comprehension
listening: dictation and spelling check
oral fluency: discussion based on information in the table prepared in Part 1 above
language focus (Wind Power Phones): selecting words appropriate to the context

Theme
computers

▶ Unit 1: Introducing Computers

preparation
language focus (vocabulary): accurate definitions; multiple meanings; compound nouns
oral fluency: making comparisons; discussion

part 1
language focus: accurate definitions
writing (Are Computers Better than Human Brains?): channel conversion from table to explanatory text

part 2
reading ('IT for all': only a slogan?): detailed reading
oral fluency: role-play (Explaining Computers): (explaining and convincing)

follow-up
language focus (eLearning) (grammar)
identifying and correcting mistakes
writing: writing a simple description with the help of a diagram

▶ Unit 2: New Frontiers

preparation
language focus: pronunciation (pre-reading exercise)
oral fluency: discussion on ways of classifying something
language focus: meanings of expressions

part 1
reading (Science Fiction)
language focus (Robots): appropriate vocabulary
writing writing about future needs

part 2
listening (Silicon Valley and Apple): note-taking

follow-up
oral fluency (Myths of Artificial Intelligence)
language focus: grammar (modals)
oral fluency talking about the future

▶ unit 3: Computers in India

preparation
oral fluency: discussion
language focus (vocabulary): working out meaning from context
reading: reading with vocabulary prediction
writing: definitions

part 1
language focus (grammar): making compound adjectives
reading (Employing Computers) prediction of content and skimming; comprehension check

part 2
reading (Call it e-Philanthropy): scanning and comprehension check

follow-up
language focus (grammar): contrasting the simple past
and the present perfect
oral fluency: role-play

Theme
transport

▶ Unit 1: Problems and Solutions

preparation
language focus (vocabulary) prefixes
oral fluency discussing problems and solutions

part 1
reading and oral fluency (Travelling by Bus; Transport by Autorickshaw)
comprehension and information transfer to other formats
(e.g. a flow-chart), discussion

part 2
reading (Road Safety) pre-reading discussion followed by scanning of text
listening (Suspended Animation) accuracy in listening
oral fluency (Improving Road Safety) role-play featuring representatives
of various groups

follow-up
oral fluency: discussion
reading comprehension check
language focus (vocabulary) fixed expressions
writing discussing the relative benefits of something

▶ Unit 2: Transport Tomorrow

preparation
language focus (vocabulary) pre-reading task
language focus (grammar) verbs

part 1
language focus (mechanics)
oral fluency discussion in groups
reading (Looking down the Track…) skimming, post-reading comprehension check

part 2
language focus (If Travel were a Pleasure…) (grammar): conditional clauses
reading (The Automated Freeway) skimming and post-reading comprehension check
writing (Solving a Traffic Problem) proposing a solution

Theme transport

follow-up
language focus (grammar) adjectives
reading comprehension check
writing suggesting solutions and evaluating their benefits

Unit 3: Travel for Pleasure

preparation
language focus (grammar) gerunds; (vocabulary): words/phrases associated with travel and tourism

part 1
oral fluency (On your Own Two Feet) pre-reading discussion
reading (Mountaineering and Trekking) intensive reading
writing comparing two activities

part 2
reading (Journeys) skimming
listening (Hassles in the Air) note taking

follow-up
language focus (vocabulary) cloze task
writing: suggesting ways of dealing with problems of health

Theme technology

Unit 1: Appropriate Technology

preparation
language focus vocabulary orientation and prefixes with *self*
oral fluency discussing a definition
writing paragraphs from points

part 1
listening while-listening note-taking
reading (Pedal power) sequencing text
(A Bicycle-operated Domestic Pump) intensive reading
oral fluency discussion

part 2
language focus (Cement from Rice Husk) verbs in the passive (modified cloze)
writing: describing the process indicated in a flowchart
reading (Find your Feet) intensive reading
oral fluency discussion

follow-up
language focus (vocabulary) modified cloze
reading comprehension check
writing developing ideas into a paragraph

Theme
technology

▶ Unit 2: Printing

preparation
language focus (grammar) discourse-markers for sequences of action;
pre-reading the vocabulary of printing: familiarisation task

part 1
reading (Traditional Printing Methods) comparing accuracy of information in the flowchart and text which follows
listening while-listening task: completing table
reading reading advertisements and formulating reasons for buying the product

part 2
reading (Excellence in Adversity) reading with the help of text-anticipating questions

follow-up
language focus (vocabulary) working out meanings from context; using appropriate words
writing Inkjet or Laser Printer?

▶ Unit 3: Evaluating Technology

preparation
language focus working out meanings
reading predicting content from initial sentences
writing paragraph-writing assessing problems/benefits

part 1
oral fluency discussion
reading (Solar Cookers) predicting content, reading comprehension

part 2
reading (A Fable for Tomorrow) comprehension, literal and inferential
language focus (Policy on Technology) constructing sentences from a substitution table
reading (Goodbye Pictures, Hello Pixels): detailed reading
writing writing about future changes/developments
reading (Mass Production or Production by the Masses?): predicting content; completing sentences as evidence of accurate comprehension of text

follow-up
reading: comprehension
language focus: using appropriate words

Theme
communication

▶ Unit 1: Language

preparation
language focus (vocabulary): identifying objects and their use; sentences expressing purpose/use
oral fluency: country–language–native vocabulary; describing languages and language communities

Theme
communication

reading (The English Language) comprehension
listening while-listening note-taking
writing comparisons

part 1
oral fluency discussion
language focus appropriate words
listening while-listening categorisation of data in tables

part 2
language focus word puzzle with words ending in -ity
reading (Symbols: Towards Universal Understanding)
comprehension of detail and analytical reading
writing writing a reply to a letter (to the editor of a newspaper)
expressing a point of view
language focus non verbal communication

follow-up
language focus (grammar): constructing mirror sentences; adjectives
oral fluency discussion of attitudes to English

▶ Unit 2: The Media

preparation
oral fluency warming-up activity
language focus matching words and meanings
eading showing understanding of intended content (completing sentences)

part 1
reading (Will Newspapers Survive?) skimming followed by while-reading
note-making
writing paragraph based on discussion

part 2
language focus (grammar) structures which express purpose
and means (e.g. in order to);
language focus (Preserving Traditions) (grammar) filling in prepositions
reading (Building an Internet Culture) showing understanding of intended content
oral fluency group discussion

follow-up
language focus (grammar) appropriate prepositions and adverbs
writing (based on earlier reading and tasks)

Theme
environment

▶ Unit 1: Pollution

preparation
language focus stressed and unstressed syllables
writing ordering and sequencing based on vocabulary or context clues
listening while-listening completion of notes

Theme environment

part 1
reading (Cleaning the Heights) reading based on content guidelines
oral fluency role play: offering solutions
writing writing a report of the proceedings of a meeting (simulated by the role play task)

part 2
reading (Climate Change in Short) discussion on theme as anticipation of ideas in text to follow; text comprehension
language focus (vocabulary and grammar) appropriate words
listening while-listening notes o **writing**: offering recommendations to solve a problem

follow-up
reading comprehension based on re-reading of text in Part 1
oral fluency role play: discussing an issue
writing letter of complaint to a newspaper

Unit 2: Ecology versus Development

preparation
language focus prefixes and suffixes; grammatical forms of the same word
oral fluency discussion in small groups

part 1
reading (Bamboo Forests) content- and vocabulary prediction followed by detailed reading and comprehension
language focus placing words in text
writing making recommendations

part 2
reading (Bags of Rubbish) reading with pre-reading guidelines
writing expressing views
oral fluency role play: interview to seek opinion

follow-up
reading comprehension
writing using notes made in listening exercise to write a paragraph
oral fluency asking and answering questions to elicit/offer information
language focus (grammar) structures expressing cause and effect

Unit 3: Our Living Environment

preparation
language focus accurate comprehension
oral fluency role play communicating disapproval with reasons, and responding to this; group discussion followed by presentation of views
writing description of animals based on hints

part 1
language focus reading a story and reconstructing it from a point of view
reading intensive reading and comprehension check

part 2
reading (Vanishing Animals) reading with text-predict prompts followed by comprehension check

follow-up
reading (Animals at Night) intensive reading and comprehension
writing writing based on hints
oral fluency agreeing and disagreeing with statements

Theme
industry

Unit 1: Personnel And Production

preparation
oral fluency discussion
writing genre analysis of letter-writing conventions; completing a biodata sheet; writing a letter of application with a biodata sheet

part 1
reading (The Dry Cell Battery) understanding the text and suggesting points of paragraphing

part 2
reading (Virtual Reality) detailed reading followed by comprehension
listening while-listening completion of steps of a process

follow-up
language focus prefixes
reading intensive reading followed by a range of comprehension formats including a table

Unit 2: Safety And Training

preparation
oral fluency discussing safety measures
writing public warnings and notices
language focus prepositions

part 1
reading (Personal versus Professional Relationships) while-reading notes
listening completing fishbone diagram
writing preparing a report

part 2
oral fluency discussion
reading (Training in Industrial Organisations) reading and comprehension check
writing preparing safety checklists
language focus other grammatical forms of words

follow-up
reading comprehension check (the detection of toxic gases): making a diagram following text
writing writing a proposal

Unit 3: Selling Products

preparation
oral fluency group discussion and presentation of ideas
language focus matching words and meanings
reading reading and understanding opinions and views from experts
writing instructions and warnings

part 1
reading (The Deadly Sins of Customer Service): reading followed by discussion based on comprehension
listening while-listening completion of information

part 2
reading (Selling New Products) analysing product information literature
writing paragraph from hints describing an event
oral fluency discussing advertisements

follow-up
oral fluency role-play (asking for and giving product information)
writing writing based on texts
language focus matching products with messages

contents

Resources

Unit 1: Water
Preparation 3
Part 1 7
Part 2 9
Follow-up 10

Unit 2: Gold and Silver
Preparation 13
Part 1 15
Part 2 19
Follow-up 22

Unit 3: Human Resources
Preparation 23
Part 1 26
Part 2 28
Follow-up 31

Energy

Unit 1: Oil
Preparation 35
Part 1 38
Part 2 39
Follow-up 40

Unit 2: Nuclear Power
Preparation 41
Part 1 43
Part 2 47
Follow-up 49

Unit 3: Alternative Sources
Preparation 50
Part 1 52
Part 2 54
Follow-up 57

Computers

Unit 1: Introducing Computers
Preparation 61
Part 1 63
Part 2 65
Follow-up 67

Unit 2: New Frontiers
Preparation 68
Part 1 69
Part 2 71
Follow-up 73

Unit 3: Computers in India
Preparation 74
Part 1 76
Part 2 80
Follow-up 81

Transport

Unit 1: Problems and Solutions
Preparation 85
Part 1 87
Part 2 89
Follow-up 92

Unit 2: Transport Tomorrow
Preparation 94
Part 1 95
Part 2 98
Follow-up 100

Unit 3: Travel for Pleasure
Preparation 101
Part 1 102
Part 2 106
Follow-up 106

Technology

Unit 1: Appropriate Technology
Preparation 109
Part 1 111
Part 2 113
Follow-up 116

Unit 2: Printing
Preparation 117
Part 1 119
Part 2 123
Follow-up 124

Unit 3: Evaluating Technology
Preparation 126
Part 1 127
Part 2 129
Follow-up 135

Communication

Unit 1: Language
Preparation 139
Part 1 142
Part 2 144
Follow-up 148

Unit 2: The Media
Preparation 149
Part 1 150
Part 2 153
Follow-up 155

english for engineers and technologists
Volumes 1 and 2 (Combined Edition)

contents

Environment

Unit 1: Pollution
Preparation 159
Part 1 161
Part 2 164
Follow-up 168

Unit 2: Ecology versus Development
Preparation 170
Part 1 172
Part 2 175
Follow-up 177

Unit 3: Our Living Environment
Preparation 178
Part 1 179
Part 2 183
Follow-up 185

Industry

Unit 1: Personnel and Production
Preparation 189
Part 1 195
Part 2 196
Follow-up 198

Unit 2 : Safety and Training
Preparation 201
Part 1 203
Part 2 204
Follow-up 207

Unit 3: Selling Products
Preparation 209
Part 1 211
Part 2 212
Follow-up 216

english for engineers and technologists
Volumes 1 and 2 (Combined Edition)

THEME
resources

1
WATER

🌢 Reading skills development

Preparation

Read these three short texts very quickly and guess who is speaking in each case.

a farmer?
an officer at Metro Water?
the Director General of Meteorology?

> The weather forecast covers the entire part of the country. Even within the region which has received the normal rainfall there will be drought.

> The cyclical shortages of water have prompted Metro Water to think in terms of permanent solutions such as the sinking of 70 borewells in the Palar river bed, the installation of sewerage treatment plants and the desalination of water.

> The rain god has failed us once again. The earth is hard and dry. The paddy crops are dying. I am afraid there will not even be one grain of rice at home, at the time of Pongal, the harvest festival.

Oral practice

- The availability of water varies from place to place.
- When there isn't enough water, we say it is **scarce**.
- When there is just enough (but no extra), we say it is **sufficient**.
- When there is more than enough, we say it is **plentiful**.

a
Using the three words in bold discuss with your partner the availability of water during the different seasons of the year in any three parts of India.

b
The table below should show sources of water and devices for obtaining it from each source. Discuss the entries with your partner and complete the table.

	sources	devices
1	well	suction pump
2		
3		
4		

c
The reading text on page 7 of this Unit is about rainwater harvesting. Why do you think the word 'harvesting' is used for this idea?

d
Working in small groups, describe the processes of collecting water that are used in villages. How are those different from what is used in cities?

Language development

This exercise will help you with some of the vocabulary you will come across in the reading text.

a
Look at the ten words in column A. If you know the word, mark it ( ). If you don't know it, write ( ). If you're not sure of what it means, put in a question mark (?).

A	B
com__plex__	use
de__vice__	__in__crease
di__ver__sion	a__bil__ity
ca__pa__city	__pas__sing through
e__ro__sion	__in__strument
__per__meability	__mar__kedly
sig__ni__ficantly	tool
augmen__ta__tion	__in__tricate
__im__plement	__tur__ning aside
con__sump__tion	__wea__ring away

Now compare your work with your partner.

b
For each word in column A, there is a word in column B which has a similar meaning. Find the matching words. Work with a partner. When you have finished, your teacher will review the answers with you, and help you with the correct pronunciation of these words.
The stress is on the syllables which are underlined

c
Use the appropriate form of the words in column A to fill the gaps in the following paragraph.
Rainwater can be collected using simple techniques such as pots and jars as well as through more .... techniques. Commonly used systems are constructed of three components:

Resources: Water

the catchment area, the collection
...................., and the conveyance system.
In the catchment areas, the .... of
rainwater from gutters to containers is done to
settle the particulates. In land surface catchment
areas, the runoff .... of the land
surface is improved. Clearing vegetation can
cause soil .... Chemical applications
with soil treatments can .... reduce
soil .... Rainwater harvesting is
a freshwater .... technology in
Asia. Local people can be trained to ....
harvesting technologies. This method provides
water at the point of ....

Check your work with another student's.
Now your teacher will check answers with
the class.

Reading skills development

Before each paragraph in this reading text, you will find a question. Try to answer this question as you read the paragraph.
Read as fast as you can.

WATER: THE ELIXIR OF LIFE

* **Why is water such an important substance in life?**

This common substance called water, which we take for granted in our everyday life, is the most potent and the most wonderful thing on the face of our earth. It has played a vast role in shaping the course of the earth's history and continues to play a leading role in human life.

* **What kind of preservation of water takes place in South India?**

There is nothing which adds so much to the beauty of the countryside as water. The rainfed tanks that are so common in South India are a cheering sight when they are full. They are, of course, shallow, but this is less evident since the water is silt laden and throws the light back, and the bottom does not therefore show up. These tanks play a vital role in South Indian agriculture. In Mysore, for example, much of the rice is grown under them. Some of these tanks are surprisingly large and it is a beautiful sight to see the sun rise or set over one of them.

* **What happens when particles are carried through in flowing water?**

One of the most remarkable facts about water is its power to carry silt or finely divided soil in suspension. This is the origin of the characteristic colour of the water in rainfed tanks. This colour varies with the nature of the earth in the catchment area and is most vivid immediately after a fresh inflow following rain. Swiftly flowing water can carry fairly large and heavy particles. The finest particles, however, remain floating within the liquid in spite of their greater density and are carried to great distances. Such particles are, of course, extremely small, but their number is also great and incredibly large amounts of solid matter can be transported in this way. When silt-laden water mixes with the salt water of the sea, there is a rapid precipitation of the suspended matter. The colour of the water changes successively from the muddy red or brown of silt through varying shades of yellow and green finally to the blue of the deep sea. That great tracts of land have been formed by silt thus deposited is evident on an examination of the soil in alluvial areas. Such land, consisting as it does of finely divided matter, is usually very fertile.

What are the benefits and disadvantages of the flow of water?

The flow of water has undoubtedly played a great part and a beneficent one in the geological processes by which the soil on the earth's surface has been formed from the rocks of its crust. The same agency, however, under appropriate conditions, can also play a destructive part and wash away the soil, and if allowed to proceed unchecked can have the most disastrous effects on life. Soil erosion occurs in successive steps, the earliest of which may easily pass unnoticed. In the later stages, the cutting up and washing away of the earth is only too apparent in the formation of deep gullies and ravines which make all agriculture impossible.

What are the principal factors in soil erosion? What are the contributory causes for soil erosion?

Sudden bursts of excessively heavy rain resulting in a large run of surplus water are the principal factors in causing soil erosion. Contributory causes are the slope of the land, removal of the natural protective coat of vegetation, the existence of ruts along which the water can flow with rapidly gathering momentum, and the absence of any checks of such flow. Incredibly large quantities of precious soil can be washed away if such conditions exist, as is unhappily too often the case.

C V Raman

❋ Writing skills development

Look back at the paragraphs and list the causes for soil erosion. Write five sentences describing the process of soil erosion. Try not to copy words from the text.

Part 1

Reading

AN INTRODUCTION TO RAINWATER HARVESTING

Rainwater harvesting is a technology used for collecting and storing rainwater from rooftops, the land surface or rock catchments using simple techniques such as jars and pots as well as more complex techniques such as underground check dams. The techniques usually found in Asia and Africa arise from practices employed by ancient civilisations within these regions and still serve as a major source of drinking water supply in rural areas. Commonly used systems are constructed of three principal components: namely, the catchment area, the collection device, and the conveyance system.

CATCHMENT AREAS

Rooftop catchments:

In the most basic form of this technology, rainwater is collected in simple vessels at the edge of the roof. Variations on this basic approach include collection of rainwater in gutters which drain to the collection vessel through down-pipes constructed for this purpose, and/or the diversion of rainwater from the gutters to containers for settling particulates before being conveyed to the storage container for domestic use.

Land surface catchments:

Rainwater harvesting using ground or land surface catchment areas is less complex way of collecting rainwater. It involves improving runoff capacity of the land surface through various techniques including collection of runoff with drain pipes and storage of collected water.

Clearing or altering vegetation cover:

Clearing vegetation from the ground can increase surface runoff but also can induce more soil erosion. Use of dense vegetation cover such as grass is usually suggested as it helps to both maintain a high rate of runoff and minimise soil erosion. Increasing slope: Steeper slopes can allow rapid runoff of rainfall to the collector. Use of plastic sheets, asphalt or tiles along with slope can further increase efficiency by reducing both evaporative losses and soil erosion.

Soil compaction by physical means:

This involves smoothing and compacting of soil surface using equipment such as graders and rollers.

Soil compaction by chemical treatments:

In addition to clearing, shaping and compacting a catchment area, chemical applications with such soil treatments as sodium can significantly reduce the soil permeability.

COLLECTION DEVICES

Storage tanks:

Storage tanks for collecting rainwater may be either above or below the ground.
Rainfall water containers: As an alternative to storage tanks, battery tanks (i.e., interconnected tanks) made of pottery, ferrocement, or polyethylene may be suitable.

CONVEYANCE SYSTEMS

Conveyance systems are required to transfer the rainwater collected on the rooftops to the storage tanks. This is usually accomplished by making connections to one or more down-pipes connected to the rooftop gutters.

Rainwater harvesting is an accepted freshwater augmentation technology in Asia. While the bacteriological quality of rainwater collected from ground catchments is poor, that from properly maintained rooftop catchment systems, equipped with storage tanks having good covers and taps, is generally suitable for drinking, and frequently meets WHO drinking water standards.

Rainwater harvesting technologies are simple to instal and operate. Local people can be easily trained to implement such technologies, and construction materials are also readily available. Rainwater harvesting is convenient in the sense that it provides water at the point of consumption, and family members have full control of their own systems, which greatly reduces operation and maintenance problems.

Rainwater harvesting appears to be one of the most promising alternatives for supplying fresh water in the face of increasing water scarcity and escalating demand.
(Source: Hari Srinivas: hsrinivas@gdcr.org)

a
What is the prime importance of rainwater harvesting as seen in this short piece?

b
Have you heard about rainwater harvesting? Why do you think it is important?

c
Read these four questions below, then look at the text quickly to find out which paragraph (s) answers each question. Do not waste time reading carefully. Try to finish this task in three minutes, then check with another student. Your teacher will check with the class as a whole.

i. What is the main reason for the introduction of rainwater harvesting?

ii. What are the chief catchment areas for the collection of water?

iii. Name two major collection devices for rainwater.

iv. What are the ways in which rainwater harvesting can meet WHO requirements?

Learner Awareness

What you have been doing is scanning, or reading a text quickly to look for specific bits of information.

Work in pairs:

d

You will be given one of the four questions listed above. Read the paragraph in the text which answers the question you have been given. Jot down the main points of each paragraph. If you finish quickly, move on to another paragraph to read and summarise. Wait for instructions.

e

Write down two or three words you are familiar with, but which you think are important in the paragraphs you have just read. Try to guess their meaning from their spelling or from the general context.

f

Look at the text again, and write two more 'scanning' questions. Then give your questions to your partner, who must scan for the answers. Which question was easier? Say why.

Role play

Rainwater harvesting techniques

You and your partner are in English-speaking Africa.

Student A

You are a marketing engineer for a company that advises people on the advantages of rainwater harvesting. To prepare yourself, read the last two paragraphs and make a list of the advantages of rainwater harvesting.

Student B

You are the leader of the village. You are very happy about the technology of rooftop catchments. How will you convince your village to try this out?

To prepare yourself, read paragraph 2 and make a list of the possible drawbacks of this system.

Begin when both of you are ready.

Part 2

Listening

The water we need

In this class you will practise listening for specific information. All the information you need to listen for is in the form of numbers. Before your teacher gives the talk, read through the exercises below to make sure you understand them. If you are not sure about any of the questions, your teacher will explain them. Can you guess the answers to any of these questions before you hear the talk?
Your teacher will stop and check the answer at the end of each section of the talk.

a

Fill in the gaps in the sentences below.

.... of our body weight and .... of its volume is water. That is why water is essential for life. People can survive for upto .... without food, but will die within .... water.

b

Match A with B by drawing arrows (---->) between the boxes.

A	B
amount of water needed per person per day for cooking and eating	15 litres
amount of water needed per person per day to stay healthy	5 litres
amount of water a person can carry at one time	25-45 litres

c

Complete this.

Situation	Approximate Consumption per day
A. no tap or standpipe	........................litres
B. standpipe only	........................litres
C. single house tap	........................litres
D. several house taps	........................litres

d

At the end of section c use the figures you noted down to complete the bar chart below. How much water do people living in modern houses use?

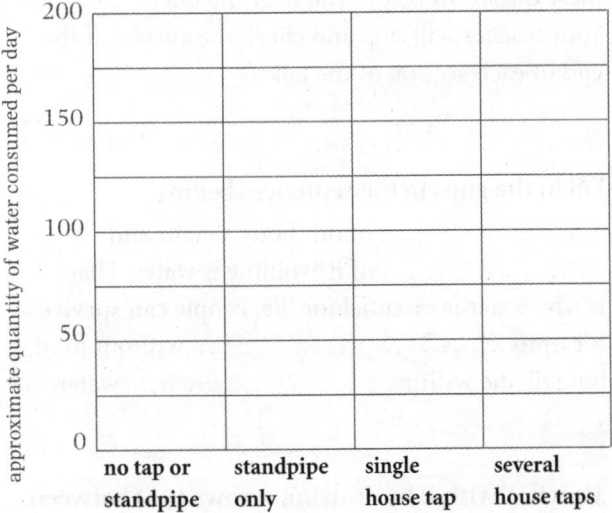

Which of these activities do you think uses the most and the least water?
While you are listening fill in the amounts.

   i. flushing a toilet: .... litres
   ii. filling a basin to wash face: .... litres
   iii. cleaning teeth with tap running: .... litres
   iv. having a shower: .... litres
   v. having a bath: .... litres

☀ Discussion

Saving water

Work in groups.

a

Think of the ways an educational institution or a public place could save water. Your teacher will write the best suggestions on the board.

b

Think of a device or invention which would help people to save water. Tell the class about your device.

Follow-up

☀ Language check

There are ten spelling mistakes in the following paragraph. How many can you find?

In the most basic from of this technology, rainwater is collectd in simple vassals at the ege of the roof. Varishions on this basic approach include collaection of rainwater in guttars which drane to the collection vessel through down-pipes constructed for this purpose, and/or the divertion of rainwater from the gutters to containars for settling particulates.

Now look back to the reading text in WATER, Part I, paragraph 2, to check. Rewrite the paragraph, correcting all the spelling mistakes.

❋ Language development

Many nouns can be made from verbs by adding these suffixes:

| -tion | -ment | -ence | -ance |

e.g. to develop ⟶ development
    to collect ⟶ collection

a

Make nouns from these verbs. Look back to the reading text on pages 7–8 to check when necessary.

(*para 2*) collect ....

(*para 1*) convey ....

(*para 1*) civilise ....

(*para 7*) treat ....

(*para 2*) divert ....

(*para 4*) erode ....

(*para 6*) equip ....

(*para 7*) apply ....

(*para 11*) construct ....

b

Now use some of the nouns you have just made to complete these sentences.

i. The................of water is a permanent problem in rural areas.

ii. Chemical applications with soil .... like sodium can reduce the permeability of soil.

iii. Commonly used systems are made of three principal components: namely, the catchment area, the collection device, and the .... system.

iv. Clearing vegetation can cause soil ....

v. The ....of rainwater from the gutters to containers is done to settle particulates.

❋ Oral practice

Try to answer these questions as quickly and clearly as you can.

a. Can you describe rainwater harvesting?
b. Why is it useful/important?
c. Where is it used?
d. What are some of the equipment required for this?

❋ Language check

Using the points in a–f below, write six sentences describing rainwater harvesting. Put each verb in the passive. Be careful with word order.

> **Learner Awarness**
>
> Remember, the passive is often used for description in scientific or technical texts.

a. Rainwater harvesting (use) for collecting and storing rainwater.

b. Commonly used systems (constructed) of three principal components.

c. Rainwater (collect) in simple vessels at the edge of the roof.

d. Use of vegetation cover such as grass (suggest) to maintain a high rate of runoff.

e. Local people can be (train) to implement these technologies.

f. Rainwater harvesting technologies (instal and operate) very easily.

The passive voice is used to do one of the following

1. to avoid mention of the name of the doer of the action

2. to stress the recipient of the action

3. to make a general statement.

In converting from active to passive forms, some points have to be remembered:

▸ If there are two objects, one can use either of them as the subject in the passive voice. For example,

- Ravi gave Ram a writing pad. (active)
- Ram was given a writing pad by Ravi. (passive)
- A writing pad was given to Ram by Ravi. (passive)

When there is a prepositional phrase in the active voice, the preposition is to be retained.
For example,
- They gave up the project. (active)
- The project was given up by them. (passive)

The passive voice is used for impersonal statements. For example,
- It is hoped that she will come.
- It is believed that rainwater harvesting is a good method.

Writing skills development

The following sentences are taken from paragraph of the reading text on page 7 but they are in the wrong order. Put the sentences in the correct order by numbering them. Sentence b is the first one.

a. The techniques usually found in Asia and Africa arise from practices employed by ancient civilisations.

b. Rainwater harvesting is a technology for collecting and storing water.

c. Commonly used systems are constructed of three principal components.

d. Rainwater is collected from rooftops, the land surface or rock catchments using simple techniques.

Now look back at the reading text to check your order.

2
Gold and Silver

Preparation

✻ Oral practice

a

Silver and gold are often mentioned together. Can you say why this is so?

b

Name some articles made of gold that you would find in Indian homes.

c

What use do the following people make of gold or silver?

    an artisan

    a bride or bridegroom

    a jeweller

    a smuggler

✻ Language development

a

The following paragraph describes gold. Select adjectives from the list in the box to fill the gaps in the paragraph. The words and phrases should help you.

precious	expensive	indestructible
prevalent	unique	exquisite
exceptional	excellent	criminal

13 | Resources: Gold and Silver

Gold is …………….. among metals since it possesses certain properties not found in any other metal. It is a rare metal with a beautiful yellow colour. It is not affected even by strong acids. The only liquid which can dissolve gold is a mixture of hydrochloric acid and nitric acid; one can, therefore, say that gold is nearly ………… .

It has certain …………….. qualities which make it an ……………………. substance for jewellery. Skilled goldsmiths can make gold ornaments of …………………. workmanship. Gold jewellery is …………………. and people often show off their wealth by wearing ornaments of gold. Some people collect gold for its own sake. Gold, being a ……………… metal, inspires human greed. It gives rise to ……………………… acts like theft, robbery and even murder. Another crime that is ……………… in India is the smuggling of gold into the country.

b
Are the words in column A familiar to you? If not, try to guess their meanings.

c
Match the words in column A with their meanings in column B. Check your answers with your partner. (The underlined syllables are stressed.)

A	B
extraction	property pledged by a borrower
col<u>la</u>teral	bringing together
flo<u>ta</u>tion	suffering
de<u>fault</u>	process of treating something with a cyanide compound
<u>stag</u>nant	remaining on the surface
amalga<u>ma</u>tion	taking out
dis<u>tress</u>	in the absence of an alternative
cyani<u>da</u>tion	not moving or changing

Language development

※ You can form adjectives from nouns by adding suffixes like -al, -ic and -ical.

Add a suitable ending to each of the following words to form an adjective.

| metal | nature | chemistry |
| physics | profession | industry |

Which of the words above have to be modified before the ending is added?

※ Some nouns are formed by adding suffixes to adjectives or verbs. Some of the common endings used to form nouns are **-ity, -cy** and **-ce**.

14 | Resources: Gold and Silver

Add the appropriate endings to the following adjectives to make nouns.

rare	impure	indestructible
ductile	important	reliable
malleable	abnormal	frequent

Which of the words above have to be modified before the ending is added?

✷ Writing skills development

a

Make a list of adjectives and phrases which can be used to describe silver (look back over this lesson for ideas).
Check your list with your partner.

b

Write a short description of silver. Begin like this:

Silver is a precious metal. It

....
....
....
....
....

Learner Awareness

To enrich your vocabulary: learn ten new words every day and try and use them in conversation or in your work.

Part 1

✷ Language focus

The importance of gold

a

Here is an incomplete paragraph on gold. As you read it, fill in the gaps with the appropriate form of the words in the brackets.

Since ancient times, gold has caught the … (imagine)… of people by its unique qualities. What makes it so …(fascinate)… is not just its …(rare)…. and beauty, but also some of its …(chemistry)… properties. For example, there is only one liquid that can …(dissolve)… gold, a …(mix)… of hydrochloric acid and nitric acid. This gives it the quality of near…(destroy)….

15 | Resources: Gold and Silver

It is possible that gold is the first metal that humans …(discover)… . In nature, gold occurs in the …(metal)… state, almost as though waiting to be picked up by us. The …(extract)… of gold is, therefore, a simple process. Most of the …(pure)… can be removed from the freshly mined metal by a simple …(physics)… process.

Check your answers.

b

In the paragraph below, change active verbs into the passive where necessary. If you like, work with a partner.

The Egyptians knew the art of jewellery making as early as 3,000 B.C. In ancient India too, skilled artisans made exquisite gold ornaments. Gold is important for another reason. The nations of the world accept it as a medium of international exchange.

Although we do not use gold for coinage nowadays, there was a time when gold coins were in use. The Greeks developed the art of coin-making to a high degree of skill. Gold possesses two properties which make it easy for the artisan to work on it. It is malleable and we can, therefore, change its shape by pressing or hammering. It is also ductile; this means that we can draw it out into a wire. Today, gold has important industrial applications. We can use gold in making alloys of many kinds suitable for use in different industries.

Compare your new version of this text with the original. Which version seems
more formal?
more friendly?
more impersonal?

Listening

The uses of gold
You will hear a talk on the uses of gold. Take notes as you listen.
Use the framework below.

a

In government transactions

i. 68 per cent of gold—held by governments

ii. ……………………………………………………

iii. ……………………………………………………

iv. ……………………………………………………

b

Uses by craftspersons

i. ……………………………………………………

ii. electroplating of jewellery

iii. ……………………………………………………

c

Industrial uses

i. ……………………………………………………

ii. ……………………………………………………

iii. protective layer for satellites

iv. ……………………………………………………

d

Other uses

i. ……………………………………………………

ii. ……………………………………………………

Reading

Extraction of gold

a

Scan the following passage quickly to identify the types of mining and the ways of obtaining pure gold.

b

Now read the passage again and complete the flowchart on page 18.

The method of mining gold varies with the nature of the deposit. Two types of deposit can be considered here: one is placer deposit, which refers to the occurrence of gold in sand particles or gravel in a riverbed; the other is lode mine which refers to gold occurring as veins in gravel or rock. In placer mining, the separation of gold from gravel or other impurities is done by sifting. Hand panning is also common, in which water and gravel containing gold are swirled in a pan. Gold, being heavy, settles down, and the gravel is washed away. In lode mining, shafts are dug into the rock following the veins of gold. Using explosives, the rock is broken and the ore is obtained. The ore is then transported to mills.

In milling, the ore is first crushed using heavy machines. This is followed by sluicing, that is, using water to wash the ore into sluices or artificial water-channels in which there are grooves that trap the gold.

There are three ways in which this gold is treated to obtain pure gold. They are flotation, amalgamation and cyanidation. In the first method, a frothing agent is added to produce a foam. A collecting agent is used to produce a film on the gold, which then sticks to the air bubbles. Gold is then separated from the top. In amalgamation, the ore, mixed with water to form a pulp, is collected on a copper plate covered with mercury. The mercury is then removed, partly by squeezing it out and partly by distillation. The cyanide process is now widely used. In this process, a weak solution of sodium, potassium or calcium cyanide is used to dissolve the gold. The gold is then precipitated by the addition of zinc dust.

The gold thus obtained is smelted and cast into bars.

EXTRACTION OF GOLD

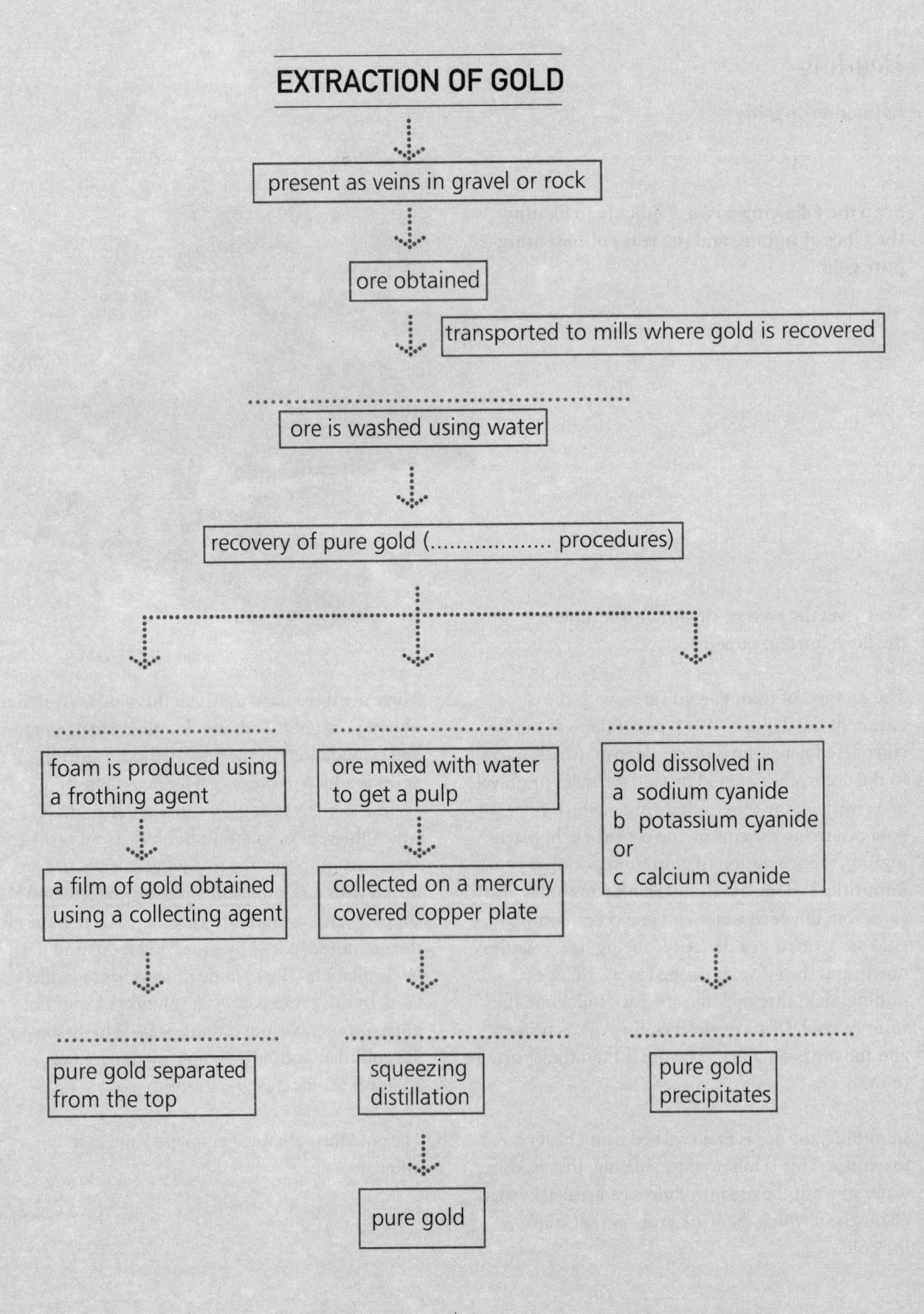

↓

present as veins in gravel or rock

↓

ore obtained

↓

transported to mills where gold is recovered

⋯⋯⋯⋯⋯⋯⋯⋯⋯⋯⋯⋯⋯⋯⋯⋯⋯⋯⋯⋯⋯⋯⋯⋯⋯⋯⋯⋯

ore is washed using water

↓

recovery of pure gold (⋯⋯⋯⋯⋯⋯ procedures)

↓ ↓ ↓

⋯⋯⋯⋯⋯⋯⋯⋯⋯⋯⋯⋯ ⋯⋯⋯⋯⋯⋯⋯⋯⋯⋯⋯ ⋯⋯⋯⋯⋯⋯⋯⋯⋯⋯⋯

| foam is produced using a frothing agent | ore mixed with water to get a pulp | gold dissolved in
a sodium cyanide
b potassium cyanide
or
c calcium cyanide |

↓ ↓ ↓

| a film of gold obtained using a collecting agent | collected on a mercury covered copper plate | |

↓ ↓ ↓

⋯⋯⋯⋯⋯⋯⋯⋯⋯⋯ ⋯⋯⋯⋯⋯⋯⋯⋯⋯⋯ ⋯⋯⋯⋯⋯⋯⋯⋯⋯⋯

| pure gold separated from the top | squeezing distillation | pure gold precipitates |

↓

pure gold

Writing

Industrial uses of gold

Write a paragraph on the industrial uses of gold, using some of the notes you took during the talk you heard.

Begin like this:

The industrial applications of gold are many. Because of its high conductivity, it is used for…………

Check the grammatical correctness of the paragraph you have written with your partner.

Part 2

Listening

You will listen to a description of the salt cellar, a famous art object in gold made by the great Italian goldsmith Cellini. As you listen, jot down the words and expressions used to describe the salt cellar.

....
....

Using the words and expressions you jotted down, present a description of the golden salt cellar made by Cellini.

Reading

a

Read the six statements below carefully. Then skim the three paragraphs for the gist and choose the statement which best summarises each one.

1. This paragraph compares the uses of gold and silver.
2. This paragraph is about supply and demand in the world silver market.
3. This paragraph is about the history of silver.
4. This paragraph is about the changes in the price of silver.
5. This paragraph is about silver in India.
6. This paragraph is about the mining of silver.

SILVER IS GOLD

One need not believe in astrology, which says that silver is governed by the moon and that any object under such an influence is *volatile* since the moon is the fastest moving body in the sky. That silver prices have undergone violent changes at times can be seen by what happened some years ago. Within a very short span of time the price of silver changed nearly four times. It leaped from Rs 2,758 per kg to Rs 3,038 per

Resources: Gold and Silver

kg to again Rs 4,108 and finally Rs 5,300. The rise in just 12 days was 92 per cent. Reportedly at that time West Asian oil producers were converting dollar holdings into precious metals and *speculators* were *hoarding*. Came a fall, and silver was again a tame Rs 2,841 per kg. During this period many speculators made millions if they pulled out fast enough, while many went broke because they didn't.

Internationally the demand for silver has been growing due to increased industrial consumption. Speculators and other investors are also responsible for the growing demand. On the supply side, however, mine production is almost *stagnant*. The gap between demand and supply is filled by what are known as secondary supplies. These include melted coins, scrap silver, and sale by governments of debtor countries like Mexico and Brazil, who are also major producers of silver. Since these secondary supplies play an important part in filling the demand supply gap, they are highly *sensitive* to changes in demand.

Although there is *virtually* no production in India, it is estimated that India has perhaps the largest *accumulated* stocks of silver in the world. This is not surprising considering that for the majority of the people who are poor and cannot afford gold, silver is the only precious metal they can invest in. Every year Indians sell about 2000 tonnes of silver. In rural areas, seasonal *abnormalities* induce *distress* sales.

During drought, famine and flood, there is a heavy flow of silver into the market. Most of the middle and lower classes, both in urban and rural areas, lack financial *assets* against which they can borrow in times of need. Since commercial banks do not lend money against silver, they have to sell.

b

Look back at the words in italics in each paragraph.

They are all examples of reference words. For each one, say what it refers to.
e.g. *it* (line 5) refers to the price of silver.

c

Explain the meanings of the words below as they are used in the text. Discuss this in pairs.

vo<u>la</u>tile (line 3)	<u>spec</u>ulators (line 13)
<u>hoard</u>ing (line 14)	<u>stag</u>nant (line 24)
<u>sen</u>sitive (to) (line 31)	<u>vir</u>tually (line 32)
ac<u>cum</u>ulated (line 34)	abnor<u>ma</u>lities (line 40)
dis<u>tress</u> (line 40)	<u>as</u>sets (line 44)

(Syllables which are stressed are underlined.)

Learner Awareness

Reference words act as signposts while reading. They provide clues to understanding the linking of ideas in the text.

❋ Language focus

a

Read the passage below. Fill each gap with an appropriate word.

WORTH A FORTUNE

In 1715, off the coast of Florida, a convoy of Spanish ships was struck by a storm. Some of the

ships sank and nearly a thousand ....
.... died. Eighteen years later, a storm struck
.... convoy which had set out from
Havana only a couple of days before. ....
..... ships were part of the convoy syatem which was
in regular operation in the .... and
eighteen centuries. There were hundreds of such ....
.... off the Florida coast, and what is more
interesting, the .... that these ships
carried remains on the ocean ....

In the early years of twentieth century, Spanish ......
.... were found on the ....
and soon a group of professional treasure hunters
launched a massive .... using

powerful .... for pumping and
dredging. What they salvaged was worth a ....
.... : coins of gold and ....,
crockery made of pewter ...., silver
and various artifacts.

The above exercise, called cloze reading is meant to help students select one word from a possible set of words of the given context which would be most appropriate to the given sentence. This requires familiarity on the part of the student, with the context and the meaning it has in relation to a set of familiar vocabulary.

Discussion

Investment in gold and silver

Discuss the wisdom of investing in articles of gold or silver as an economic proposition. Be ready to report your views to the class when your teacher asks you.

Reading

Smart materials

Read the text below and answer the questions that follow.

Smart materials with a memory, and in the form of metals and plastics which can change their shapes automatically, are emerging from their infancy. They are all set to play a key role in many aspects of everyday life early in the next century.

Research in Britain is not only finding new metallic alloys and plastic materials with even smarter capabilities, but is also identifying a rapidly growing range of uses for them that promises to bring major practical benefits, particularly in the industrial, domestic and medical environments. First discovered around thirty years ago, smart material to shape memory alloys (SMAS) can have a predetermined shape "implanted" in their structure. They can be transformed into a completely different shape to serve a particular purpose. They will only reveal their original shape when they are triggered by a specific stimulus, such as reaching a certain temperature or reacting to a particular chemical.

A new class of composite materials with unusual physical properties has also been produced by physicists at the University of California, San Diego (UCSD). While they obey the laws of physics, they are predicted to behave totally differently from normal materials and should find interesting applications. Their unusual property is essentially their ability to reverse many physical properties that govern the behaviour of materials. One such property is the Doppler effect, which makes a train whistle sound higher in pitch as it approaches and lower in pitch as it recedes. The new materials are known colloquially as left hand materials because they reverse the relation between the electric and magnetic fields and the direction of the wave velocity. What is unusual about the new class of materials produced by the UCSD team is that it acts simultaneously with a negative electro electric permittivity and a negative magnetic permeability—a combination of properties never before seen in a natural or manufactured material.

1. Will the emergence of the new metal alloys enhance the qualities of gold and silver?
2. What other factors will enhance the qualities and value of gold and silver?

Follow-up

Language development

Sometimes a prefix can be used to turn an adjective into its opposite.

Use the prefixes im-, in- and un- to find the opposites of these words.

| comfortable | pure | destructible | common |
| sensitive | skilled | exceptional | reliable |

Reading skills development

Read the text below and draw a flowchart to represent the process of extracting silver.

Silver occurs in ores of several metals. The froth process of extracting silver accounts for about 75 per cent of all silver recovered. Here the ore is ground to a powder, placed in large vats containing water suspensions of frothing agents and thoroughly agitated by jets of air. Depending on the agent used, either the silver-bearing ore or the gangue adhering to the bubbles of the froth is skimmed off and washed. The final refining is done using electrolysis.

Writing skills development

Put sentences (i)–(vii) in the right order to make a paragraph beginning with the underlined sentence. The questions in brackets should help you. Their answers should be in the sentence that follows.

The Egyptians knew the art of jewellery-making as early as 3000 B C.

i. It is malleable, and we can, therefore, change its shape by pressing and hammering. (What else?)

ii. It has been accepted by the nations of the world as a medium of international exchange. (Do we use it for money?)

iii. It is also ductile; this means that we can draw it out into a wire.

iv. In ancient India, too, exquisite gold ornaments were made by skilled craftspeople.

v. Although we do not use gold for coinage nowadays, there was a time when gold coins were in use. The Greeks developed the art of coin-making to a high degree of skill.

vi. Gold is important for another reason. (What is this reason?)

vii. Gold possesses two properties which make it easy for the artisan to work on. (What are these properties?)

To check your answer, look back at page 16.

3

HUMAN RESOURCES

Preparation

✻ Language development

a

Listed in column A are some examples of human resources. Can you match the job done by each person listed in column A?

A	B
A farmer	uses brick and mortar and builds houses
A trader	lays water and sewage pipelines
An architect	cultivates land and raises food crops
A scientist	cares for the sick or infirm
A mason	buys and sells or barters
A nurse	a person who works in a branch of science
A plumber	designs buildings and advises in their construction

b

Suggest some more examples under column A and describe the work done.

Resources: Human Resources

c

Make sure you can pronounce all the words in column A correctly. The stressed syllables are underlined. Your teacher will help you. Try to match each word in column A with a meaning from column B.

A	B
migrant	a condition caused by or as if by magical powers
rural	numerical facts systematically collected
urban	bring into a country people, goods etc. from foreign countries
cramped	relating to towns and cities
statistics	a person having an instinctive and extraordinary capacity for creative activity
recruit	relating to the countryside
import	confined within narrow limits
spell	something that rouses people to activity
genius	take people into service on contract
stimulus	a person who moves from one place to another for a limited period

The sentences that you came across at the beginning of this lesson are examples of the simple present tense. The simple present tense is used to refer to an action which is repeated, an everyday occurrence, or something which is always true.

For example,
   The carpenter **makes** articles out of wood.
   India **has** large reserves of silver.

In contrast, the present continuous tense is used to indicate an action taking place now, which is continuing. Look at the following example:

   A: Where *are* you *going*?
   B: I *am going* to the shop.

Similarly, the past continuous tense is used to refer to an action in the past extending over a period of time. Look at the following example:

   A: What were you doing yesterday?
   B: I was resting at home.

Fill in the gaps with the appropriate present or past continuous tense forms of the verbs in the brackets.
Pay attention to the proper spelling of words.

   A: What ………… you ……………………
      now? (do)
   B: I …………..………… in a factory. (work)

   A: What ………. you………………. earlier? (do)
   B: I ……………………. the lands of a
      farmer in the village. (cultivate)

   A: Are there other people here now who
      ……………………………..
      earlier in your village? (live)
   B: Yes, some of them ……….…………….. in
      this city now. (live)

   A: ………….. your wife ……………... now? (work)
   B: Yes, she ………………………. part time
      and also ………………….. after the baby
      at home. (work) (look)

❋ Oral practice

a

In pairs discuss the answers to the following questions.

i. Which are the countries that attract a large number of Indian workers?

ii. What kinds of jobs do Indians primarily seek in other countries?

iii. What are the reasons for Indians seeking employment outside the country?

b

Look at the bar charts given below and explain them.

Critical choice factors among Indian youth for selecting any job.

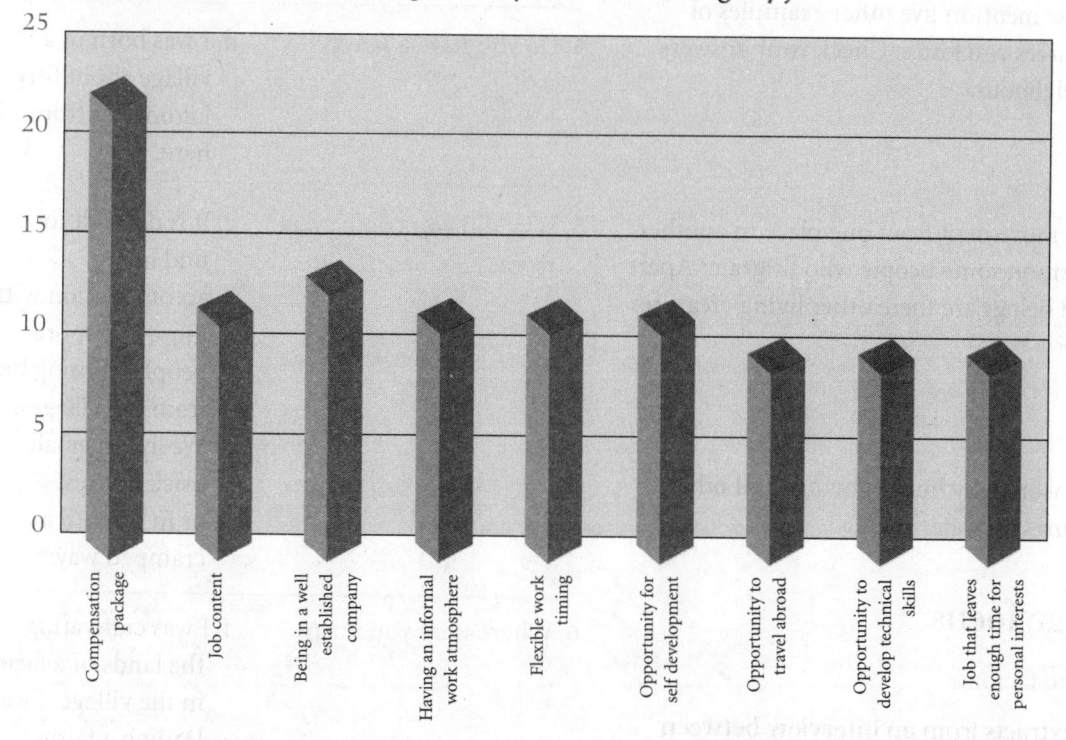

percentage going as rank 1

- Compensation package
- Job content
- Being in a well established company
- Having an informal work atmosphere
- Flexible work timing
- Opportunity for self development
- Opportunity to travel abroad
- Opportunity to develop technical skills
- Job that leaves enough time for personal interests

Industry/sector preferred by young Indians for employment.

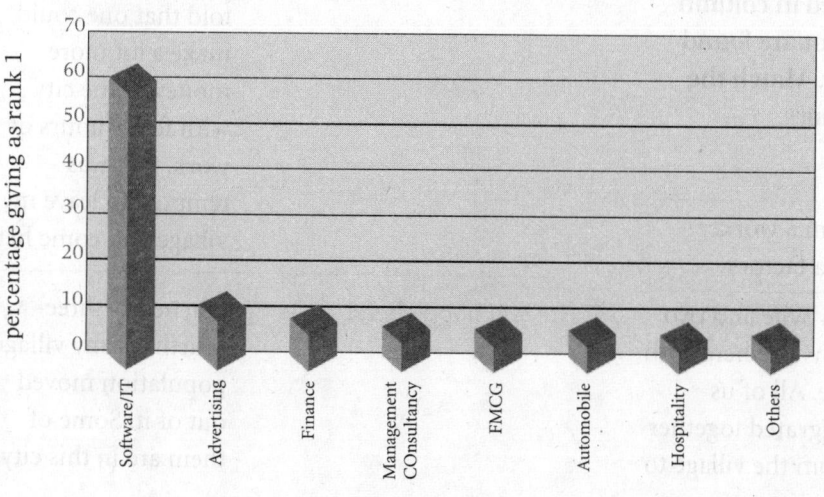

percentage giving as rank 1

- Software/IT
- Advertising
- Finance
- Management COnsultancy
- FMCG
- Automobile
- Hospitality
- Others

Resources: Human Resources

Part 1

❋ Discussion

What are human resources?

a

Human resources are human beings whose contribution society can use for different purposes. The worker in a factory is an example of a human resource. Now mention five other examples of human resources you know. Check your answers with your neighbour.

b

Migration is movement from one place to another. Can you mention some people who migrate? Apart from human beings are there other living creatures that migrate?

c

List some reasons why human beings and other living creatures migrate.

❋ Language focus

From farm to factory

Below are extracts from an interview between a journalist and a rural–urban migrant. The questions of the journalist are listed in column A, while the answers of the migrant are found in column B. They are not in order. Match the questions and answers. Work in pairs.

A	B
1. Do you have any problems here?	a. I am a worker in a factory
2. What do you do here?	b. My wife and two sons live here with me. All of us migrated together from the village to the city
3. Are there others in your village who followed your example?	c. Yes, I am. I have no regrets about my decision to come away from the village.
4. Do you have a family	d. I was born in a village about fifty kilometres from here.
5. Why did you come away from the village?	e. It is difficult to find living accomodation with more and more people coming here from the villages. We live in small brick houses, or in huts, in a cramped way.
6. Where were you born?	f. I was cultivating the lands of a farmer in the village. I was leading a fairly decent life. But I was told that one could make a lot more money in the city with fewer hours of work. So I was tempted to leave my village and come here.
7. Are you happy here?	g. Oh, nearly three-fourths of my village population moved out of it. Some of them are in this city.

Role play

Interview with Guru

Here is a letter written by a person who returned to his village for good after having migrated earlier to the city. Read the letter, then do the task which follows.

Dear Raju,

You must have been wondering what happened to me since my return to our village from the city. Perhaps you think I made a mistake in coming away from the city. Anyway, I don't think so. I am quite happy about my present lot. It is true that as a village carpenter I could not lead a successful life here before I left for the city. But the three years of my stay in the city have taught me how best to use my skills in the village with some modern implements. That is why I brought them with me to the village. Now I use them successfully to manufacture all kinds of furniture needed in the village. I am making a lot more money than ever before. I am delighted that I can be of service to the village community and contribute to the development of my village.

With love,
Guru

Now work in pairs and role-play an interview between a journalist and the writer of the letter. You may want to use some of the questions on page 26.

Reading

BPOs are now moving to villages

a

Read the following article and draw bar charts to show

i. the percentage of employees in different categories: graduates, class 12 pass, class 10 pass and others.

ii. the expenditure on salaries for the various categories

Kizhanur is like any other village in Tamil Nadu, surrounded by paddy fields and grazing cows. But look closely at No:1 Sivan Koil street which is awash with a new phenomenon – a business process outsourcing unit in a village. E-tools is a village BPO, doing coding on legal paper for a US client. It is run by an entrepreneur who supervises the Kizhanur franchisee of an end-to-end outsourcing company that has a presence in the healthcare and publishing industries.

The initiative termed 'E-tools Village BPO' is to be extended to five more locations in Tamil Nadu, Andhra Pradesh, Kerala and Karnataka by the end of 2006. Right now there are two in Kerala and one in Karnataka.

Ninety per cent of those employed by E-tools have passed class 10 or above. Out of these, five per cent have passed class 12 and the remaining five per cent are graduates.

The Kizhanur centre employs 200 people who work in three eight-hour shifts. The centres in Kerala and Karnataka employ 220 and 250 respectively.

Graduates at the Kizhanur centre are paid Rs 5000 a month, those with class 12 pass earn Rs 4000 while those with class 10 pass earn Rs 3000. The others are paid Rs 2000.

The company that runs E-tools has 60-odd centres in and around Tamil Nadu and Pondicherry, while the central hub in Chennai employs about 1000. The 60-odd centres in the rest of Tamil Nadu employ 5000 personnel. The 50 centres in Karnataka have about 2500 personnel.

Though the BPO in Kizhanur is right now only an experiment, in two years' time the shift to rural areas may become more of a necessity, as the BPO industry will be embroiled in a grim survival game.

(Source: Nelson Vinod Moses, 29 June, 2005; rediff.com India Limited, © 2005)

b

Which is the better way to present this kind of information, a text or a chart? Discuss your opinion with your neighbour.

Part 2

Reading

a

i. Have you heard of Srinivasa Ramanujan?
ii. What do you know of him?
iii. Have you come across anything named after him?

b

Now scan the passage on Srinivasa Ramanujan quickly (for not more than two minutes) and write down six key phrases or sentences from the text which help to sum up the important aspects of his life and work.

THE CONTINUING SPELL OF RAMANUJAN

Srinivasa Ramanujan, a poor, uneducated Indian, born a hundred years ago, was one of the greatest and most unusual mathematical geniuses who ever lived. Although he died young – at the age of 32 – Ramanujan left behind a collection of results that are only now beginning to be appreciated. No one has ever been able to understand the workings of Ramanujan's mind, how he came to think of his results or the source of this incredible outpouring of mathematics. His is the example of inborn mathematical ability.

Not only is Ramanujan's work meaningful and a stimulus to mathematicians today – he touched on some very fundamental problems in number theory and analysis – but his results are also relevant to problems he could have known nothing about, such as the string theory in physics and fast algorithms in computer science. G H Hardy of Cambridge University characterises Ramanujan as a very great mathematician, full of paradoxes and contradictions, who defies all judgement. Ramanujan was born in 1887 in the town of Erode, in southern India, and grew up in the town of Kumbakonam where his father was an accountant for a cloth merchant. Ramanujan, his brother, and his parents lived in a one-room house.

His entire mathematical education seems to have been gleaned from only two books, and these were books that mathematicians would not give to students today because they are not particularly good. In fact, the books were not good even in Ramanujan's day.

Ramanujan completed high school and tried twice to obtain a college education. But he failed both times because he was so obsessed by mathematics that he simply could not bring himself to spend any time on other subjects. In 1909, when he was twenty-two years old, he married nine-year-old Janaki and took a clerical position in the Madras Port Trust Office to support her and his mother, who lived with them. While he worked as a clerk, Ramanujan continued to pour out math results, using excess wrapping paper from the office to scribble down his formulas. He was so obsessed with his mathematics that he did not want to stop even to eat. His wife has said that she and Ramanujan's mother used to feed him at mealtimes so that he would be free to continue writing while he ate.

Fortunately for Ramanujan, both the chairman and the manager of the office where he worked were engineers who recognised that he seemed to have extraordinary mathematical talent. The chairman, Sir Francis Spring, was English and the manager, S N Aigar, was educated in England. Both urged Ramanujan to send some of his results to English mathematicians, who might be able to evaluate them.

Ramanujan wrote to mathematicians H F Baker and E W Hobson of Cambridge University. Both returned his letters without comment.

Then, on 16 June 1913, he wrote to G H Hardy of Cambridge University—a letter that was to change his life and Hardy's.

Hardy showed a colleague Ramanujan's strange letter, which was crammed with as many as 60 mathematical theorems and formulas, stated without any proofs. It did not take them long to realise that Ramanujan was a genius. So Hardy wrote to Ramanujan and invited him to come to England to study with him. Ramanujan accepted and arrived at Trinity College in April 1914. 'For the next three years he pitted his brains against the accumulated wisdom of Europe,' Hardy said. And Ramanujan was successful. At Cambridge, he derived outstanding results in number theory in particular.

But life in England was not easy for Ramanujan. His wife stayed behind in India and he had no one to care for him. He cared more for mathematics than for eating and sleeping. Ramanujan reportedly would work for long stretches – 24 to 36 hours – and then would collapse and sleep for twelve or more hours at a time. He was a vegetarian, which presented additional difficulties. It was difficult to get vegetarian food in England. Ramanujan would have boxes of rice sent from India and he would fry rice powder in ghee.

In May of 1917, Ramanujan came down with a mysterious illness that may well have been a vitamin B 12 deficiency caused by his poor diet while in England. Ramanujan was so weakened and incapacitated by his illness that he returned in 1919 to India, where he died a year later.

```
                                      293.458
RAMANUJAN (Aiyangar),Srinivasa:
[Werke.]Collected Papers.Ed.by G[odfrey]
H[arold] Hardy,P.V.Seshu Aiyar,and B.M.
Wilson.(Reprint.) - New York:Chelsea (1962).
XXXVI,355 S. 8°
1965:4508.                            Ga..
```

When he died, Ramanujan left behind three notebooks, which he wrote before coming to England and which are filled with as many as 4000 results, stated without proofs. He also left behind the papers he published in England, many of which were written in collaboration with Hardy. And he left behind results he discovered during the last year of his life. He mailed many of these results to Hardy, but the papers were never published. But even if the Ramanujan collection is incomplete, it has given researchers more than enough to work on. More and more often mathematicians are finding that their clever new ideas were discovered first by Ramanujan.

(Source: *The Hindu, July 1987*)

Compare what you have written with your neighbour's work to see if you agree.

c

Read the passage again and choose seven or eight words which you do not understand. Try to guess their meanings from the context. If you cannot, ask your neighbour. The teacher will then explain the meanings of some of them.

d

Write down three or four headings under which the whole passage can be organised. Work in pairs.

❋ Discussion

If Ramanujan had...

a

Do you think that Ramanujan's contribution to mathematics would have been greater if he had been exposed to the work of other great mathematicians?

b

Do you think Ramanujan would have made a greater contribution if he had never gone to England?

c

Complete the statement from the choices given

▸ **Ramanujan failed to obtain a college education because**
  i. he was poor.
  ii. he could not understand the subjects taught.
  iii. he could not spend any time on subjects other than mathematics.
  iv. he did not complete high school.

▸ **In 1913 Ramanujan wrote to G H Hardy of Cambridge University because**
  i. Hardy was his friend.
  ii. he was urged to send some of his results to English mathematicians.
  iii. he lost his position in the Madras Port Trust Office.
  iv. he wanted to make a pleasure trip to England.

▸ **Life in England was not easy for Ramanujan because**
  i. his neighbours often quarrelled with him.
  ii. the climate was very cold.
  iii. he was among strangers.
  iv. he did not eat and sleep properly and overworked himself.

▸ **Ramanujan returned in 1919 to India because**
  i. he had become very weak and physically unfit.
  ii. he was not permitted to continue to stay in England.
  iii. his mother passed away.
  iv. he had an employment offer in India.

d

What evidence do you find in the text to support the statement that Ramanujan was an unusual mathematical genius? Make notes, then write down the answer in not more than three sentences.

Work in consultation with your neighbour.

Learner Awareness

Try reading biographies and autobiographies of famous people. Besides providing inspiration they expose you to language well written. Are you aware of some famous biographies of men of science?

Follow-up

Language check

Some of the words used to indicate the time of an action are:

| while | at | for | in | when | on | ago |

Fill in the blanks in this passage using these words.

Srinivasa Ramanujan, born a hundred years ……….. was a great mathematical genius. To be exact, he was born ………… 1887. ……….. he was twenty-two years old he married Janaki. He accepted a clerical position in the Madras Port Trust Office. ………… he worked as a clerk he was engrossed in mathematics. ………….. 16 June 1913, he wrote G H Hardy of Cambridge University a letter that was to change his life. At Hardy's invitation, Ramanujan arrived in England ……… 1914. At Trinity College he worked ……. hours and hours at mathematics, often neglecting food and sleep. Unfortunately he fell ill and returned to India ……… 1919. He died a year later, ……… the age of 32.

Language focus

You would have noticed that in Ramanujan's story, the main verbs are usually in the simple past tense (wrote, would etc.)

Fill in the gaps in the text below with the correct tense and form of the verbs in brackets.

Sir Benjamin Baker (be) a British civil engineer. He (be) an expert on bridges. Before the age of twenty he (learn) all about steel and iron. A practical man, he never (leave) anything to chance. He (insist) on carrying out exact tests on every piece of steel or iron. He (write) a book about cantilever bridges. He (win) a reputation for brilliance in the engineering profession. He (help) in building new underground railways in London. He (build) the famous Aswan Dam in Egypt.

Reading skills development

Read the following text and make notes under the headings provided.

a. Types of visas to the US
b. Advantages of having a H1-B visa
c. Limitations of the H1-B visa
d. Conditions for applying for a H1-B visa

GETTING A VISA

Long before the nuclear bomb blasts put Indian scientists in the international radar top-class, Indian professionals had become the mainstay of many a major American "cutting edge" company. And the H1-B visa emerged as the crucial enabling instrument. Even now, the H1-B visa is one of the most widely used US employment visas for newly hired foreign employees in specialty occupations.

US companies engaged in cutting edge operations include those in aerospace engineering, research, biotechnology, pharmaceuticals and information technology industries. These fields rely heavily on the H1-B visa category to employ foreign professionals to meet skill shortages in the US labour market. The impact on American businesses, with key projects that are dependent upon the services of H1-B workers, is very critical.

The US government has proposed to increase the number of H1-B visas to 95,000 per year with the provisions of increasing it to 1,05,000 a year within the next five years. With the increase of H1-B visas to 95,000, it means that more people from India should logically find employment in the US under this category. However, companies can consider alternative visa categories including the B-1 (business visitor), L-1 (intra-company transferee), E (treaty trader and investor), TN (professional for Canadian or Mexican) or O-1 (extraordinary ability) visa, each of which has qualifying criteria. The privileges of H1-B visas are that they can be issued quickly and are available for accompanying relatives.

They allow travel in and out of the US and enable the visa holder to remain there continuously. They also allow the holder to work legally in the US for an H1-B sponsor. The limitations are that they cannot be held for more than six years. A holder of an H1-B visa is restricted to work only for an employer who is an H1-B visa sponsor. To change a job a new H1-B visa is needed. Also, accompanying relatives allowed to stay in the US with the visa holder are not entitled to work there.

There are five eligibility requirements for a H-1B visa.

1
The candidate must be a member of a profession with a college degree or its equivalent work experience. US immigration law is vague about the definition of 'profession' stating only that the meaning includes such occupations as architects, lawyers, physicians, engineers and teachers. Other occupations which are not specifically mentioned but routinely recognized as professions include accountants, computer systems analysts, physical therapists, chemists, medical technologists, hotel managers and upper level business managers.

2
The immigration and naturalisation service (INS) considers every three years of work experience equivalent to one year of college.

3
You must have a job offer from a qualified US employer for the work to be performed in the US.

4
The job you have been offered must be one that requires a degree of professional work. It cannot be for just any type of work. The position must really require the skills of a highly educated person. A person who is an ordinary computer operator or has merely basic knowledge about a computer will not qualify as these visas are meant for specialty occupations.

5
You must have the correct background to qualify for the job which you have been offered. If you are a qualified nuclear scientist but are offered a position of managing a US pharmaceuticals factory you will not be granted a H1-B visa.

(Source: The India Today Website)

✽ Oral practice

Role-play the interview below in pairs. Use the information in the reading text 'Getting a visa'.

✽ Student A

You are a newspaper reporter. You want to know details about the issuing of visas by the US government. Prepare a list of questions to ask an officer of the US Immigration Department.

✽ Student B

You are an officer in the US Immigration Department. You have to provide information to a reporter. Prepare a list of points about the visas issued by the US government.

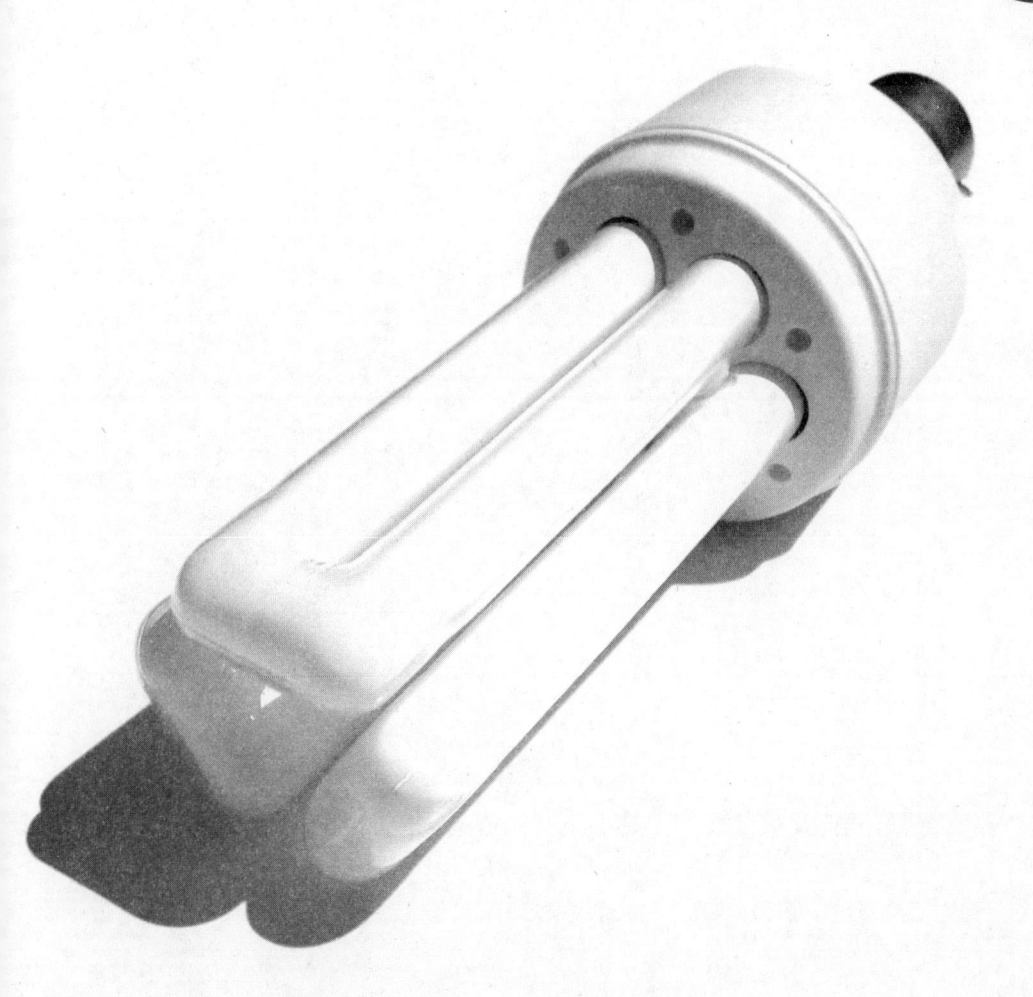

T H E M E
---
energy

1
OIL

Preparation

🌢 Oral practice

a

Interview another student about the region he or she comes from. Begin your questions like this:

Could you tell me something about your district?

- What about ....?
- Do you ....?
- How has .... developed in your ....?
- Have there been many/any changes in ....?

b

Now imagine that you are going to interview someone from the Middle East.

Write as many questions as you can, in the time given, about the development, culture and way of life. Use the questions listed above if necessary.

Energy: Oil

Reading

OIL AND ALTERNATIVE SOURCES

Speaker X: How will we meet our energy needs in the future?
We cannot have oil for all time.

Speaker Y: We appear to be entering a particularly innovative period, with more than one path to a sustainable energy system.

Speaker X: Predicting the future is easy – getting it right is the hard part. Twenty-five years after the automobile was invented, we are still continuing to ask searching questions about the world's future energy needs.

Speaker Y: We can think about the different choices and possibilities that might arise within the commercial energy system during the next 50 years and develop scenarios to help us understand how energy systems could evolve during that time. This is the approach we should use to think about how today's energy industry might evolve.

Speaker X: Energy development has always depended on choices – by consumers, producers, governments and society. This has brought about an energy system based on those sources seen as most satisfactory in terms of cost, quality, reliability, security, convenience and social impact. In thinking about the future of that system, we need to examine the key drivers of fundamental change – resource constraints, technology development, and changing social and political priorities.

Speaker Y: There are a number of key questions:
- When will oil and gas resources cease to meet rising energy demand, and what will replace oil in transport?
- Which technology will win the race to improve the environmental standards of vehicles?
- How will demand for distributed power shape the energy system? Who will drive the market growth and cost reduction of renewable energy sources, and how will energy storage for intermittent renewables like solar and wind be solved?
- How will emerging economies balance rapidly growing energy needs with rising import dependence and environmental effects?
- Where will social and personal priorities lie and how will these affect energy choices?

Speaker X: In particular, we have to address the overarching question: What energy needs, choices and possibilities will shape a global energy system which halts the rise in human-induced carbon dioxide emissions within the next 50 years without jeopardising economic development?

Speaker Y: Advances in biotechnology, materials technology such as carbon nano-fibres, and information and communications technology will support development of bio-fuels, fuel cells, new energy carriers such as hydrogen, micro-power networks, and new generations of solar technologies.

(Adapted from www.bbc news.com)

Read the text and answer the questions.

a. How do you think energy systems can evolve during the future?

b. How has the present energy system evolved? What is it based on?

c. List at least two questions which arise in this discussion of energy needs.

d. What kind of energy needs, choices and possibilities will shape a global energy system for the future which will halt the rise in carbon-dioxide emissions?

Language development

Look at these examples of words with the prefixes **micro-** and **under-**

▼ A **micro-power** network is one that carries very little power.

▼ A country which is not very highly developed is an **underdeveloped** country.

a

Now complete these sentences with words which have the prefix micro- or under-

i. A processor which is made on a very small scale is a ....

ii. A living creature which is too small to be seen is ....

iii. A person who does not have enough nourishment is ....

iv. An employed person who does not have enough work is ....

v. Engineering on a very small scale is called................................ .

vi. When you think someone's abilities are less than they actually are, you have .... them.

b

Read the words below. Note the stressed syllables.

surfaces	exploit	oil-rich	feasible
conservation	feedstock	crude oil	columns
lubrication	consumption		

Fill in the blanks with the appropriate word.

1. Many Arab countries are ....
2. Petrol leaves the ground in the form of ....
3. Friction is reduced by ....
4. Bitumen or tar is used for road ....
5. Figures in log tables are arranged in horizontal rows and vertical ....
6. Our .... of food must be limited to suit our digestive system.
7. .... of energy will reduce demands for energy.
8. Some selfish employers try to .... their employees.
9. Before undertaking an adventurous project, one must consider if it is ....
10. Material which is fed into an industrial process is called ....

c

Strike out the word that does not belong to the group. Say why it is different from the other words.

For example: **doctor, nurse, hospital, x-ray, nomad**

Answer: **All the other words are about health, but *nomad* is not.**

i. economy, per capita income, wealth, treasure
ii. industrial, rates of production, prices, dramatic, consumption
iii. schools, deserts, universities, academics, colleges
iv. swords, standstill, muskets, arms, weapons
v. business, ransom, commodity, scarce, costly
vi. tents, palaces, homes, camels

If you are unsure of any word, ask your teacher.

Reading

Solar Energy

a

Before you read the text, answer these questions.

i. Name some of the sources of energy humankind has been using over the years.

---

37 | Energy: Oil

ii. Can you think of the benefits of solar technology?

iii. Where do you think solar energy is derived from, and do you think this will last?

Part 1

SOLAR ENERGY

Solar technologies use the sun's energy and light to provide heat, light, hot water, electricity, and even cooling, for homes, businesses, and industry.

Photovoltaic solar cells, which directly convert sunlight into electricity, are made of semiconducting materials. The simplest cells power watches and calculators and the like, while more complex systems can light houses and provide power to the electric grid.

Buildings designed for passive solar and daylighting incorporate design features such as large south-facing windows and building materials that absorb and slowly release the sun's heat. No mechanical means are employed in passive solar heating. Incorporating passive solar designs can reduce heating bills as much as 50 per cent. Passive solar designs can also include natural ventilation for cooling.

Concentrating solar power technologies use reflective materials such as mirrors to concentrate the sun's energy. This concentrated heat energy is then converted into electricity.

Solar hot water heaters use the sun to heat either water or a heat-transfer fluid in collectors. A typical system will reduce the need for conventional water heating by about two-thirds. High-temperature solar water heaters can provide energy-efficient hot water and hot water heat for large commercial and industrial facilities.

The availability or access to unobstructed sunlight for use both in passive solar designs and active systems is protected by zoning laws and ordinances in many communities.

Consumer demand for clean renewable energy and the deregulation of the utilities industry have spurred growth in green power, solar, wind, geothermal steam, biomass, and small-scale hydroelectric sources of power. Small commercial solar power plants have begun serving some energy markets.

Read the report, and say whether the following statements are true or false.

i. Solar energy is derived from the light and heat of the sun.

ii. Buildings can be designed to absorb and release the sun's heat as required.

iii. There are levels of complexity in the intensity of light of photovoltaic solar cells.

iv. Concentrated heat energy derived from the sun can be converted into electrical energy.

v. Solar water heaters can use the heat of the sun to heat water or even large commercial establishments.

vi. Some laws and governances do govern access to and availability of sunlight.

vii. Growth in green power, solar power, wind power etc. is the result of consumer demands.

Language Focus

Correct the errors in the following passage. Underline the errors first and then do the corrections.

Concentrated heat energy converts to electricity. Solar water heaters use sun to heat water or a heat-transfer fluid. A typical system reduces need for conventional water heating into two-thirds. High temperature heaters can provides hot water and heat in commercial and industrial facilities. The access of unobstructed sunlight in active and passive solar designs protected by zoning laws. Consumer's demand has spurred growth to green power, solar, wind, steam etc. powers. Small commercial solar power plants have begun serve energy markets.

Part 2

Language focus

Prospecting for oil

a

The sentences in task b below are not in the right sequence. Read each sentence and underline the reference words (it, they, etc.). Then do task b.

b

Sequence these sentences to make a paragraph about prospecting for oil. The words that you underlined in task a should help.

i. If that strikes oil, then production wells can be drilled.

ii. They carry out surveys from the ground and from the air using a variety of instruments, and they bore into the rocks to take samples.

iii. When petroleum engineers search for oil, they look for certain types of rock layers, or strata, which they know from past experience can trap oil.

iv. If it indicates that oil may be present, a test well is drilled.

v. Oil is found underground trapped in the layers of rock.

vi. When all the information is collected and analysed, a picture of the underground strata is obtained.

vii. They also set off explosions in the ground and record the waves reflected from the underground rock layers.

viii. This is called seismic surveying.

c

Now decide what each of your underlined reference words actually refers to. Check your answers with a partner.

Discussion

A world without oil

What would the world be like if our supplies of oil were to run out (or become unobtainable)?

a

Make a list of all the things you can think of which come from crude oil, not forgetting the products of petrochemical industries.

b Classify the uses of your listed items using general headings such as domestic, industrial, transportation, chemical.

Writing

A world without oil

Imagine it is now 50 years in the future. There is very little oil left. Write a paragraph telling young people how life was better, because of oil, in the twentieth century.

Begin: In my day, oil was plentiful, we could... but these days we cannot...

Follow-up

Language development

- Comparison is expressed by adding the endings **-er** and **-est** to adjectives. With certain adjectives we use **more** and **most** instead of -er and -est. For some adjectives, completely different words are used. For example **bad, worse**.

Study the sentences given below. Underline the comparative adjectives. Find out how these adjectives are modified in English to denote comparison.

i. Saudi Arabia was more reluctant to increase oil production than many other countries.

ii. Venezuela is closer to the equator than Bolivia.

iii. Dealers feel that the sale of four-wheelers will definitely be better in the future than it is now.

iv. 24-carat gold is purer than 22-carat gold.

v. His clothes have become wetter than they were before because of his walk in the rain.

vi. The dependence on alternative power sources is heavier in developing countries than in developed countries.

Look at the following comparative adjectives and put them into groups according to how they are formed.

larger	easier	wealthier
more important	more powerful	worse
more interested	cheaper	heavier
higher	better	
more traditional	bigger	wetter

Write the comparative forms of the following adjectives.

dry	sturdy	valuable	simple
greedy	feasible	good	beautiful
professional	reliable		

2

Nuclear Power

Preparation

🌸 Oral practice

Work in pairs.

a

What do you understand by the term 'nuclear energy'?

b

What are the uses of nuclear energy?

c

Are there any dangers involved in the use of nuclear energy?

d

Do you know of any recent accidents involving nuclear energy?

🌸 Language development

a

Look at the words in column A in task b on the next page and make sure you can pronounce them properly. Then do task b.

41 | Energy: Nuclear Power

b

Match the word in column A, with its meaning in column B.

A	B
nucleus	division of the atom
uranium	getting rid of
fission	pollution
disposal	central part of the atom
core	producer
coolant	metallic element
breeder	giving out rays
radiation	danger
hazard	cooling fluid
contamination	the innermost part

c

Guess the meanings of these words and phrases (if you do not know them already).

derived from	consumption	generated by
depleted	disaster	more difficult
abuse	expensive	radioactive

Now use the words/phrases to complete the sentences below.

i. In hydel units, electricity is .... heating water.

ii. Vast quantities of energy can be .... a very small quantity of nuclear fuel.

iii. The existing coal reserves will fast become .... if we continue to use such a large amount of coal.

iv. Our present .... of oil and gas exceeds the present production levels.

v. An accident in a nuclear power station can lead to a great ....

vi. Causing destruction through atom bombs is a clear example of .... of scientific knowledge.

vii. Prospecting for oil is in many ways .... than extracting it.

viii. Uranium and plutonium are .... nuclear fuels.

ix. When oil becomes .... many countries consider using alternative energy sources for economic reasons.

d

Underline all the phrases in the text which are used to make recommendations.
For example, It is necessary to ....
A coolant channel replacement machine (CCRM) should be developed to carry out large scale replacement of pressure tubes in Pressurised Heavy Water Reactors Servomanipulators. Images have to be incorporated in the system. Since many challenges are foreseen in the area, the engineers ought to prepare themselves for the task. It is necessary to set up fast breeder reactors to multiply fissile material inventory.

Part I

Reading

US and India seal Nuclear Accord

a

i. What does energy mean to people in India? Think of three people from different walks of life. How would they respond to this question?

ii. What do you know about nuclear power? Why do you think it is called this? What do you know about nuclear fuels?

iii. The reading text on the next page is about the accord signed between India and the U. S. for sharing of nuclear power. What do you think the impact of this would be? Make a list.

b

i. Reading the first sentence of a paragraph can often give you an idea of what the whole paragraph is about. Try out this technique with the paragraphs on the next page. Make a note of what you think each paragraph is about.

ii. Which part of the text gives you India's 3-stage nuclear power programme? Make a list of these stages.

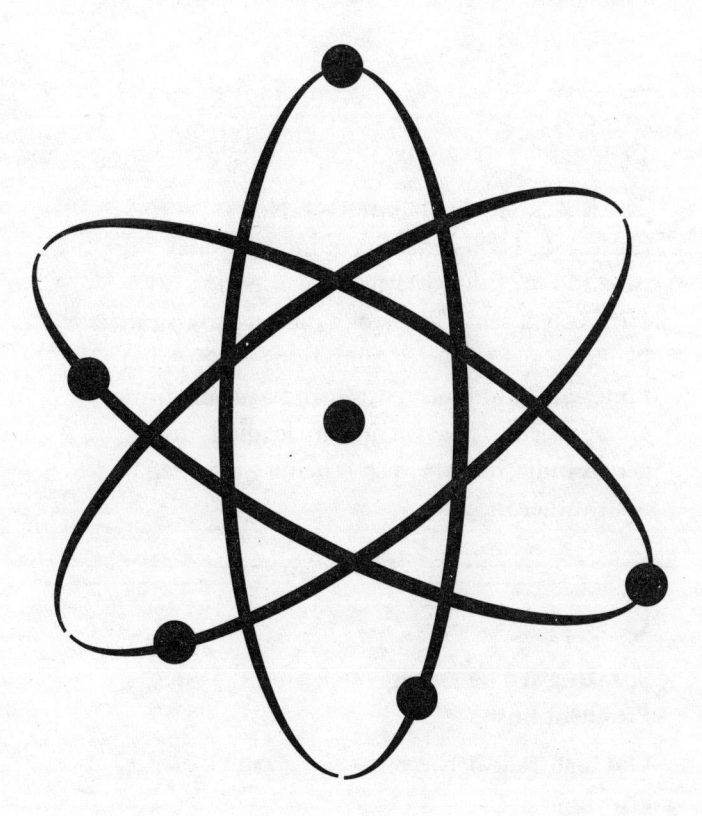

c

Work in pairs. Read each paragraph on the next page. Think of sub-headings that you can insert in the text in consultation with your partner. Be ready to report back when the teacher asks you to do so.

US and India seal nuclear accord

A

The US and India have finalised a controversial nuclear deal after talks in Delhi between President George W Bush and Indian Prime Minister Manmohan Singh. Energy-hungry India will get access to US civil nuclear technology and open its nuclear facilities to inspection.

Mr Bush, on his first visit to India, called the deal 'historic'. But he said it might be hard to get it through the US Congress, which must ratify it. India has not signed the Nuclear Non-Proliferation Treaty (NPT).

B

The BBC's Sanjoy Majumder in Delhi says the nuclear deal will end years of international isolation for India over its nuclear policy. But critics say it sends the wrong message to countries like Iran, whose nuclear ambitions Washington opposes. Communist parties and Muslim groups are opposed to the visit and are leading protests across India, but Mr Bush is being welcomed by many other Indians.

C

Speaking at a news conference after the talks, President Bush

- said that trade between the two countries was growing;
- promised to share information on terrorism and cooperate militarily;
- encouraged India and Pakistan to resolve the Kashmir dispute;
- joined India in criticising the human rights situation in Burma.

D

Nuclear Power in India

India has 14 reactors in commercial operation and nine under construction. Nuclear power supplies about 3% of India's electricity. By 2050, nuclear power is expected to provide 25% of the country's electricity. India has limited coal and uranium reserves. Its huge thorium reserves - about 25% of the world's total - are expected to fuel its nuclear power programme long-term.

E

Dr Manmohan Singh said India had finalised a plan to separate its military and civilian nuclear facilities, a move contingent on the deal going through. 'We have made history today,' he said, praising Mr Bush's personal efforts to secure the accord. Under the agreement, India will classify 14 of its 22 nuclear facilities as being for civilian use, and thus open to inspection. France, which signed a similar deal of its own with India last month, said the accord would help fight climate change and non-proliferation efforts..

F

Those opposed to the deal, in the US Congress and elsewhere, disagree. Many supporters of the NPT believe the deal ignores India's nuclear weapons programme. In India, too, critics have alleged that the country's tradition of non-alignment is being eroded as it forges closer ties with the US. India's traditional rival, Pakistan, indicated that it wanted a similar agreement.

'Pakistan believes that we also have a claim, an expectation for international cooperation under safeguards for nuclear power generation,' Pakistani foreign ministry spokeswoman Tasnim Aslam said.

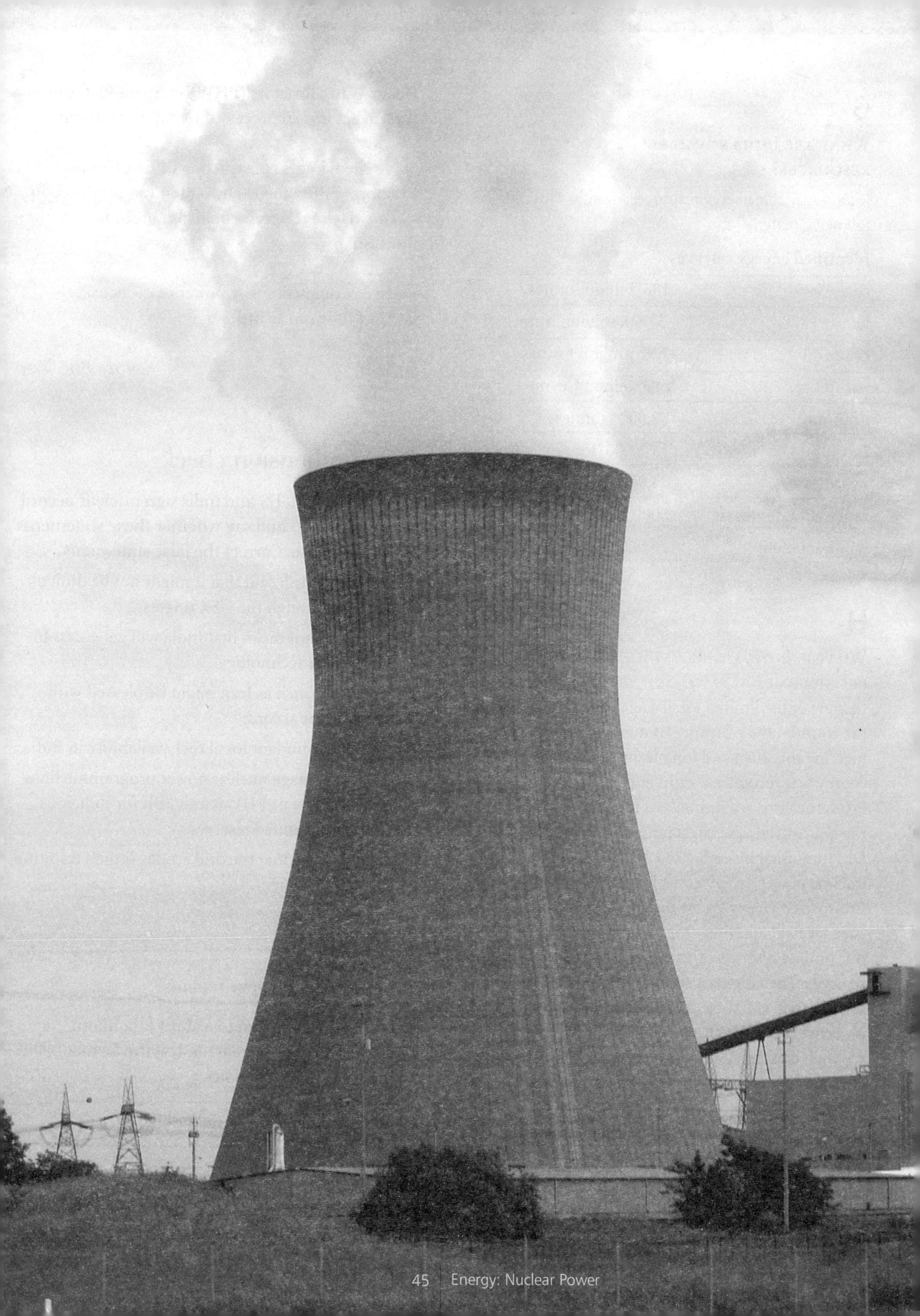

G

WHAT ARE INDIA'S AVAILABLE ENERGY RESOURCES?

India's available energy resources are shown in the following table:

Identified energy reserves

coal	186 billion tonnes
lignite	5,060 million tonnes
crude oil	728 million tonnes
natural gas	686 billion Cu-m
uranium	78,000 tonnes
thorium	3,63,000 tonnes
hydro	84,000 MW at 60 % PLF
renewables biomass	6000 MWe
wind, solar etc.	20,000 MWe

H

WHAT IS INDIA'S THREE-STAGE NUCLEAR POWER PROGRAMME?

In view of the limited fossil fuel availability with the country, the relevance of nuclear power in meeting the short and long term needs of our energy was recognised right at the initial stage. From the very beginning, as a long term strategy, the Nuclear Power Programme formulated by Dr Homi Bhabha embarked on the three stage nuclear power programme, linking the fuel cycle of Pressurised Heavy Water Reactor (PHWR) and Fast Breeder Reactor (FBR) for judicious utilisation of our limited reserves of uranium and vast thorium reserves. The emphasis of the programme was self-reliance and thorium utilisation as a long term objective. The PHWR was chosen due to extensive research and development facilities covering diverse areas for supporting technology absorption.

The three-stage of our nuclear power programme are:

Stage 1: envisages construction of natural uranium, heavy water moderated and cooled Pressurised Heavy Water Reactors (PHWRs). Spent fuel from these reactors is reprocessed to obtain plutonium.

Stage 2: envisages construction of Fast Breeder Reactors (FBRs) fuelled by plutonium produced in stage 1. These reactors would also breed U-233 from thorium.

Stage 3: would comprise power reactors using U-233 / thorium as fuel.

Source: BBC News

Comprehension check

Look at the text 'US and Indis sign nuclear accord' on pages 44-46 and say whether these statements are true or false. Correct the false statements.

i. President Bush said that it might not be difficult to get it through the US Congress.

ii. This does not mean that India will get access to US nuclear technology.

iii. Countries such as Iran might be pleased with this nuclear accord.

iv. There is abundant fossil fuel availability in India.

v. The three-stage nuclear power programme links the fuel cycle of PHWR and FBR for judicious use of our limited reserves.

vi. Critics allege that the deal erodes India's tradition of non-alignment.

Listening

Two kinds of nuclear reactor

You are going to listen to a short talk about two types of nuclear reactor. Use the format below to help you write the notes.

	1	2
types of reactor		

reason for name	
coolant system	
relative merits	
other information	

Using the notes you have made, decide which type of nuclear reactor you would recommend, and make out a case for it. Then defend your choice to your partner. (For a better discussion, don't choose the same reactor as your partner!)

Part 2

✺ Reading

Dangers and disasters

a

Make brief notes to answer these questions.

   i. What dangers do you think can arise from the use of nuclear power?

   ii. Can you think of any possible abuse of nuclear power?

   iii. What instances can you recall of a disaster involving nuclear power?

   iv. What safety measures do you think should be adopted while dealing with nuclear power?

b

Now quickly skim the text below entitled 'Dangers and Disasters' and suggest a suitable heading for each paragraph.

DANGERS AND DISASTERS

A

Nuclear fuels such as uranium and plutonium are radioactive. They give out dangerous and very penetrative radiation. During fission even more radiation is produced. This radiation is harmful even in small quantities. It attacks living tissues and it can alter the genes in body cells. Such mutation can affect later generations. In large quantities its effect is lethal.

B

Nuclear reactors produce wastes which remain dangerously radioactive for hundreds or perhaps thousands of years. The disposal of these wastes is a serious problem. At present, they are often stored in underground tanks or sealed in containers and dropped into deep ocean trenches. Neither method is very satisfactory. The threat of environmental pollution is always there.

C

Nuclear plants need to be suitably located away from densely populated areas. Adequate waste disposal facilities must be available. The reactor ought to be surrounded by concrete and steel walls thick enough to prevent any escape of radiation. The working of the reactor should be slowed down by inserting control rods, also known as neutron absorbing rods, into the core. It is necessary that the reactor has emergency systems to cope with any unexpected failure of the fuel elements of the cooling system. Workers at the plants must protect themselves against possible contamination by using gloves, overshoes, respirators etc. Radiation measuring instruments have to be used to monitor radiation levels in and around the plants. It should be ensured that all releases into air and water are kept well below permissible levels.

c

Does the text answer all the questions in a above?

✱ Language focus

Safety in nuclear plants

a

Underline all the phrases in the third paragraph of the text above which express recommendations (e.g. It should be ensured that ….).

b

Work in pairs. Using the expressions you have just underlined, ask and answer questions about safety measures in nuclear power plants.

Reading

Leaks at India's Nuclear Power Plants

The text below describes the inherent dangers in India's nuclear power reactors in comparison with international standards.

   a. Skim the text for gist. (1 minute)

   b. Read the text quickly, noting which sections discuss the status of India's nuclear power plants.

   c. Make notes about these factors under the headings 'Dangers', 'Standards' and 'Precautions to be taken'.

LEAKS AT INDIA'S NUCLEAR-POWER PLANTS: CAUSE FOR CONCERN?

Even the country's safest reactors do not meet international standards, according to its atomic regulations agency.

Kakrapara Atomic Power Station (KAPS), in the western city of Surat, is India's well-groomed nuclear workhorse. When it comes to controlling radiation leakage, KAPS is 'our best station,' says S.P. Sukhatme, chairman of India's Atomic Energy Regulatory Board (AERB).

That, it turns out, is bad news. KAPS may be India's prized nuclear plant, but radiation emitted from its reactors is three times as much as the international norm, says Mr Sukhatme.

It is a shocking admission that puts the rest of the country's nuclear-power plants in grave perspective. 'The main implication is that other nuclear-power plants are much worse than even Kakrapar,' says Suren Gadekar, considered to be India's top anti-nuclear activist.

There has always been this worry about the possibility of two nuclear-weapons rivals, India and Pakistan, approaching the brink of war. That problem apparently on hold, India's nuclear scientists say the country could still face an equally devastating nuclear catastrophe without a shot being fired.

This time, the threat is not Pakistan or terrorists, but India's power plants themselves. Some scientists say that the plants are so poorly built and maintained and so a Chernobyl-style disaster may be just a matter of time.

'The fact that India's nuclear regulator acknowledges that reactors in India are not operated to the standards of reactors in the US and

Energy: Nuclear Power

Europe is not much of a surprise,' says Christopher Sherry, research director of the Safe Energy Communication Council in Washington. 'But it is very disturbing.' Today, India has 14 nuclear power reactors including two at KAPS. Most are modelled after a design first built in Pennsylvania in 1957. However only three of those nuclear reactors fall under International Atomic Energy Agency (IAEA) standards. The rest, which were built with local technology, are accountable only to national standards set by the AERB.

When the reactor in the state of Rajasthan that first put India on the nuclear world map developed a series of defects, starting with 'turbine-blade failures', the AERB ordered its closure. While the government releases no information about leaks or accidents at its nuclear power plants, Dhirendra Sharma, a scientist who has written extensively on India's atomic-power projects, has compiled figures based on his own reporting. 'An estimated 300 incidents of a serious nature have occurred, causing radiation leaks and physical damage to workers,' he says. 'These have so far remained official secrets.'

The chairman of India's Atomic Energy Commission, Anil Kakodkar, has repeatedly asserted that his group is doing what it can to ensure that the country's power plants are safe. Still, leaks continue to raise serious questions about safety.

Part of the problem, says a former manufacturer of nuclear reactor components, is that well-connected manufacturers are able to cut deals with politicians in India's Department of Energy, often selling defective parts, which are then used to build reactors.

According to Dr Kakodkar, India should not be held accountable to international standards until the international community helps make such technology available to developing countries. 'Safety and technology cannot be divorced,' he says. (Source: V. K. Shashikumar, Special to *The Christian Science Monitor, New Delhi*)

Learner Awareness

What you have been doing is a form of study reading which is useful when you have a clear purpose for your reading.

Writing

Leaks at India's Nuclear Power Plants

Using the notes made in 'c' above, write a paragraph about the need to bring India's nuclear-power plants to required standards. Then write a list of precautions inferred from this.

Follow-up

Writing skills development

a

Use the notes you made from the listening exercise on page 46-7 to complete this paragraph comparing the two types of nuclear reactor.

One of the main differences between the pressurised heavy water reactor and the fast breeder reactor is that the PHWR uses water as a coolant while the fast breeder reactor uses liquid sodium metal for this purpose.

Also…………………. smaller……………..
Therefore…………… more compact………….
……………… higher power density ………….
……………………… lower capital costs ……….
But,…………………. more efficient ……………….
……………………….. twice as much ……………..

b

Write a short paragraph of five sentences expressing your views on the nuclear tests conducted at Pokhran on 11 May 1998.

Energy: Nuclear Power

3

ALTERNATIVE SOURCES

Preparation

✱ Language development

a

Choose suitable words from the box to fill in the gaps in this passage. Use each word only once. The underline indicates stress.

gl<u>o</u>bal	c<u>au</u>sing	ig<u>ni</u>te	pl<u>a</u>gued
spont<u>a</u>neously	contr<u>i</u>buting	part<u>i</u>cularly	d<u>ou</u>sed
geol<u>o</u>gical	disc<u>ar</u>ding		

Scientists warn that wild coal fires are a .... catastrophe, burning hundreds of millions of tonnes of coal every year and .... to climate change and damaging human health.

These fires can rage both above and below ground and may contribute to more than three per cent of the world's annual carbon dioxide emissions, which are thought to be .... global warming.

Coal fires occur wherever there is coal, but major fires blaze in Indonesia, China, India and the US. Underground fires can be .... dangerous as they can burn for decades and .... forest fires in times of drought. Surface fires tend to be .... eventually by rains, but underground fires burn until they exhaust the coal or hit the water table, he said.

Indonesia has been .... with coal fires for two decades, ever since a drought induced by the weather phenomenon El Niño in 1982.

50 | Energy: Alternative Power

Although coal seam fires have occurred .... far back into .... history, they are much more common now. Mining activities like welding, using explosives, or miners simply .... cigarette butts can ignite them. It's almost always someone's hand that does it. Currently 63 fires are being monitored in the US.

b

i. For each word in column A, find a word in column B with the opposite meaning.

A	B
ab<u>un</u>dant	<u>sim</u>ple
arti<u>fi</u>cial	<u>de</u>salination
<u>for</u>mer	<u>na</u>tural
so<u>phis</u>ticated	<u>lat</u>ter
sali<u>na</u>tion	<u>li</u>mited

Learn the correct pronunciation of the words in A and B with your teacher's help.

c

Now complete these sentences with the words in B above.

i. Since the reserves of oil and .... gas are .... we have to look for other energy sources.

ii. The developed countries should help the developing countries so that the .... can meet the basic necessities of their people.

iii. The gobar gas plant, or biogas generator, is a .... apparatus when compared to a nuclear reactor, which is far more ....

iv. In spite of the higher cost involved in the process of ...., it is used on a large scale in many oil-producing countries because there is an acute shortage of water.

Oral practice

Look at the following points. Now tick (✓) those items in the list below that you consider to be the advantages of alternative sources of energy.

causes atmospheric pollution	easily available
renewable	less expensive
involves high technology	can be quickly exhausted

Compare your list with a partner's.

Now say which of the advantages of using alternative source of energy make them appropriate for India. Offer examples to support your opinion.

Be ready to say what you think when your teacher asks you.

Language development

a

Make nouns of the following verbs by adding the suffix -tion.

For example, salinate → salination.

construct	pollute	conserve	destroy
compose	electrify	irrigate	ferment

b

- Make as many words as you can from the following by adding different endings.
- Make sure that you know the meanings of all the words.
- Be ready to put them in sentences to show their meanings when your teacher asks you.

Energy: Alternative Power

e.g. science ⇢ scientific, scientist

   i. photo ⇢ ....
  ii. maintain ⇢ ....
 iii. alternate ⇢ ....
 iv. renew ⇢ ....
  v. inferior ⇢ ....

Part 1

Language focus

Alternative energy sources

a

Complete the text below by selecting the most appropriate word or phrase from the alternatives given in the right-hand column.

The use of alternative .... sources of energy is attractive because of the high price and .... availability of oil, the pollution that is associated with the burning of fossil fuels, the tremendous expense and .... of nuclear power, and a variety of other reasons. In .... countries, their initial development came at a time of relatively plentiful oil supplies at .... cost. This resulted in their being more .... this single source of energy than is true in the ....,.... countries.	artificial/natural abundant/limited dangers/uses developing/ developed lower/higher independent of/ reliant on developing / developed

b

Check your answers with a partner before your teacher checks with the class.

Discussion

Drawbacks of electricity

a

Work in pairs.
List the problems involved in producing and using electricity in India.

b

Read each of the following statements and decide if you think they are true or false. State your reasons.

    i. Alternative natural sources of energy are so cheap, there is no need to use them carefully.
   ii. There are only three renewable sources of energy.
  iii. Energy conservation is cheaper than extra energy production.
  iv. Alternative sources of energy involve little or no environmental pollution or destruction.
   v. These alternative energy technologies are relatively simple in construction and maintenance.
  vi. Alternative energy technologies have a stigma of technical inferiority since they are applicable only to small scale industries.
 vii. The power needs of larger industries can be met by alternative energy units.
viii. Energy from natural sources is not sufficient to meet the fuel needs of the rural masses in India.

Reading

Two alternative energy devices

a

Below are descriptions of two alternative energy devices. One is used in a developing country, the

Philippines, and the other was in common use in a developed country, the United States.
After reading the passages you will be asked to choose the device you feel would be more suitable for use in India.

Pedal Power

Pedalling is probably the most efficient use of the muscles of the human body. Pedal power, using either a bicycle-like pedal arrangement or a treadle mechanism, can be used to power a range of agricultural equipment, water pumps, grinders and electric generators.

At the International Rice Research Institute in the Philippines, engineers have developed a small, lightweight, inexpensive foot-powered pump that will lift large quantities of water several feet, using only moderate amounts of human power. The operator simply stands on two footrests at either end of the pump and rocks back and forth. This effect compresses a diaphragm which forces water from the outlet valve. By operating the pump in a rhythmic manner, a continuous flow of water is pumped.

The Case for Wind Power

For human development to continue, we will ultimately need to find sources of renewable energy. It is difficult to imagine this, but even if we find several hundred or even thousand years of coal and natural gas supplies, what will humans do for the next 250,000 years or so after they are depleted?

There's a lot of underlying popular support for wind energy and the other renewables in the United States. But there's also a lot of apathy as well. We are gulping down the few remaining years of cheap natural gas and Mid East oil. As we do this, the inertia of global warming is inexorably building.

What drives the continued development of mechanical devices like wind turbines in the face of this widespread lack of support? In the case of wind turbine technology, part of the reason for persistence of this vision is how accessible wind turbines are to the understanding. They are personal in a way that almost no other form of power generation is.

Wind energy conversion is a fascinating field because its past has been so checkered and its exact future is so uncertain. Unlike the aerospace industry, the computer industry, and almost any other successful industry you can name, wind energy -- the leading mechanically-based renewable energy for much of man's history-- it has been around for thousands of years.

It's a technology that has been reinvented numerous times. And so, we are left with the promise that there will be success with wind power because of this.

(Source: http://telosnet.com/wind/The Case for Wind Power; © 2002 Darrell Dodge and TelosNet Web Development)

b

Complete this chart with information from the texts you have just read.

	pedal power	windmill
resources needed		
machinery needed		
possible uses		

Writing

A device for rural India

Consider both pedal and wind power in the context of rural India. Fill in the chart below to help you compare their relative merits.

in the rural Indian context	pedal power	wind power
necessary resources available?		
necessary machinery available?		
machinery sufficiently familiar?		
local construction possible?		
maintenance simple enough?		
uses required?		

Now use the chart you have just completed to write a paragraph explaining which of these devices would be more suitable for use in rural India. Plan your paragraph with the help of the chart.

Part 2

Discussion

Energy for cooking

In pairs, decide what energy source might be used for cooking in the following places:

a five-star hotel   a houseboat in Kashmir
a village hotel   an open-air tea shop
a mountain region   an apartment in New York
an industrial canteen   a fast-food place

Reading

Alternative sources of energy

a

Take a quick glance (1 minute only) at the texts on pages 54-6, and then decide whether they come from

  i. an advertisement
  ii. a government handbook, or
  iii. a magazine.

b

Here are six titles. Match each one with the relevant text on the next page. After completing this task, check your answers with a partner.

  i. Wave Power from the West
  ii. Biogas Plants
  iii. Seaweed Power
  iv. Iceland's Economy
  v. Offshore Wind
  vi. Solar-powered Car Sets New World Record

A

A team of Canadian students from Ontario, has set a new world record for the longest distance travelled in a solar-powered vehicle. Over 30 days, driving at average speeds of 80 kmph, the sleek, aerodynamic car, Radiance, travelled 7,044 kilometres from Halifax, Nova Scotia, to Vancouver, British Columbia.

The Sun Trek 2000 expedition hoped to demonstrate the potential of renewable energy to communities along their route. During the month-long trip Radiance used the equivalent of just £4 worth of electricity compared with over £600 in diesel fuel for a support vehicle.

According to the project's designers, the vehicle's solar panels worked well, powering the electric motor and storing excess energy in batteries for cloudy days.

B

Iceland is making plans to become the world's first hydrogen-powered economy. With backing from the Icelandic government, a consortium is using Iceland as the testing ground for a new generation of hydrogen-powered cars and buses. At present 70 per cent of the primary energy supply and 99.9 per cent of the country's electricity is produced by geothermal energy and hydropower. Iceland, however, consumes more oil per capita than any other country in the world, and the next challenge is to convert the transportation economy to renewable energy. By 2002 the country's first fuel cells will run three Reykjavik buses at a cost of $1.25 million each, with plans to eventually power the city's 100 buses by hydrogen fuel-cell technology.

Iceland currently produces 2,000 tons of hydrogen annually, primarily to produce ammonia for making fertiliser. Between 80,000 to 90,000 tons would be needed to power the country's entire transportation sector and fishing fleets. "We believe that we can eliminate most of our dependence on oil by 2030," Hjalmar Arnason, chairman of the Icelandic government's committee for alternative fuel is reported as saying. Reducing its annual oil bill to almost zero would have a significant impact on the Icelandic economy, and could transform the already wealthy Icelanders into hydrogen sheiks of the future.

C

Two of the world's most powerful wind turbines are to be raised off the UK coast by the consortium Blyth Offshore Wind Limited. Each turbine is capable of generating two megawatts of electricity and in total will provide enough electricity to power 3,000 households annually.

The turbines will be the largest ever to be erected offshore and will also be the first to be placed in such a demanding position, subject to the full forces of the North Sea. The twin turbines are due to be installed a kilometre or so from the coast of Northumberland in the summer, and will start generating electricity in August. The turbines will be installed at an average depth of eight metres by the marine division of AMEC Capital Projects and Seacore.

The UK is one of the windiest countries in Europe, with the offshore resource theoretically sufficient to supply the UK's current electricity needs three times over.

D

Considering that 680 million cars and lorries now cram our roads worldwide, the need for alternative energy sources is greater than ever before. Biomass fuel is a source of energy derived from living organisms, commonly plant residue (dried, burned or processed into solid, liquid or gaseous fuels). The global potential of biomass energy has been estimated at 100 million megawatts per year, 35 per cent of which is from marine biomass. Marine biomass can be used to produce electricity and fuels with the added advantage of being grown in the ocean, freeing valuable agricultural land. More than five million tons of seaweed is farmed in China, Japan and the Philippines for biomass every year. The ocean is the only region that has space and sufficient water for large-scale cultivation of new primary biomass, and efforts are under way to develop marine cultivation as well as realise its limitations and constraints.

E

The biogas generator is a simple apparatus for turning animal dung into biogas and nitrogen fertiliser. Animal dung can be supplemented by organic wastes, water hyacinth, corn stalks, wild grass and aquatic weeds.

Biogas is a gas mixture containing about 60 per cent methane and 40 per cent carbondioxide. The mixing of equal parts of animal dung, water hyacinth and algae results in upto 70 per cent of methane being produced. A one-acre plot of water hyacinth would yield 1100 cu ft of gas per day or 400,000 cu ft/yr which is equivalent to 60 MW power. Biogas can be used as a fuel for domestic cooking or for running diesel engines.

F

A team of European researchers and small businesses, coordinated by the University of Plymouth, have invented a new device for harnessing the power of the waves.

The new 'Wave Energy Device' comprises a column or cylinder, five metres in diameter, which extends some 14 metres below the surface of the sea. The device is based on the principle of multiple water columns which oscillate owing to the movement of the waves. Air in the columns, under pressure from the water below, drives a turbine to generate power.

In the short term the device could supply energy to remote islands and offshore installations with a future potential to supply coastal communities.

G

Now read the passages again more carefully in order to answer the following questions. Use the titles to help you find the relevant part of the passage for each question.

i. List the element(s) from which each different source of energy is being derived. What do they have in common?

ii. Why is such intensive research being carried out to discover viable alternative sources of energy?

iii. Is there a direct link between a country's consumption of fossil fuels and its quest for alternatives?

iv. Which of the above sources would have universal application and which would not? State the reasons for your answer.

v. Is development a major factor in the adoption of an alternative energy source?

Role play

Renewable energy sources

Student A

You are a journalist writing a feature article on a village that makes productive use of alternative energy sources. The people of the village are proud of their self-reliance. Prepare a list of questions to ask the sarpanch of the village as well as a few other villagers.

Student B

You are the sarpanch of a village that is becoming famous for its use of alternative sources of energy. You and some other villagers are going to be interviewed by a journalist. Prepare a list of points that will help you to answer questions. Be as imaginative as possible.

Start when you are both ready.

Try to keep the interview quite formal.

Energy: Alternative Power

Writing

Energy for India

Choose a form of energy which you consider to be suitable for further development in India. You may look back at the work of the last three weeks for ideas. Write three short paragraphs in the way described below.

paragraph 1 : Introduce India's energy needs.

paragraph 2 : Compare your choice with other alternatives.

paragraph 3 : Summarise the advantages of your chosen form of energy.

Follow-up

Comprehension check

a

Before your teacher talks to you about pedal power, read these sentences.

i. Pedal power can only be used for one type of agricultural equipment.
ii. The foot-powered pump developed in the Philippines will lift large quantities of water.
iii. This pump needs a great amount of human power.
iv. It does not weigh very much but it is expensive.
v. It is not possible to pump a continuous flow of water using this pump.

b

Now listen to your teacher and decide if the sentences are true or false.

Language check

Your teacher will dictate a passage to you about wind power. Check your spelling and punctuation carefully with reference to the text on page 53.

Oral practice

a

Using the chart you prepared on page 54 ask and answer questions. Work with another student.

b

Say which of these devices would be more suitable for use in rural India. State your reasons. Try and make use of appropriate comparative adjectives.

Language check

Wind power phones

Choose words from the box and fill in the appropriate blanks in the passage.

protect	wind	energy
source	conventional	power
constant	operate	damage
environment	quietest	cheaper

One 2 One is a mobile phone company based in the United Kingdom. It is taking the lead in testing the use of .... turbines to power its base stations in remote parts of the country in a move to .... the environment.

The first mobile phone base station in the UK to use the wind as an .... has been erected by One 2 one at Cairnsaigh Hill in Scotland.

The 7.5-meter-high wind turbine can provide all the .... needed by the base station. Unlike the .... stations, where winter power failures may require the use of diesel generators, the wind turbine can .... all year round, however strong the wind. A unique blade-feathering device keeps the blades spinning at a .... speed no matter how strong the wind gets.

The wind turbine provides free, reliable, ... friendly power and also avoids .... caused to the health of people when electricity cables are installed.

"Under the right conditions a turbine can be considerably .... than mains power", said Greg Mould, One 2 one's health, safety and environment adviser. "In addition, its environmental impact is about as small as it's possible to get".

A low rotor speed makes it one of the .... wind turbines in the world and a patented polypropylene blade design allows the turbine to function at full power in speeds of upto 240 kilometers (150 miles) per hour.

58 | Resources: Water

THEME

computers

1

Introducing Computers

Preparation

✺ Language development

a

In any science, it is vital to be precise about terminology. Definitions of key terms are needed.

Decide which of the following are definitions, and which are not.

i. A laboratory is a room which is used for experimenting.

ii. A computer is an expensive machine.

iii. A calculator is a machine which can perform arithmetical and some other logical operations.

iv. Mathematics is a very ancient subject.

v. Petroleum is a fuel used by motor engines such as buses and cars.

✺ A good definition should be precise, and it should identify the item you are defining beyond any doubt. In a formal definition the term being defined is first assigned to a class or group to which it belongs and is then set apart from other terms in the class. For example, an expensive machine in the sentence 'A computer is an expensive 'machine' could be a car, a space rocket or many other things. A good definition is completed by some form of restriction clause and has the structure shown below.

(A) (**term**) is (a) (**class**) which or that (**specific detail**)

Using this formula we can define the following:

- A solar cell is a device which converts the energy of sunlight into electrical energy.
- A camera is an instrument that is used for taking photographs.
- An endoscope is an instrument that doctors use to look inside the body.

Now, try to write definitions of an abacus, log tables, a telephone and a compact disc. Use the pattern given above.

b

Try to guess the meanings of the words in capital letters by looking at the examples.

SCREEN	a cinema screen – a TV screen
SOURCE	an energy source – the source of the Ganga – the source of the problem
CAPACITY	a one-litre capacity bottle – capacity of bus: 70 passengers
DEVICE	a measuring device – a device for heating food – a balancing device
DISPLAY	food on display in a market – an aeronautics display – a display of skill
MEMORY	a memory like an elephant – a calculator with a memory – a short memory
POWER	electric power – nuclear power – wind power – political power

Make sure you can pronounce all these words correctly. Your teacher will help you.

Compound nouns are made by putting two suitable nouns together:

power source	a source of power
arithmetic unit	a unit in which arithmetic is performed
mains electricity	electricity which comes from the mains

c

Discuss these compound nouns with your partner and then explain them.

energy source	control centre
cassette tape	calculator memory
calculation speed	video screen
machine language	data input
word processor	keyboard
disk drive	item code

✼ Oral practice

✼ When you compare two things, you do so on the basis of features, or parameters applicable to both. It is important to remember that things are explained through comparison and also defined by comparison. Thus, you may compare a person with an elephant on the basis of weight or lifespan and say,

The elephant is heavier than a human.

The elephant lives longer than a human.

a

Suppose you want to compare logarithm tables with a pocket calculator. With your partner first decide on some features you want to compare, such as cost or energy source. Once you find at least three items, fill in the second and third columns.

62 | Computers: Introducing Computers

Parameters for comparison	Log Tables	Calculator
cost		
energy source		

b

Using the table, compare log tables with calculators, like this:

A What about an energy source?

B Well... log tables... but calculators ...

Writing skills development

a

The words *but*, *however*, *whereas* and *while* have something in common. What is it?

Decide whether each of these words can be used:

  only at the beginning of a sentence

  only in the middle of a two-clause sentence

  in either position

b

Use your comparison table to write a paragraph comparing log tables with calculators. Write one or two sentences for each line of your chart. Use the words you studied in b on page 62.

Part 1

Discussion

Information processing

A living brain can be thought of as a device for processing information. Information reaches the brain through, for example, the eye.

Name other ways in which input about the world reaches the brain. What is the output of a brain?

Listening

A computer is an artificial device for processing information. There are several ways in which computers are able to obtain input, and several ways in which output can be produced.

You're going to listen to a short talk about these input and output devices. Before you start to listen, copy the diagram below into your notebook, leaving space to write where you see the dotted lines.

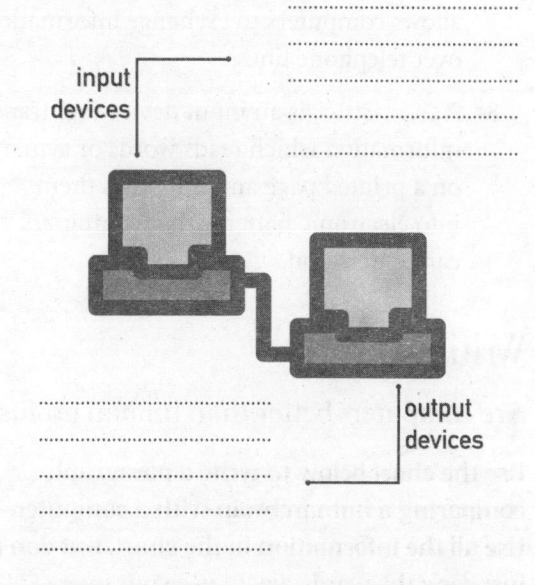

Now check your answers carefully (including your spelling!) with your partner.

Language focus

Computer hardware

Using intelligent guesswork, complete these definitions of some of the items you have just listed. Write them in your notebook.

1. A ………….. is an input device that is used in computer games to move the cursor or other objects on the VDU.
2. A ………….. is an input device which is used to type in information.
3. A ………….. is an ………….. device which can be used to write directly on the monitor screen and read information from bar codes.
4. A ………….. is an input device which moves over a surface and gives instruction to computers.
5. A ………….. is an ………….. device which displays characters and graphics on a television-like screen.
6. A ………….. is an output device which puts the data for the computer on paper or in special film.
7. A ………….. is an output device which allows computers to exchange information over telephone lines.
8. A ………….. is an input device that transfers information which reads words or symbols on a printed page and translates them into electronic patterns that computers can understand.

Writing

Are computers better than human brains?

Use the chart below to write a paragraph comparing a human brain with a computer. Use all the information in the chart, but don't just copy the words: try to use your own. Use the words *however*, *while* and *whereas* to make your comparisons clearer.

	the human	a computer brain
WEIGHT	about 1.5 kg	from a few grams to tons
ENERGY SOURCES	blood glucose	electricity
TEMPERATURE NEEDED	fairly steady	not very sensitive to change
NO. OF PARTS	approx 10^{11}	approx 10^{11}
LOCATION OF PARTS	inside skull	could even be in different countries
MEMORY	probably unlimited capacity	capacity limited by technology
SPEED OF CALCULATION	slow compared to a computer	extremely fast

64 | Computers: Introducing Computers

Part 2

Reading

'IT for all'—only a slogan?

This is an extract from 'Can Information Technology Help Transform India?' by Ashok Jhunjhunwala. Read it carefully and answer the questions that follow.

What is normally regarded as India's greatest weakness – the large population – can also be a strength. It represents a large potential market. This potential can be converted into reality only if IT products are affordable to a large section of its people, and this is indeed a difficult task. This is one of the reasons why India is yet to be converted into a large internal market in which Indian companies can learn and consolidate. Without this, it is difficult to compete in the world market.

After a new product is introduced in the West, it is continuously innovated upon to bring down the price till it is widely affordable. Beyond this, there is little motivation to further bring down the price. All innovations thereafter are geared to improve features while the price is kept constant. Unfortunately, this affordable price level in the West is affordable to only the top few of the population in a country like India.

To make it affordable to a larger cross-section, innovations different from those pursued in the West are required. The price of the product has to be brought down to a third or a fourth of its price in the West to make it affordable to even 20 per cent of the Indian population. However, 20 per cent of the Indian population is a large market, and can fuel unprecedented growth.

Without such steps, "IT for all" will remain a slogan used as a cover for policies to enrich the lives of a few. It is not that IT has made no difference so far in India. The introduction of IT has made some noticeable differences—railway ticket bookings is probably the most visible example. Small shops and offices are now installing computers. There are many small software companies located in garages. They have served the Indian market, and have gradually grown.

However, it is Internet access which has transformed computers from mere computing machines to drivers of the information age. The problem however, is that widespread Internet access pre-supposes a widespread telecom network and access to telephones. It is generally not known that a telephone in India costs upwards of Rs 30,000 to instal. Taking a mere 15 per cent as yearly finance charges on investment, and 15 per cent as yearly operation, maintenance and obsolescence charges, an operator requires a minimum revenue of 30 per cent of Rs 30,000, or Rs 9,000, a year from each telephone to break even. This implies that our telephone bills need to exceed Rs 9,000 per year. Even with cross-subsidy (a smaller number of people generating much higher revenues) not more than 3-4 per cent of the people in India could afford telephones.

How do we talk about providing Internet for all without facing this basic issue?

Why is the cost of installing a basic telephone in India as high as Rs 30,000? This is because this cost, in the West, amounts to an easily affordable $800. The West has little motivation to significantly bring down the cost any further. The emphasis, instead, is on adding features, while keeping the cost constant.

It is here that scientists from countries like India have to wrest the initiative, and aim to reduce the per-line cost of telephone and Internet access to a much lower value, say Rs 10,000. At such levels, it would be immediately affordable to over 15 per cent of population, and with cross-subsidy, to a much larger percentage.

The task is not merely to free the corporate sector and some of those who can benefit from the removal of various regulations currently slowing them down. We need to analyse what needs to be done to have IT in the hands of hundreds of millions of people. A concrete program has to be made so that in some time frame (say 10 years), IT is looked upon by a large section of people as liberating, rather than as yet another technology that pushes them into the category of have-nots. It will not do if the country has to depend for ever on imported high-cost telecom infrastructure—the $50 billion software export goal should not be based on a $50 billion import. Unless various sections of our people from all walks of life, from the towns as well as the villages, participate in this effort, the IT industry will remain a small part of our relatively small economy.

a

Say which words in the above passage convey the following meanings?

strengthen	takes as a given
basic requirements	new features
grab	apparent
well-planned	ageing

b

Which sentences in the passage tell you that

i. Western technology is constantly working to improve an invention.
ii. Unless prices in India are brought down, innovations will remain out of the reach of most people.
iii. However, IT has definitely changed the Indian scenario.
iv. Telephone bills have to be very high in order for the network to be viable.
v. India should become technologically self-sufficient.

Role play

Explaining computers

Work in pairs.

Student A

You are a schoolmaster, and you have heard that next year your school will be given a computer. You are not at all sure what that is, or what the school will use it for. Prepare a list of questions to ask your son, who is on holiday from his studies at university.

Student B

You are an engineering student visiting your schoolmaster father. You expect he will ask you to tell him about computers. Prepare what you can tell him.

Start when you both are ready.

Follow-up

✱ Language check

e-Learning

There are some mistakes in the language in this passage. Find them and correct them.

eLearning is a activity that utilise electronic technology, such as email, websites, multimedia, information from the Internet, etc. To be very specific, it is a tool and method for providing instructional content or various learning experiences through an electronic network, which can be customised for specific business needs. This differs from conventional training in many ways. eLearning can be interactive, which generates an atmosphere that is more appropriate to learning for employees. By engaging directly, employees are more willing to participate. eLearning is memorable and easy to understand. With the ability to organise material into level-specific topics, employees know better what their employers expect them to learn and can spend more time focused on those issues identified as high priority.eLearning is adjustable and flexible. Not all employees are created equal. Therefore it would difficult to assume that one training module will fit all equally. The customisation of eLearning tools allows employers to account for different levels of competence and knowledge.eLearning is resourceful in nature. In the normal and usual classroom training module an instructor is not able to provide attention support to all students whereas eLearning tools are direct and are utilised at the individual's pace. eLearning is easily accessible, which would be the most valuable function of tool. With large number of workers access to computers while on the job, trainees can go through training sessions at their own pace and on their own schedule. Because of this feature employees need not leave their existing jobs unattended while receiving training. In most of the cases, employees are granted permission to take the courses on their personal computers at home.

This can save corporations huge amounts of money in efficiency and overtime.In kind of system, the costs of rent, cost of tuition for each employee related to infrastructure, etc. are all done away. And most of the time, the absence of employees must be filled with overtime worker which certainly add to the cost.

(Source: info@techsers.com; © 1999–2004 Techsers and/or its affiliates)

✱ Writing skills development

You have been asked to write a short and simple explanation of what a computer is, for a children's book. Write about sixty words, and draw a simple diagram to illustrate the definition. Write your explanation in the present tense, and make your sentences short.

2
NEW FRONTIERS

Preparation

✻ Language development

a

First, make sure that you can pronounce all the words in column A correctly. Then try to match each word in column A with its meaning in column B. Work with a partner.

A	B
fi̱ction	not belonging to the earth
fa̱ntasy	electronic device producing awareness of the surroundings
extrarre̱strial	device composed of silicon
ro̱bot	not factual
se̱nsor	material whose conductivity at room temperature lies between that of metals and insulators
na̱tural la̱nguage	wild imagination
artifi̱cial	the faculty of verbal expression and the use
inte̱lligence	of words in human communication
chip	machine which can perform some of the actions of a human being or animal
semicondu̱ctor	electronic device which can perform a range of basic logical functions upon given signals
microproce̱ssor	the capacity of a computer for learning and decision taking similar to human intelligence

b

You have just looked at the words *microprocessor* and *semiconductor*. The prefix **micro-** means *small* and the prefix **semi-** means *half*. Think of six other words, three with the prefix **micro-** and three with the prefix **semi-**. Use them in sentences of your own. Compare your work with your partner.

Oral practice

Classification is the systematic arrangement of persons or things in groups or under specific headings, based on features, characteristics, etc.
For example, **stone**, **water** and **oxygen** can be classified under the headings **solid**, **liquid** and **gas**, respectively. **Iron** and **wood** can be classified under the headings **metallic substances** and **non-metallic substances**. Similarly, animals can be classified into **domestic** and **wild** categories.

Now try to to classify computers under different headings. State the basis of the classification. Work in consultation with your partner. If you have any difficulty, your teacher will help you.

Language development

Here is a list of useful expressions. Make sure you know what each one means.

orientation towards	in view of
call for	on the part of
on the lines of	resort to

Now use the above expressions to complete the text below.

Computer education in universities and colleges today leaves much to be desired. .... the importance of the subject, much thought needs to be given to the improvement of computer education at these levels. It is of little use teaching computing .... the traditional, theoretical approach to the subject. On the contrary, it .... a great deal of imagination .... computer lecturers to present their subject in a clear and interesting way. Rather than theorise about computing principles, they must .... actual demonstrations and hands-on experience in the classroom. The really valuable part of computer learning is an .... the quick solution of everyday problems.

Discussion

Work in groups of two or three.

a

What are some of the areas of activity in which computers are being used today?

b

Are you aware of some specific uses to which computers are put?

c

What possible directions do you think computer development will take in the future in India?

Part 1

Reading

Science fiction

a

Read the text on science fiction and note down your answers to these questions.

   i. Name some writers of science fiction.
   ii. What are some of the themes in science fiction?
   iii. Do you think that science fiction could have any harmful effects on society?
   iv. Does science fiction sometimes come true?

b

Skim the text on SCIENCE FICTION and locate

i. the phrase which indicates that this is science fiction.
ii. sentences or phrases which may not belong in other kinds of fiction.

Try to do this in less than two minutes.

Science fiction is one of the most popular forms of literature. It commands a very wide reading public. Many writers all over the world are trying to produce it. As the name itself indicates, it is a mixture of fiction and reality where adventures are set against the background of tomorrow. It is this orientation towards the future which endears it to young people and those in the forefront of science. Some of the greatest writers of science fiction such as Arthur Clarke, Isaac Asimov, Robert Heinlein, Johan Taine, Edward Smith, Leo Szilard, Otto Frisch, Fred Hoyle, Chad Oliver, Stanislaw Lem and Norbert Wiener were themselves renowned scientists or engineers.

Some of the major themes dealt with by science fiction are space travel to and from other planets, solar systems and galaxies; exploration, settlement and exploitation of other worlds; encounters with or between extraterrestrial life forms; time travel to the future or the past; psychological and biological changes in humans brought about by nature or science and similar changes in other species; supernatural powers and talents achieved either through technology or the advancement of such 'fringe sciences' as parapsychology; and science, applied directly or indirectly, to human relations for either constructive or destructive purposes.

Language focus

Robots

Robots were once fictional. Now, computerisation has made them a reality. Read the text below carefully once, then try to fill in the gaps with the most appropriate word from those given.

person	sequence	commonly
sensors	benevolent	efficiency
version	limited	mechanical
malevolent	past	future
react	gripping	artificial
numerous	sense	correspond
refer	machine	

A robot is a ……………………. which can perform some of the actions of a human being or animal.

The kind of robot that is now ……………. in use is a machine which carries out a …………… of operations under computer control. The association of robots with science fiction has served to project them as nightmarish, ………………….. automatons. But the industrial robots now in use seem anything but dreadful. They can tirelessly perform monotonous and exhausting physical tasks with maximum ………………………. and minimum supervision.

A newer …………………… of robots is the one with electronic 'senses'. The robot is fitted with ………………………………. in the form of radar devices and microphones with which it can detect movements and hear noises. The robot's radar and microphones ……………………… to human eyes and ears. In addition to 'sight' and 'hearing' the robot can have a ………………………. of 'touch', too, via pressure pads which show how tightly they are ……………………. something, and can also sense heat and cold. Though human beings can …………………………. in a great number of ways to the information supplied to the brain through the senses, a robot's responses are …………………………. .

Robots of the ……………………….. might be endowed with ……………………. intelligence. They would then perform not merely mechanical operations, but react to unforeseen circumstances and make decisions. They might play games, solve problems and use natural language.

Check your answers with your partner.

Writing

Robots

Do task a or b.

a

Write a paragraph about robots. In your first sentence, define a robot. Then classify robots on the basis of the information in the text.

b

It is some time in the not-too-distant future, and you have decided to order a household robot which will be designed to suit your requirements. First, list the household tasks which you expect the robot to perform, then sort these tasks into broad categories.

Write a paragraph (which is part of a letter) to the robot factory stating what you require. Begin like this:

There are several types of tasks my robot must be able to perform.
Firstly, …

Part 2

Listening

Silicon Valley and Apple

a

You are going to listen to a talk about Silicon Valley and Apple. In pairs quickly discuss what you know about Silicon Valley and Apple.

b

Listen carefully and take notes. If you need help, a chart like this may help you organise your notes:

Silicon Valley	Apple
‣ where located	‣ what it is
‣ why so called	‣ its co-founder and chairman
‣ what it was 50 years ago	‣ his background
‣ what it is now	‣ his contribution
‣ its economic status	‣ its economic status
‣ how it can be described	‣ its impact

Computers: New Frontiers

Discussion

The myths of artificial intelligence

Every decade technology and science provide us with new keywords and terms such as 'virtual reality', 'fuzzy logic', 'artificial intelligence' and many others. Among these, 'artificial intelligence', the idea of making computers and machinery think, learn and even correct itself from its own mistakes, just like human beings, is a concept that may have brought about countless discussions, disagreements, arguments, misunderstandings and wrong hopes. Myths and fiction influence persons who regard the computer as an almighty tool. Since these people usually do not know much about computers and algorithms, it is necessary to present what is really happening behind the scenes of this scientific discipline. The fact that even experts are split into two schools of thought does not make it easier to discuss the real essence of artificial intelligence.

Some believe in artificial intelligence and are convinced that it will exist soon. Others argue against it and regard it as impossible to make computers act intelligently. All misunderstandings are due to different points of view and different definitions of intelligence. Considering the true and deep meaning of intelligence, it is obvious that computers can never act intelligently.

We could discuss the definitions of intelligence to understand these opinions. We might say that intelligence refers to a large collection of data, a compilation of knowledge, as may be maintained by the CIA (Central Intelligence Agency), for example. This definition might justify the point of view of experts arguing for artificial intelligence. Others may say that true intelligence cannot be presented without consciousness.

Of course, advanced computer systems may even be capable of successfully passing intelligence tests.

If we discuss the etymological background of the word 'intelligence' we would understand its real meaning.

The word 'intelligence' is derived from the Latin word 'intellegere', to understand, to perceive, to recognise and to realise.

Dividing the word into its two parts would reveal further details. 'Legere', the second part of the word by itself means to select, to choose and to gather. The first part of the word comes from the prefix 'inter-', which generally means 'between'. Interpreting the combination of these words could indicate that intelligence is the ability to establish abstract links between details that do not necessarily have any obvious relationship.

When people refer to a computer programme as being intelligent, what is it that may make it appear so? There are certain qualities of the computer that make its actions or responses seem intelligent. Most essentially, a computer is much faster than the human brain when it comes to searching data, number crunching, playing a game, applying rules or finding general solutions to a problem. A computer may appear to be intelligent, because only meaningful responses or solutions to a specific question are filtered out and displayed. Due to the speed, it seems as if the algorithm is not even considering any obviously wrong attempts. That, of course, is not true. In most cases the programme will consider every possibility, even those that are destined to fail right from the beginning.

(Source: Judea Pearl, Heuristics, *Reading, Massachusetts: Addison-Wesley, 1984. Web Page created in February 1995 by Attila Narin http://www.narin.com/attila © 1993, 1995 Attila Narin*)

Follow-up

Language development

Look back at the text 'Myths of Artificial Intelligence' and notice how the following modal verbs are used.

modals	use
can	
could	
would	
may	
might	

Classify them according to the degree of probability they express:

    definite (100% probability)
    probable
    possible
    impossible (0% probability)

Learner Awareness

In English, modals are used to express certain moods for which the language has no inflected verb forms. We can express such concepts as ability (*can, could*), possibility (*may, might*), permission (*may, might, can* and *could*) or obligation (*must* and *ought*).

Modals go along with the base form of a verb. For example, *She cannot sing*. Modals cannot take the 's' form in the third person singular and also the 'ing' or 'ed' forms. For example, *He can do the task./ They must go there*. Modals are used in question tags:
You will come, won't you?
She can write well, can't she?
Questions are formed by placing the modal before the subject: *Could you please shut the door?/May I leave now?*

Oral practice

Look at the following headlines.

- **COMPUTERS REPLACE CHILD'S REAL PARENTS**
  - **METEOROLOGISTS REDUNDANT. COMPUTERS TAKE OVER**
- **COMPUTERS TO REPLACE MARRIAGE BROKERS**
  - **PERFECT SPELLING BY COMPUTER**
- **COMPUTERS DECLARE STRIKE**
  - **COMPUTER DIAGNOSIS MORE ACCURATE THAN DOCTORS**
- **COMPUTER AWARDED Ph.D.**

Using the modal verbs you have studied, make statements expressing how probable you think these events are. For example:
A computer can never replace a child's real parents.

3
COMPUTERS IN INDIA

Preparation

✼ Oral practice

In pairs, discuss the following.

a

Has the introduction of computers affected the employment situation in India?

b

Do you know any examples of large-scale computerisation in India?

c

Do you think that computers may eventually replace teachers in classrooms? If yes, mention some reasons.

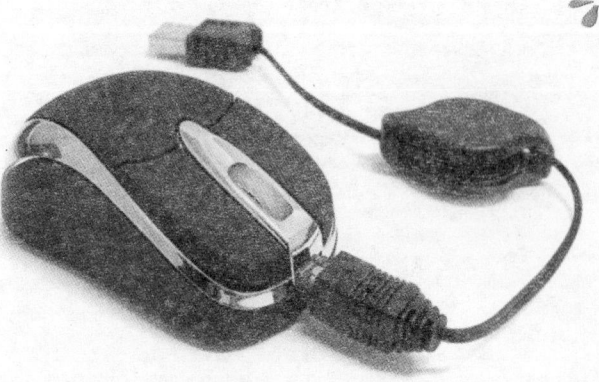

✼ Language development

Work in pairs. Try to guess the meanings of the word underlined in each of these sentences. The context will help you.

a

Some people argue that computerisation will <u>aggravate</u> the unemployment problem.

b

One of India's <u>priorities</u> is to grow more food.

c

There are <u>countless</u> opportunities for work for qualified computer personnel.

d

The crux of the matter is training. Without adequate training the Indian industry cannot progress.

e

Many projects are being held up owing to a paucity of funds.

f

The Indian government is taking steps to streamline the working of the railways through computerisation.

g

Indian agriculture is affected by the vagaries of weather so even computers cannot produce accurate production forecasts.

h

To deepen our understanding, we need to look at problems from different perspectives.

> **Learner Awareness**
>
> When you come across a word whose meaning you do not know, the context will often help you guess the approximate meaning.

Reading skills development

a

Before reading the following text, make a list of things which you feel may have been made possible by the introduction of computers in Indian Airlines.

b

As you read the text, go through your list. Place a tick ( ) by the items you had thought of, and add to your list any points mentioned in the text which you had not thought of.

Today seats can be reserved on IA flights instantly with the aid of a computer at the international and domestic airports. The remaining stations in the country are connected to the central system by teletype links. Tickets are printed automatically in the major cities.

Another facility that has been made possible by computerisation is the Flight Information System which provides updated information of the departure and arrival times of flights. This information can be displayed on screens in the passenger lounges.

Meteorological information is of vital importance to a flight; the crew will find such information most useful, since flights may have to be delayed or cancelled or diverted if the weather does not permit safe landing or take-off. The computer provides up-to-the-minute information on the conditions in the airports, and the information can be displayed on the screen at any airport from where a plane is due to take off.

c

Did your list help you to read more efficiently?

Writing skills development

Write definitions of the words in the first column by using words and expressions from the second and third columns.

an arithmetic unit	a chart	which can perform some of the movements of a person or animal
a computer	a device	which shows the sequence of steps in a programme for solving a problem on a computer
a flow chart	a machine	which tells the computer what to do
a microprocessor	a part of the computer	which can accept and process data and give an output of the result
a printer	a set of instructions	in which calculations are done
a programme	a silicon chip	which can print out information from a computer.
a robot		which can do the same jobs as the parts inside a computer

---

Part 1

Language focus

An adjective inventing task.

Look at the following expressions.

voltage-controlled oscillator

time-consuming process

ferrous-oxide-coated tape

Notice how the past participle (**-ed**) and present participle (**-ing**) forms of verbs are used to form compound adjectives.

a

The first of these expressions means 'an oscillator which is controlled by voltage'.
What do the other two mean?

b

What is the difference between

a computer-controlled machine

and   a computer-controlling machine

c

Now make similar, meaningful expressions by choosing one item from each column. How many expressions can you make?

binary	-aided	circuits
card	-coded	decimal
computer	-coupled	design
data	-loading	logic
emitter	-made	machine
ready	-processing	packages
self	-punching	systems

d

Can you think of any more examples from the field of computer science?

Reading

Employing computers

a

Discuss the following in small groups.

1. Do you think that the introduction of computers has lead to unemployment?

2. Are there any advantages in the computerisation of work in large establishments? If so, what are they?

3. Do you know of any Indian organisations which have introduced computerisation? In which area would computerisation be useful?

b

Skim the text below and

1. Say which of these describes the name of the text:

    descriptive
    expository
    argumentative
    narrative

2. Choose the best alternative to complete this statement.

    ▼ The aim of the author is to compare the computer revolution with the Industrial Revolution.

    ▼ to suggest a solution to the problem of unemployment.

    ▼ to describe the benefits of computerisation.

3. Now read the text more carefully and answer the questions which follow it.

EMPLOYING COMPUTERS

Some time ago the most <u>vehement</u> opposition to computerisation came from people who believed that it would lead to unemployment. The <u>hue and cry</u> was based on the argument that computers would <u>aggravate</u> the unemployment situation by taking jobs away from human beings.

However, the year 2001 tells a different story. The cause of unemployment is not a matter of too few jobs for too many people. There are many people without work and yet <u>countless</u> jobs that need to be done. It is imperative that India – with its population crossing the one billion mark – fulfils the basic requirements of the poor and homeless, <u>improve</u> its infrastructure and yet be on par with global standards of technology.

It has been established that the computerisation of an economy increases its <u>efficiency</u> and productivity while bringing about savings in cost; funds are generated and additional employment is created. But the paradox of India is its millions of poor people lacking the basic means of survival even while the rest of the world recognises the invaluable worth of its technological industry.

India's track record in the field of technology is now well known. There is a great demand for software professionals from India. At the same time there is a great deal of foreign investment in the technology sector.

Computers are now <u>extensively</u> employed in private and government sectors like banks, hotels, airlines, media, multinational business houses. Videsh Sanchar Nigam Limited (VSNL) supports infrastructure for most nationalised banks, smallscale industries and for the individual user as well. Many of these companies use networking systems like Wide Area Network (WAN) and

Local Area Network (LAN) extensively. More recently in India, GenPact and Office Tiger have gone to the extent of maintaining their own lease
40 lines to <u>enhance</u> business. Another feature in communication that multinational businesses and media houses have is the intranet facility which links their offices globally. Nuclear and defence establishments use supercomputers to manage vast
45 amounts of data. Software packages are created for a particular kind of industry, <u>tailored</u> to meet their special needs. Schools and other educational institutions have introduced computers as a subject. Private institutions that train students
50 in programming are <u>thriving</u> because of the demand for more and more computer analysts and programmers. More than 70,000 computer professionals graduate every year.

India has also got well and truly caught up in the
55 Internet revolution. Cyber cafés have sprouted up in nooks and crannies in towns and cities across the country. The Indian IT industry is aggressively pursuing Internet and e-commerce opportunities. Indian firms design multimedia content for
60 Hollywood animation movies. Technology parks have been set up in the metro cities because India is considered the top destination for software outsourcing.

The question now is no longer whether computers
65 are here to stay, but how much they contribute to the development of a country. Calamities such as droughts, floods and earthquakes are a reminder that these problems have to be addressed.

c

Explain what the following items refer to:
it (line 3)
its (line 11)
these companies (line 35)
they (line 65)

d

What is a paradox? Explain the paradox mentioned in paragraph 3. Can you give an example of a paradox from your own knowledge or experience?

e

How many examples of the use of the computer are given? What are they?

f

The fourth paragraph discusses India's position in the field of computers. However, the text ends on a negative note. Can you explain it?

g

Look at the words underlined in the text. Match each word with one of the meanings given below:

   i. widely
   ii. specially made
   iii. make worse; make more serious
   iv. degree of performance till the present time
   v. to increase in strength or amount
   vi. to develop well and be successful
   vii. numerous, a very large number of
   viii. loud protest, or expression of alarm or opposition
   ix. forceful
   x. become better than before

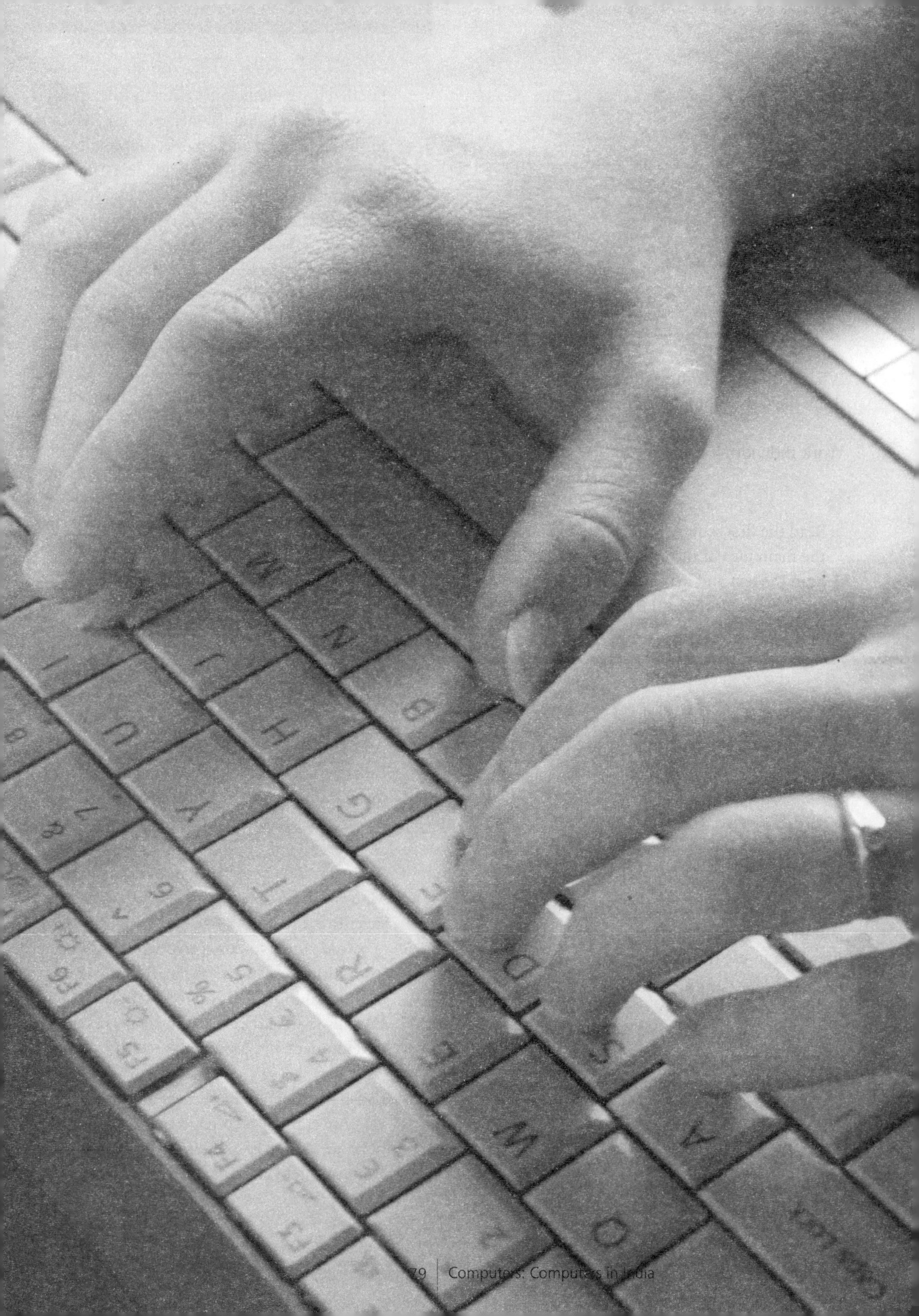

Part 2

✳ Reading

Call it e-philanthropy

Work in pairs.

a

What does 'philanthropy' mean? What do you think the term 'e-philanthropy' refers to?

Work individually.

b

i. Read the first sentence quickly. Can you guess the main idea of the article.
ii. Scan the text and list the advantages of computerisation and the Internet mentioned in the text.

CALL IT E-PHILANTHROPY

by Lakshmi Chaudhry
11 July 2000

Some Seattle-based techies are dreaming up an ambitious initiative to fight global poverty. And they plan to use the Internet to do it.

Digital Partners [http://www.digitaldivide.org] says
5 it wants to change the definition of philanthropy. The group will not give food, clothing, or shelter to the poor. It will offer them online content instead.

"We're looking to put together creative applications of the Internet that will provide immediate benefits
10 for the poorest of the poor," president Craig Smith said. "This is not trickle-down economics."

Funded by the Kellogg, Ford, and Rockefeller foundations, Digital Partners was formed last year to cultivate talent and other resources designed
15 to narrow the global digital divide. Last month, at a meeting in Redmond hosted by Microsoft, it launched a five-year global plan, which will begin with the India Initiative. The organisation has created a working group of 65 India-born
20 technology entrepreneurs, who will brainstorm to come up with a series of Internet-focused proposals.

The idea is to use the wealth and expertise of the extensive network of Indian engineers and
25 entrepreneurs to help the nearly 330 million Indians who live in abject poverty. One of the main reasons Digital Partners picked India as its first target country is the presence of a large Indian community in the United States. It's a
30 community that is closely knit, highly skilled, and financially sound.

"Forty per cent of all new startups are run by Indians. Together they account for nearly $ 235 billion in market capitalisation," Smith said.

35 And more than half of all H-1B visas go to Indian engineers. Better yet, the current crop of immigrants also has strong business and social connections to their country of birth.

"Most of these people live in two worlds.
40 Many of them have a branch office in India," executive director Akhtar Badshah said. "This is a way for them to develop local talent for their own businesses and markets. And unlike the traditional Indian elite, they want to use their
45 IT skills to develop a brand new approach to development and economic growth."

Badshah points to the success of Grameen Bank – a project that first offered micro-loans to women in Bangladesh – as an example of how economic
50 empowerment can be lucrative business.

Digital Partners hopes to jump-start the process by creating a social venture fund that will contribute to both companies and nonprofit organisations that produce online content for poor people. For now, the fund will focus on three main areas: literacy, healthcare, and micro-enterprise, especially for women.

"We want to help a village gain access to information that has perhaps been kept from them to keep them back," Smith said.

Women, for example, could learn more about healthcare. Or a farmer can get more accurate information on prevailing market prices for farm products. It may seem outlandish to propose using the Internet in a country with such a poorly developed infrastructure. Many Indian villages often lack more basic resources, such as electricity or running water.

But many development agencies working in India are already using information technology to help the poor. There are several microprojects in place to wire rural areas using solar panels. Others are turning to cellphones to connect villages that have never seen a telephone line. The India Initiative hopes to build on and perhaps reorganise the various IT initiatives that are already in place.

(Source: www.bytesforall.org)

c

Now answer these questions.
1. Look at the words which are underlined in lines 1 to 22. Say what they refer to.
2. Whom does the title 'Digital Partners' refer to? What is their ambition?
3. What kind of resources can this organisation command?
4. What kind of information can be provided by the organisation?
5. Explain the following terms in your own words.
   ambitious initiative (line 2)

online content (line 7)

trickle-down economics (line 11)

brainstorm (line 20)

brand new approach (line 45)

jump-start the process (line 51)

Follow-up

Language development

a

Rewrite the following sentences using 'because of', 'on account of', 'owing to', 'due to' paying careful attention to any necessary changes in grammar.

   i. The computer produced nonsense because there was a mistake in the programming.
  ii. The information was easily stolen because there were no security checks in the system. (Use the word *lack*.)
 iii. Silicon is used in computer chips because it has some special electrical properties.
  iv. The VDU quality was poor because there was a loose connection.
   v. Computers are widely used because they can process a vast amount of information at great speed. (Use the word *capacity*.)
  vi. The trade unions fear that computerisation will lead to large-scale retrenchment.
 vii. All the data was lost because the power supply was interrupted.

Both the present perfect and simple past tense indicate an action completed in the past. But the present perfect relates it to the present situation. If a definite point of time in the past is indicated, the verb is in the simple past tense and not in the present perfect tense.

Examples: More than twenty years ago Indian Airlines decided to computerise some of their operations. (**simple past**)

By linking unemployment with computerisation they *have created* a valid issue to serve their vested interests perfectly. (**present perfect**)

b

Rewrite the following sentences using the present perfect or simple past tense forms of the verbs in the brackets.
   i. Indian Railways (introduce) the automatic printing of tickets in major cities.
   ii. In 1971 Indian Airlines (acquire) one more IBM 1401 system.
   iii. The number of jobs (increase) in the technology sector.
   iv. Last year Indian Airlines (arrange) for provision of data on a day-to-day basis.
   v. Indian banks (become) very efficient.

❋ Oral practice

Work in pairs. Start when you are both ready. Pay attention to your grammar.

❋ Student A

You are a reporter interested in the effects of computerisation on Indian Railways. Prepare to ask questions about efficiency, profitability, safety, freight, passenger services and so on, such as 'Have the railways become more efficient?'

❋ Student B

You are a publicity officer with Indian Railways. You want to make a good impression on the reporter. So you will give answers such as 'Efficiency has improved'. Prepare to answer questions, using the present prefect tense.

Learner Awareness

Whatever profession you choose to follow, you will have to produce written English in your work. To create a good impression, your written English should be clearly expressed, free from errors, and appropriate to its audience and purpose. Be critical of your own written work—there will almost always be room for improvement!

❋ ❋ ❋ ❋ ❋ ❋

Computers: Computers in India

THEME

transport

1

Problems and Solutions

Preparation

Language development

The prefix **trans-** means 'across', 'through', 'to the other side', etc.

Can you think of five other words with the prefix **trans-** besides transport? Use each word in a sentence of your own.

a

Make sure you can pronounce the words in column A correctly.

Look at the form of each word. Can you say whether the word is a noun, a verb, or an adjective?

Now try to match each word in column A with its meaning in column B.

A	B
plying	non-observance (of rules etc)
enforce	danger
fatal	moving between places
violation	a person who walks (and is not driving a bus, riding a bicycle etc)
pedestrian	severe

Transport: Problems and Solutions

- stringent
- regulations
- stray
- congestion
- hazard

- abnormal accumulation of people, traffic
- resulting in death
- make sure something is followed
- rules
- wandering

b

Use the words in column A above to fill in the gaps in the paragraph.

Vehicles ………………… the roads of India have been on the increase in recent years. These have contributed in a great measure to the ……………… of traffic on the roads, especially during the peak hours. The more disturbing aspect of the transport scene is the increasing number of accidents. ……………………………….. of traffic ………………… by drivers results quite often in ………… mishaps. The drivers are often guilty of overspeeding, rash and negligent driving and reckless overtaking on narrow stretches of roads. They are not afraid of ………………… punishment since they believe the authorities will not …………… the laws strictly. Other factors that cause traffic ……………… are …………… cattle on the road and the …………….. who refuses to use the subway for crossing the road, but just darts across it.

Check your work with your partner. Now your teacher will check with the class.

❊ Oral practice

a

Transport involves problems, and these problems require solutions. Below, you will find some of the problems listed in one column and the possible solutions in the other.
Which is the solution for which problem?
Consult your neighbour.

Problems	Solutions
accidents	staggering hours of work in offices and educational institutions
pollution	banning slow-moving vehicles on main roads
traffic jams	insisting on strict observance of traffic regulations
peak hour traffic	insisting that vehicles are in perfect condition

b

Having organised the information given above, use it to ask questions and get answers, like this:

> A: How would you solve the problem of …?
> B: By …

Now B will ask questions and A will answer.

❊ Reading skills development

Look back at the text in b in the previous column, and list the traffic problems mentioned. Check your answer with another student.

86 | Transport: Problems and Solutions

Part 1

Reading

Transport by autorickshaw

a

Read this imaginary letter to the editor of a newspaper and list the problems faced by autorickshaw users in a certain metro.

Dear editor—I am writing on behalf of all my fellow commuters about the problems we face with autorickshaw drivers. The general public is resigned to the demands that auto drivers make. There are over 3,000 autos in this metro city but we do not feel their presence.

In spite of the government order regarding the fitting of electronic meters, the old meters are still in use. Some kind of bargaining has to take place. The auto drivers are difficult and ask for a flat rate or a sum over and above the charge on the meter. Very often one has to pay double or triple the normal charge to travel a very short distance. Waiting charges are paid according to the whim or impatience of an auto driver. People in a hurry to reach a hospital or the railway station are charged high amounts.

We seem to be at the mercy of the auto drivers because buses are either packed at all hours or are very infrequent.

The Minister for Transport suggested recently that the public should complain to the police when they are thus harassed. I for one can say (speaking from bitter experience) that this is no solution.

The answer seems to be to throw open the transport sector to private operators who can provide minibuses or minicabs in all main areas.

Once profit is the aim, courtesy and reasonable fares might also follow.

an affected citizen

b

i. What solution to these problems is suggested by the writer?

ii. What solution was suggested by the Transport Minister?

iii. What does the writer think of the Minister's solution?

iv. Is the writer confident that his own solution is a good one?

v. The Transport Minister's proposal is to tackle the problem using legal procedures. How would you classify the writer's proposed solution?

c

Now read the following letter, published the same day, and complete the diagram below with details from the letter:

Dear Editor—I agree with the writer about the trouble we are having with autorickshaws. The police seem to be helpless. But surely the law can be enforced if autorickshaws have to have electronic meters installed. This device shows the distance travelled and the length of waiting time so the correct rate can be charged.

Early action needs to be taken to solve this problem. Increasing the minimum rate is not going to help as this will not make autorickshaw drivers follow regulations. The public can complain but only if there is a special cell to redress their grievances. There must also be surprise checks on the meters so the drivers are wary of tampering with the meter.

an affected citizen

	Solutions	Will this be effective?
	1. enforce rules	No
Problem	2.	No
	3.	Yes
	4. penalty	

Discussion

Transport by autorickshaw

a

The letters above presented the views of two dissatisfied passengers.

Do you agree with these views? What are the views of autorickshaw drivers likely to be in this matter? Consider, for example,
- the cost of petrol
- the cost of rental from the autorickshaw owner
- the hazards of the job

Work in pairs. Think of a solution acceptable to both passengers and drivers.

Reading

Travelling by bus

Bus services, including a new series of limited stop buses, called 'PP' services introduced in a metro by the Metropolitan Transport Corporation MTC, came in for appreciation as well as complaints from the public.

a

Read the three letters to the editor below and fill in first three columns of a chart like this one:

complaints	evidence	suggested solutions	Is the solution a good one
Letter A			
Letter B			
Letter C			

Letter A

Dear Editor—The yellow board MTC buses seem to dominate our roads of late. Their drivers act as if there are no other vehicles on the roads and are always in a hurry to the point of overtaking all other vehicles, so much so they never slow down even near schools where they catch children unawares. May I offer a few suggestions? The 'PP' services ought to be discontinued right away. If this is impossible then the speed limit for such buses should be fixed at 30–35 kmph. Speed controlling devices ought to be installed in every bus. And the blaring horns should be toned down considerably in volume.

MTC Commuter 1

Letter B

Dear Editor —We are said to have one of the best managed State transport systems in the country.

But this reputation is not likely to last unless the drivers curb the tendency to take too many things for granted. Being a commuter on these buses, I cannot ignore certain facts which are detrimental to the MTC's efficient functioning. You may go well in advance, even to the bus terminus, and would be happy to find a number of buses (invariably more than two) with the same route number lined up (to confuse rather than help). One can never guess for certain which of the buses will leave first.

Once you are in the bus, you are again on your own—now starts the hide and seek, with the conductor always playing hard to get. But it keeps you fit all the same—wriggling through the vast mass of humanity in search of the man, or trying to find your way about. Then comes the grand finale—the stop has finally come, but the bus does not stop. It keeps moving and you are expected to try your talent at calisthenics – the emphasis is on physical fitness – 'Keep fit MTC style', perhaps!

MTC Commuter 2

Letter C

Dear Editor—This is with reference to the news item regarding MTC's plan to extend 'PP' services to 30 more routes.

Since the inception of these services on the existing routes, many overzealous drivers, to keep up to the running time schedule, indulge in over-speeding, hazardous over-takings and blowing of horns, throwing all traffic regulations to the wind. This results in frequent, avoidable accidents. It is, therefore, in the interests of safety that the authorities, while fixing the time schedule for each route, take into account the prescribed speed limit, density of traffic along the route, the number of road intersections and signal points. Within the city the journey time should be saved only by cutting out the number of stops and not by over-speeding.

MTC Commuter 3

b
Use your own opinion to fill the final column of the chart.
Then see if your neighbour agrees with you.

c
Which of the three letters did you find the most effective?
Can you say why?

Part 2

Reading

Improving road safety

a

Working with a partner, consider the problem of road safety in any large Indian city. Prepare a chart like this one:

Problems	Solutions		
	engineering	legislation	education
i.			
ii.			
iii.			
etc.			

In the first column, list at least eight road-safety problems e.g. stray cattle, overloaded vehicles.

Next, decide on the best way to solve each of your problems. Put a tick under one or more of the SOLUTIONS columns.

Transport: Problems and Solutions

b

The article which follows is about the need for action on road safety.

Scan the article and locate the paragraph or paragraphs which,
i. tells you why we need to take action about accidents.
ii. explains why safety should be made a priority wherever there is motorised travel.
iii. gives you some statistics about road deaths.
iv. looks at variations that may be necessary in handling road accidents.
v. suggests ways of providing for road safety.

ROAD SAFETY
A PUBLIC HEALTH ISSUE

On busy streets, pedestrians and motorcyclists are particularly vulnerable to road traffic injuries.

At the inquest into the world's first road traffic death in 1896, the coroner was reported to have said all this must never happen again. More than a century later, 1.2 million people are killed on roads every year and up to 50 million more are injured. These casualties of the road will increase if action is not taken.

Throughout the world, roads are bustling with cars, buses, trucks, motorcycles, mopeds and other types of two- and three-wheelers. By making the transportation of goods and people faster and more efficient, these vehicles support economic and social development in many countries. But while motorised travel provides many benefits, it can also do serious harm unless safety is made a priority. Pedestrians and cyclists using roads are particularly at risk. Crashes are frequent. Deaths and injuries are common.

If current trends continue, the number of people killed and injured on the world's roads will rise by more than 60% between 2000 and 2020. Most of these injuries will occur in developing countries where more and more people are using motorised transport. In these countries, cyclists, motorcyclists, users of public transport, and pedestrians are especially vulnerable to road traffic injuries.

Road deaths and injuries are preventable. There are solutions to the road safety problem. A wide range of effective interventions exist, and experience in countries with long histories of motorised travel has shown that a scientific systems approach to road safety is essential to tackling the problem. This approach addresses the traffic system as a whole and looks at the interactions between vehicles, road users and the road infrastructure to identify solutions.

There is no single blueprint for road safety. Interventions and strategies that work in one setting may need to be adapted elsewhere. WHO focuses specifically on interventions relating to five of the many factors that cause road traffic deaths and injuries.

WHO and the World Bank have launched the world report on road traffic injury prevention, which presents current knowledge of the global road traffic injury problem and offers science-based evidence and solutions to address it. Global road safety campaigns aim to promote action to prevent road injuries.

The loss and suffering associated with road traffic deaths and injuries are preventable. With firm political will and an integrated approach that addresses vehicles, the people who use roads, and the road infrastructure, roads can be made safer.

(Source: World's first road death. <http://www.roadpeace.org/articles/WorldFirstDeath.html> London, RoadPeace, 29 March 2004)

c

Now read the text quickly.

d

In pairs, look back at the chart you made for a on page 88. Did you think of any problems which the text does not mention? Did you think of any other solutions not mentioned in the text? Be prepared to report back when your teacher asks you.

Listening

Suspended animation

Listen carefully to the information you are going to receive from the teacher on 'Suspended animation' and complete the tasks according to the instructions given for each division.

a

Place a tick mark (✔) against the correct answer.

i. The sanctioned amount for the Skybus Metro project is
   A. Rs 25,000 crores
   B. Rs 50,000 crores
   C. Rs 10,000 crores

ii. The project will operate in
   A. 3 cities
   B. 5 cities
   C. 7 cities

iii. The maximum speed of the skybus is
   A. 225 km per hour
   B. 200 km per hour
   C. 100 km per hour

iv. The quantity of carbon emission that would be saved by the use of skybus per day is
   A. 1750 tonnes
   B. 1750 litres
   C. 1750 kg

v. The introduction of the skybus would help the government to save on fuel import costs by
   A. Rs 20,000 crores
   B. Rs 100,000 crores
   C. Rs 10,000 crores

b

Say whether the statements listed below are true or false.

i. The installation of the skybus project does not need the acquisition of land.

ii. The underground transport system is cheaper and more efficient than the skybus mode.

iii. The potential capacity of the skybus is one lakh passengers per hour.

iv. The pillars on which the system is built occupy space on the road.

v. Skybuses are not accident prone.

c

Write sentences with appropriate information drawn from your listening activity.

The advantages of the skybus are

1 no crisscrossing
2 ....
3 .... ballast ....
4 ....
5 in case of an emergency ....
6 ....
7 suspension links ....
8 (any other advantage) ....

Role play

Improving road safety

Hold a meeting to discuss how road safety can be improved. By the end of your meeting, you should have a concrete proposal.
Before you hold your meeting, spend five minutes preparing what you will say.

Writing

The hazards of walking

Student A

You are an official from the Finance Department and are not very enthusiastic about spending a lot of money on road safety schemes. You feel that a few road safety posters on the main roads are sufficient.

Student B

You are an official from the Transport Department and want to spend money on improving road intersections and on a new bypass.

Student C

You are an official from the police department. You want to double the number of traffic policemen so that laws can be enforced with on-the-spot fines.

Student D

You are a representative of the Citizen's Welfare Association, and would like to introduce a road safety training week in all schools, colleges, factories and offices.

Follow-up

Oral practice

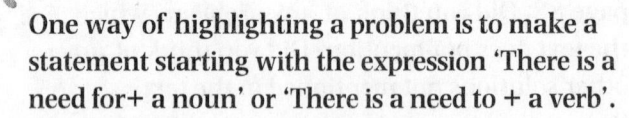

One way of highlighting a problem is to make a statement starting with the expression 'There is a need for + a noun' or 'There is a need to + a verb'.

For example

> A: What does the problem of increasing accidents imply?
>
> B: There is a need for strict enforcement of traffic rules and regulations.
> (OR)
> There is a need to enforce traffic rules and regulations strictly.

Now use the information on problems and solutions found in section a on page 89, to ask and answer questions as indicated above. Take turns to ask questions and give answers.

Comprehension check

Look back at the article about 'Road Safety' on page 90. Use your answers to question b (a scanning exercise) on page 90 to help you find the paragraph in the text which tells you that

a. one of the problems is the particular vulnerability of pedestrians and motorcyclists.

b. casualties will increase if proper steps are not taken.

c. a scientific systems approach to road safety is essential.

d. interventions and strategies need to be adapted for different settings.

e. it is possible to prevent loss and suffering associated with road traffic.

Language check

Here is a list of useful expressions. Make sure you can pronounce the words. Note the stressed syllables.

- to lodge a com<u>plaint</u>
- to prefer to re<u>main</u>
- to dic<u>tate</u> terms
- to pro<u>vide</u> with
- to a<u>dhere</u> to
- to a<u>ccount</u> for
- to take for <u>granted</u>

Make sure you understand the phrases above. Complete the sentences below with these expressions, using the appropriate verb forms and splitting the expression where necessary.

a. When the Mass Rapid Transit System starts functioning, it will .... the public .... a faster means of transport.

b. There is a tendency on the part of transport authorities .... that all is well on the transport scene.

c. Severe action can be taken against erring auto and taxi drivers only if people come forward .... against them.

d. It has been estimated that rash driving .... many deaths.

e. People who are in a desperate hurry to reach their destinations are at the mercy of unscrupulous auto and taxi drivers who .... to them.

f. Even people who are in a position to present evidence in a criminal case, generally................... silent in order to avoid the bother of turning up at courts.

g. Cyclists often show scant regard for traffic regulations. They do not .... their lanes.

Check your answers with your partner.

Writing skills development

Use the notes you have taken down on the Skybus project (page 91) and write a paragraph comparing the skybus transport system with the existing modes of ground transport in terms of cost of travel, time for travel and safety in travel.

Transport: Problems and Solutions

2

Transport Tomorrow

Preparation

✺ Language development

a

Explain the meaning of the underlined verb in each sentence. Some details (for example, 'bullet train', 'TGV' and 'maglev') will become clear when you read the text on pages 96-8 later.

  i. The bullet train <u>averages</u> 262 kilometres per hour.

  ii. The bicycle is a popular mode of travel that <u>caters</u> to the needs of many people.

  iii. The TGV has <u>clocked</u> 515 kilometres per hour in test runs.

  iv. The maglev <u>differs</u> radically from its more conventional high-speed cousins.

  v. The motor that <u>propels</u> the maglev is in the special track.

  vi. Electromagnets are <u>mounted</u> on the train and in the track.

  vii. The electromagnets <u>levitate</u>, guide and propel the train along the guideway.

b

Read the sentences below, and note the words underlined. Then match the words with the meanings in the box.

i. On many railways, <u>ballast</u> is used to pack the space below the rails and sleepers.

ii. Several <u>innovations</u> have been introduced in the design of the latest automobile.

iii. The <u>conventional</u> sources of energy used by trains are steam, diesel, and electricity.

iv. The <u>sophistication</u> of the modern petrol engine has led to greater fuel efficiency.

v. India should depend on <u>indigenous</u> technology and not on imported technology.

vi. He <u>inadvertently</u> boarded the wrong train and had to get down at the first stop.

vii. If the drivers do not obey traffic rules, the lives of their passengers will be in <u>jeopardy</u>.

A	introduction of new things or changes
B	without paying attention; thoughtlessly, not on purpose
C	usual or traditional
D	crushed rock or gravel
E	danger
F	complexity; having the latest improvements, or advanced methods
G	native of or belonging to a region; local; not imported

Language development

Many verbs are formed by adding the suffixes -ise/-ize, -fy, or -en to adjectives.

a

Make a verb from each of the following adjectives.

specific	special	electric	fresh
final	broad	central	simple

b

Look at these nouns:

freshness, finali**sation**

Now make nouns from the other words given above.

Part 1

Discussion

Tackling the traffic problem

The increased traffic in our towns and cities will create more problems until something is done. In groups, list the five most serious problems caused by the growth in traffic. Then list some solutions.

Reading

Looking down the track...

a

In pairs, consider the problems of constructing a 'railway underground'. Make a list of the most serious problems.

b

Skim the text to see which of the problems you listed are dealt with in the text.

c

Now read the text through once and answer the questions which follow it.

Looking down the track at very fast trains

by Alastair Sarre

The fastest trains in commercial operation today are the French *train à grand vitesse* (TGV), the Japanese *shinkansen* (or bullet train) and the German *Inter City Express* (ICE).
The TGV routinely travels at 300 kilometres per hour through the French countryside and has been clocked at 515 kilometres per hour in test runs. The bullet train averages 262 kilometres per hour between stations and has recorded 443 kilometres per hour in test runs, while the ICE has a top operational speed of 280 kilometres per hour and has recorded 408 kilometres per hour in trials.

These trains have several things in common:

- They all use electric motors (some very fast trains still run on diesel, but these are slower than their electric counterparts).
- They all have steel wheels that run on steel tracks.
- They have aerodynamic designs to decrease wind resistance—in some ways they look like long, thin aeroplanes without wings.
- They all require special lines to achieve their maximum operating speeds—in particular, these need to be as straight as possible, because very fast trains and tight bends don't mix well. Nevertheless, these trains can also run on conventional lines at reduced speeds, a great advantage when approaching major urban centres.

Innovations in the TGV

Many of the innovative aspects of the TGV are in the design and placement of **bogies**. Bogies consist of two or more pairs of wheels, their axles and a connecting frame that supports the carriages (usually called cars) above. At high speeds, the vibrations produced by contact between the wheels and the rails increase dramatically. This can cause the bogies to sway from side to side, which in turn can damage the track and, in severe cases, derail the train.

While developing the TGV, engineers found that increasing the distance between axles in the bogies could reduce this instability. In addition, since instability increased with increasing bogie weight, they moved the electric motors, usually mounted on the bogies, and suspended them from the bottom of the cars.

Bogie placement was also changed. Conventional train carriages have two bogies each, one towards each end. In the TGV, cars are attached to each other semi-permanently, with the front end of one car and the back end of the next car resting on a common bogie. In this way, each car effectively uses only one bogie (two halves).

Efforts are continually being made to reduce the overall weight of the train, largely because the lighter the train, the less stress there is on the track (therefore lowering maintenance costs). Reducing the number of bogies saves weight.

In addition, new, lighter materials are used in the construction of the trains. Even the seats are now made of lightweight carbon fibres, magnesium and composite materials.

While the TGV, the bullet train and the ICE all use established technology – electric motors and steel wheels – revolutionary technology has produced a high speed train which floats on a magnetic cushion of air above a special track.

The maglev differs radically from its more conventional high-speed cousins. It doesn't have wheels and it doesn't run on a steel track. It doesn't even have an on-board motor. The motor that propels the maglev is in the special track, and the propulsion comes from magnets.

In maglev technology, electromagnets (devices that become magnetic when fed an electric current) are mounted on the train and in the track (usually called a guideway). The electromagnets levitate, guide and propel the train along the guideway.

Maglev technology has several theoretical advantages over conventional high-speed trains. Since there is no wheel-to-track contact, less energy is lost due to friction and the trains create less noise. Maglevs also use less energy to achieve the same speed as conventional fast trains.

In addition, since the motor is in the guideway rather than on the train, it is possible to increase its power on steep sections. This means that maglevs can climb steeper grades than conventional high-speed trains, reducing the need for tunnels.

Despite such advantages, maglevs remain commercially unproven. In comparison, trains like the TGV, the bullet train and the ICE have been formidably successful. Millions of people have travelled on them; hundreds of thousands use them each day. Each new generation of train gets faster, and they boast an impressive safety record.

One of the biggest barriers to maglevs is the need for a whole new infrastructure. Their guideways need to be constructed from scratch, a costly and financially risky venture, at least in the early stages. In contrast, conventional high-speed trains can run on existing tracks through urban areas, and the high-speed portions can be constructed in stages.

Very fast trains are safe compared to most other forms of motorised transport. For example, the TGV, which commenced operation in 1981, travels about 10 million passenger kilometres each year. It is yet to have an onboard fatality, although a number of people have died in collisions at road crossings.

But this is not to say that major disasters are impossible. In June 1998, an *Inter City Express*, travelling at about 200 kilometres per hour, derailed near Eschede in Germany, killing 102 people and injuring hundreds more. The cause of the accident is still under investigation.

Commentators seem to agree that very fast trains – the conventional ones, at least – will form a significant part of the international transportation scene in coming decades.

(Source: www.science.org.au)

d

i. Note down the main topic of each paragraph. Group these topics under three or four sub-headings.
ii. Using the information in the first paragraph, name the fastest trains in operation today and list the things they have in common.
iii. What innovative aspects were considered while the TGV was being developed?
iv. Prepare a table comparing the established technology used for the TGV and the revolutionary technology that produced the maglev.
v. What are the barriers to maglevs being used commercially?
vi. Read the last sentence of the text. What evidence do you find in the text to support this statement? What other points can you think of?

Part 2

✳ Language focus

If travel were a pleasure, not a pain

Look at the following sentence:

If the damaged bridge is opened to traffic, it will collapse.

In this type of sentence, the if- clause indicates the conditions in which something will happen.

a

Complete the following sentences.

i. If drivers do not obey traffic regulations, . . .
ii. If . . . , the tyre will be damaged.
iii. If the engine is serviced regularly, . . .
iv. If the battery of the car is 'down', . . .
v. If passengers stand on the footboards of buses, . . .
vi. If . . . , the aeroplane cannot take off.

Look at the use of the if- clause in the two sentences given below:

If there are more pedestrians on the roads, there will be more accidents.

If there were no pedestrians on the roads, there would be fewer accidents.

✳ In the first sentence, the condition in the if- clause is likely to be true; the if- clause in the second sentence describes a condition that is improbable.

b

Complete the following sentences, making it clear if the if- clause is likely to be true or improbable.

i. If so many people (board) the boat, ...
ii. If the authorities (increase) security at airports, ...
iii. If all traffic policemen (dismiss), ...
iv. If a metro (build) in Bombay, ...
v. If the bus service (not improve), ...
vi. If auto and taxi meters (check), more frequently, ...

Reading

The automated freeway

a

Skim this text and note which part explains the problem, which offers the solution, and which presents an evaluation of the solution.

In the coming decades road transport will face serious problems. The density of automobile traffic in the cities will be so high that the roads will hardly be able to accommodate them. Bumper-to-bumper movement of cars and frequent snarl-ups will delay traffic, which will include not only cars but also trucks and trailers.

It is to find an answer to this problem that the 'automated freeway' is designed. The cars crowding the roads of the city and polluting the air with noxious gases will be removed to a freeway, where they will be controlled by a computer control system which ensures quick and safe movement of the cars to their destination.

The roads of the city will be connected to the freeway by entrance ramps at different points. The car is first driven through the city roads to the nearest entrance to the freeway. Once it has entered the freeway, it no longer depends on its own fuel, but draws its power from an electric supply line.

For this purpose, the car is fitted with a retractable arm which can establish contact with a rail from which it can draw its power. From now on the car is under automatic control. The driver telephones the computer control system to let it know his or her destination. The computer takes over and decides on the best route to follow. It ensures that space is available on the freeway for the car till it reaches its destination. In the meantime, drivers relax in their seats. When it is time to get off the freeway, they hear a buzzer. Each driver then takes an exit to join the traffic on the road. He or she leaves the car at some specified spot, where some other person can use it.

Today's conventional road can carry up to 2,000 cars per hour; an automated freeway can handle five times the number.

b

Using the information in the text, make eight sentences by matching the noun phrases in column A with corresponding phrases in column B, and supplying the necessary verbs.

A	B
i. The car on the city's road	to the entrance ramp
ii. The car in the freeway	the route to be taken by the car
iii. The driver of the car	its own power
iv. The automated freeway	pollution
v. A retractable arm	a rent for the car
vi. The computer control system	upto 10,000 vehicles per hour
vii. People who use the automated freeway	2,000 vehicles per hour
viii. Today's freeway	a rail to draw electric power

Writing

Solving a traffic problem

Write three short paragraphs proposing a solution to a current traffic problem in your area. You could choose, for instance, an area of congestion.

first paragraph	—	explain the problem
second paragraph	—	offer your solution
third paragraph	—	evaluate your solution

Follow-up

Language development

Here are some words you will have come across in your reading. Add a suitable ending to each to form an adjective.

The endings you will need are:

-able   -an   -ous   -ar
-ent   -ive   -ful   -less

advantage	continue	retract
avail	differ	suburb
care	power	vehicle
comfort	produce	vigour
compare	relate	

Comprehension check

Read the text on pages 96-8 and say which of the following statements is true. Correct the ones which are not true.

i. The very fast trains all use electric motors.

ii. These trains have aerodynamic designs to increase wind resistance.

iii. In the TGV, cars are attached to each other temporarily.

iv. Maglev trains create a lot of noise.

v. Maglevs can climb steeper grades than conventional high-speed trains.

vi. The TGV has had many on-board fatalities.

Writing skills development

In a certain small town, there are only two ways to cross the river which runs through the middle of the town. One way is to walk across the railway bridge. This is very dangerous, since there is no walkway for pedestrians. The other way is to take a small boat, which is very slow because of the current. However, many people need to cross this river each day.

Write a paragraph suggesting two engineering solutions to this problem, and evaluating each. Begin:

One solution to the problem is to . . . .

3

TRAVEL FOR PLEASURE

Preparation

❋ Language development

Look at this table.

verb	noun	(-ing) verbal noun
to ride	a rider	riding
to climb	a climber	climbing
to trek	a trekker	trekking
to run	a runner	running
	a mountaineer	mountaineering
to walk	a walker	walking
to cycle	a cyclist	cycling
to sail	a sailor	sailing

What is the difference between the two kinds of nouns?

Use words from the table to complete these sentences.

a He owned a bicycle, but didn't enjoy
   .... for long distances;
   so he took a bus.

Transport: Travel for Pleasure

b Anyone who can travel a mile on foot in less than four minutes is an excellent ………….
c A ………………….. may sometimes need extra oxygen to reach the summit if it is over 7,000 metres.
d Since she has never learnt to ………………. a horse, she should be advised to ……….. instead.

Oral practice

a

Think of five places in India which are of interest to tourists.

b

Describe how a tourist guide does his job.

c

What is trekking?

d

What do you need to carry for trekking?

Language development

a

Match the examples of journeys in column B with the categories of journey in column A. Then suggest one more example of your own for each category.

A	B
pleasure trip	going to holy places like Varanasi, Velankanni or Amritsar
pilgrimage	attempting to reach Everest, the highest peak in the world.
mountaineering	going to Nainital or Ooty during the holidays.

b

Match the words in column A with the appropriate meaning in column B. Work with your neighbour.

A	B
heritage	a complete view of a wide stretch of land; a continuously changing view or scene
intact	strange; unusual, and attractive
panorama	calm, peaceful
exotic	an object, custom or quality which is passed down over many years within a family or nation
repository	an area for wild birds or animals where they may not be hunted
lush	whole; unaffected; in one piece
spectacular	a place where things are stored
tranquil	variety; having differences
sanctuary	of grand appearance
diversity	growing thickly, very well

Part 1

Discussion

On your own two feet

In contrast to city travel and mechanised transport, travelling on foot in the countryside can be a pleasure.

a

What are the attractions of mountaineering or trekking?

What are the negative aspects?

Make a list of each.

b

What, if anything, would stop you from going on a mountaineering or trekking holiday?

Reading

Mountaineering

Read the following text carefully. Do you agree with the author? Be prepared to report back when your teacher asks you.

MOUNTAINEERING

Mountaineering is the sport of attaining great heights in mountainous regions just for the pleasure of the climb. It is different from other sports because the success of the participants rests almost entirely on their own powers of physical endurance and judgment to reach their goal. The mountain provides the field of action.

Why are people interested in mountaineering? First, they have a desire to conquer nature — to achieve the most difficult and the most impossible task. Also their spirit of adventure and interest in exploring unknown places provide the impetus to do mountaineering.

A climber must be skilled in both rock climbing and snow and ice climbing. Rock climbing is done on the uppermost slopes of a high peak after getting through the lower reaches of snow and ice. Snow and ice climbing involve greater skill and endurance. Ice axes are used to cut steps on the slopes. Cutting a step down the slope is more difficult than cutting one up.

Mountaineers should be well equipped with woollen clothes, a windproof outer garment, headgear and mittens of suitable warmth, cleated boots, heavy socks, and snow glasses. They also take with them a compass, a map, waterproof match boxes, an ice axe, a flashlight, a climbing rope, a folding lantern, a hammer, tents, a sleeping bag and cooking equipment. Skis, oxygen-tanks, a camera, an aneroid barometer, a walkie-talkie, and an avalanche-gun also become part of a mountaineer's luggage.

In spite of having to carry varied items of equipment they manage to overcome all the hazards on the way and reach their goal. This requires a supreme kind of skill. In fact, it demands of its adherents not only great physical strength, but also great mental qualities such as courage, endurance and determination. These towerless snowy peaks sometimes lure people to death—perhaps that is the cost nature demands of the mountaineers in their exhilarating attempt to unlock mystery! Nevertheless mountain lovers do not hesitate to pay the cost because this sport is worth the risk involved.

Trekking

a

Read the following text and make notes of at least three attractions and three negative aspects of trekking. If you have time, note down any other attractions and negative aspects mentioned in the text.

TREKKING

In spite of the various fast and well-developed transport systems of the modern era, trekking has its own fun and attracts many people. Bent under the weight of their rucksacks, struggling up deserted slopes, thousands of people doggedly raid India's mountains in droves. Trekking for these people is more than just a holiday; for most, it is one of the few adventures that they can act out in their otherwise drab, regulated urban lives. What is more, it can come with additional excitement, be it rappelling (descending a cliff) or the act of crossing a swift-flowing river.

Many organisations representing this new eagerness for trekking have come into being. Most of the uninitiated find it hard to understand what motivates a trekker. Why should a person actually want to sweat, risk foot sores and aching limbs, on a well-earned holiday? The reason is simple and uncomplicated; it could be the sight of an unusual flower, or a snowladen mountain or any such simple pleasure. The trekkers swear that the special satisfaction of panting slowly to the top of a ridge or having a cup of tea in a sun-drenched valley engulfed in silence, or of simply sitting on a river bank watching the water rush by, can be rivalled by few city pleasures.

The desire to trek has been helped along by the fact that although rucksacks, tents and sleeping bags are still hard to find, trekking is cheaper than a holiday to a regular resort. In India, a Central Government regulation granting one month's special casual leave to employees wanting to go on treks approved by the IMF has also provided an impetus. Although the infrastructure for trekking is still meagre, the hordes of willing walkers do not mind the inconveniences that would upset them at any other time. Because, that, in any case, is half the fun.

Writing

Trekking and mountaineering compared

a

Make a comparison of mountaineering and trekking by completing the chart given below with relevant information from the texts and your own knowledge. Work in pairs.

	mountaineering	trekking
i. experience needed		
ii. cost involved		
iii. places in India where you can go		
iv. qualities you need to have		
v. things needed		
vi. problems to be faced		

b

Your uncle has offered to sponsor you on a three-week activity holiday with some training. You have to choose between mountaineering and trekking. Which would you choose? Using the chart you have completed, write a paragraph of a letter to your uncle justifying your choice.

c

Show your letter to another student. Does he (or she) find it convincing? How could you improve your letter?

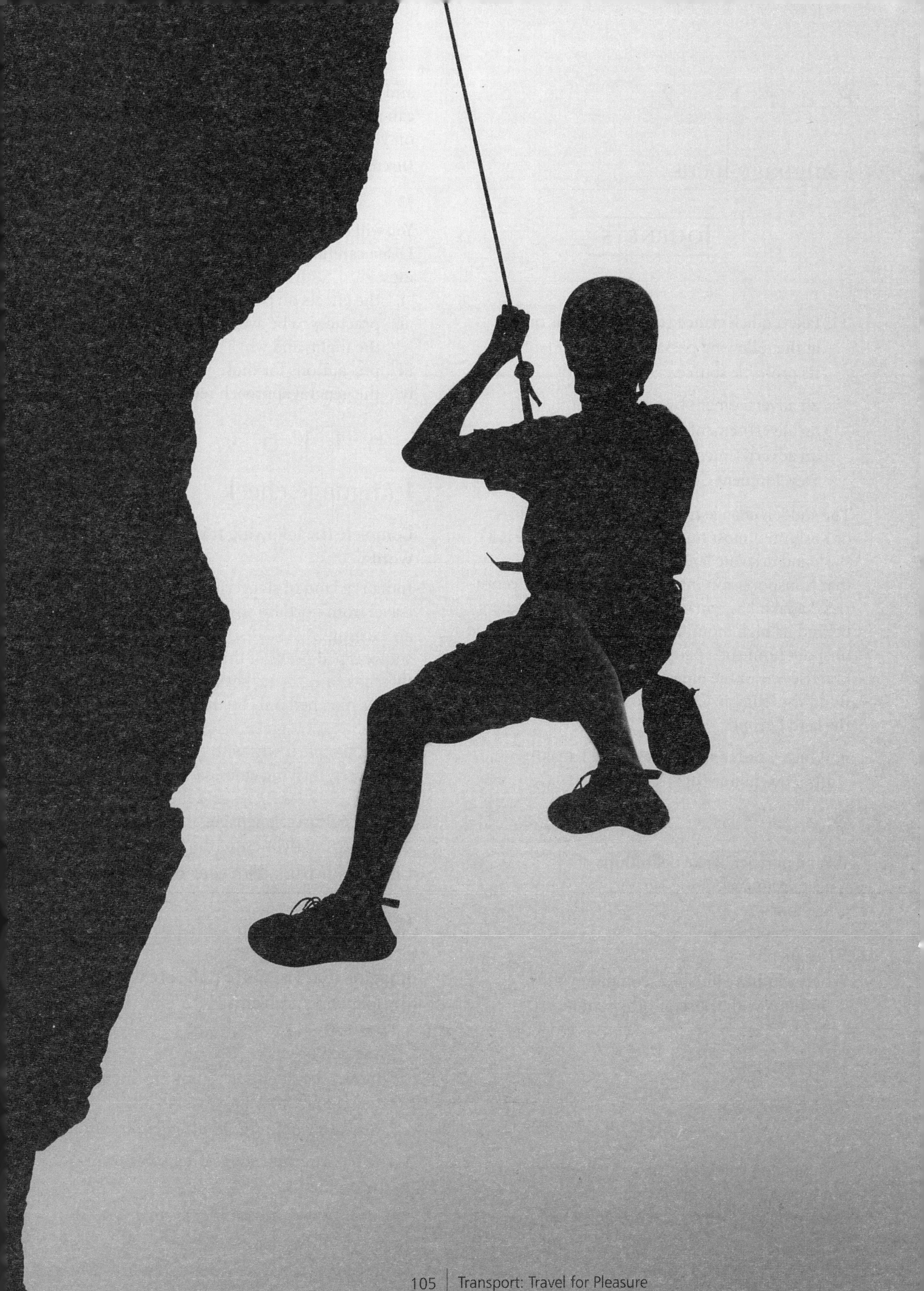

Part 2

Language focus

JOURNEYS

a

i. Take a quick glance (twenty seconds only) at the following passage and then identify its probable source.
- an advertisement by a hotel
- an advertisement by a private company
- an advertisement by the India Tourism Development Corporation.

The sudden change from the lush green valleys of Kashmir almost numbs your senses. Here is a stark and desolate landscape of incredible beauty that transports you into another world. For centuries, Ladakh has remained hidden from travellers behind its high mountain passes—the pristine and unspoilt home of a people close to nature, who still practise one of the oldest and purest forms of the Buddhist religion. Come, cross the Himalayas to the land beyond.

ii. Which words and phrases make Ladakh sound attractive to tourists?

b

With a partner, write definitions of
i. a pilgrimage
ii. a tour
iii. an expedition
iv. a picnic

When you have finished, compare your definitions with those of other students.

Listening

Hassles in the air

a

Imagine that you are going to Australia by plane, but have never travelled by plane before. Can you guess how the flight is likely to affect you physically and mentally? Do you know of any measures you can adopt to counter the adverse impact of a flight on your health?

Discuss this in pairs.

b

You will now listen to a short talk 'Hassles in the air'. Listen carefully and take down notes under these headings:
i. the effects on body and mind, and why
ii. practices to be avoided before, during and after the flight, and why
iii. precautions for those with ill-health
iv. the general approach recommended

Follow-up

Language check

Complete the following text with appropriate words.

India is a land of staggering .... As you travel from north to south or from west to east, an exciting .... unfolds itself. The snowcapped peaks of the Himalayas impress with their .... beauty. Their .... view is matched only by the grandeur of the vast plains. .... green fields and meadows, rich forests, temple towns with their .... sculptures, thriving cities, sacred rivers, unspoilt wildlife .... and the people with their varying cultures, languages and styles of dress constitute the richness of the Indian experience.

Check your work with your neighbour.

Writing skills development

Imagine that visitors to India are worried about the following problems.
- the heat
- stomach upsets
- the fact that they don't speak any Indian languages
- they cannot afford to travel in taxis
- they know nothing about Indian traditions

Write a paragraph suggesting solutions to the problems.

One solution to the problem is to ...

THEME
technology

1
Appropriate Technology

Preparation

✤ Language development

a

Match the words in column A with their meanings in column B.

A	B
i. technology	1. nourishment
ii. appropriate	2. obtaining juices by pressing, crushing, boiling
iii. exploitation	3. dry outer covering of grain, seeds, etc
iv. indigenous	4. unfit to eat
v. innovative	5. thick, sticky, solid mass
vi. porridge	6. scientific knowledge needed for industry
vii. coagulum	7. soft food made by boiling a cereal in water or milk
viii. husk	8. suitable
ix. nutrition	9. using, usually unfairly, for one's own benefit
x. extraction	10. living or growing in a place where originally from
xi. inedible	11. having the quality of introducing new things, making changes

109 | Technology: Appropriate Technology

Look at the following examples of the use of 'self' to form compound words:
   self + reliant=self-reliant
   self + sufficient=self-sufficient

b

Suggest three more expressions beginning with self and write three sentences using them.

c

Complete the following passage with the prepositions to, of, by, between and with.

Appropriate technology is technology that is developed to cater .... the basic needs .... people with low spending power. It is not low or primitive technology. Also, it is not concerned .... only small-scale technology. Appropriate technology lies somewhere .... traditional and modern technology. It is particularly easy to operate and can be maintained even .... less skilled persons. The special feature .... this technology is that it can be applied .... a variety .... rural needs.

Oral practice

Look at this definition.

* 'Appropriate technology is that technology which is affordable within the resources available, is culturally acceptable and is environmentally harmless.'

Discuss the definition with your partner and define the following. Try to use the formal language of the definition you have just read.

   i. high technology
   ii. traditional technology
   iii. laser technology

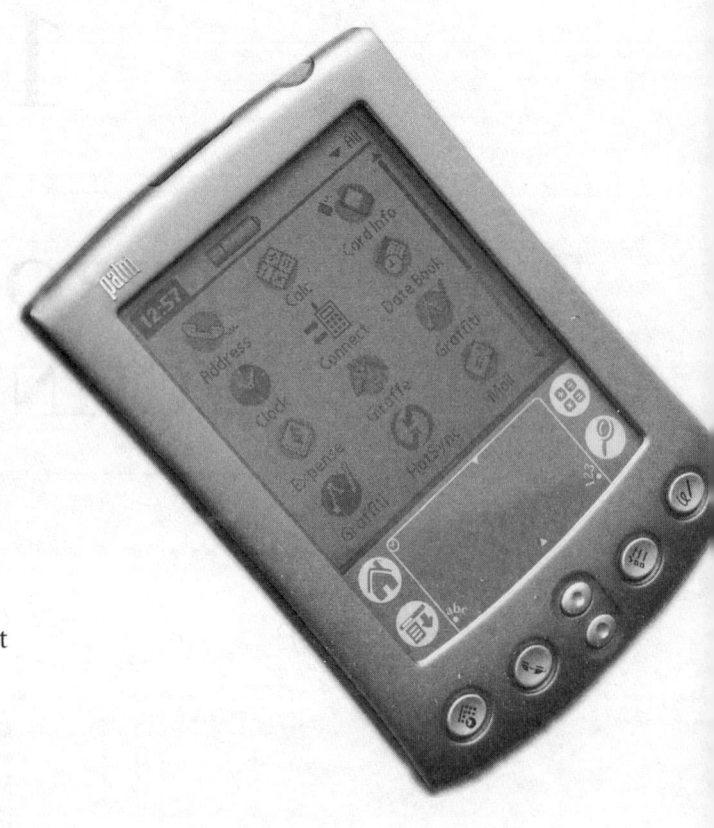

Writing skills development

Write a paragraph on appropriate technology, developing the points below.

   i. low capital investment per unit of output
   ii. small-scale operation
   iii. use of local materials wherever possible
   iv. high adaptability to local skills and labour
   v. ease of understanding and maintenance by the user without a high level of education
   vi. unpolluting and benign to the physical environment
   vii. use of natural and renewable energy sources such as wind, power, solar energy, water power, pedal power and biogas.

Part 1

Listening

Different types of technology

a

Work in small groups and try to answer these questions.

i. What is technology?

ii. Classify the different types of technology. Offer examples.

iii. What are the features of the different types of technology?

b

Listen to a brief talk about technology and take notes on the different types of technology.

Reading

Pedal power

Read the first two paragraphs of a text on pedal power below. Then arrange the twelve sentences which follow in sequence to write the next four paragraphs of the text.

Many people in India expend their muscle power every day to provide themselves with the basic necessities of life. An example is the widespread use of the bicycle. It should be noted that the power produced by a human being cannot match that produced by the internal combustion engine and electric motor. But due to the shortage of fuels and undependable electric supply, an innovative use of human energy may have to be considered seriously.

The advent of the internal combustion engine and electric motor ended the use of pedal power in small-scale industries and in agricultural processing. Even though India has abundant human power and over 40 million bicycles are used for transportation, pedal power potential has not been fully realised in small-scale agricultural activities.

1. The first type is a stationary one, in which bicycle parts like the frame, crank, chain and freewheel are used to produce a rotating motion.
2. The second type of pedal power device is a modified bicycle which can be used both as a vehicle for transportation and a prime mover.
3. This modified bicycle is called a dual-purpose bicycle.
4. There are two types of pedal power devices in existence today.
5. This rotary motion can be used to operate machines such as threshers, winnowers, pumps, woodworking lathes and metal lathes.
6. It is in fact a versatile mechanism which can be used for transportation as well as power production.
7. The dual-purpose bicycle can be used to power small-scale agricultural implements and equipment used in rural industries.
8. The dual-purpose bicycle has a permanent attachment and a modified broad stand cum carrier.
9. Some examples are paddy threshers, winnowers, groundnut shell removers, small water-pumps and grinders.
10. Thus the technologists who advocate appropriate technology are confident that the exploitation of pedal power for various uses will make many self-reliant and self-sufficient as far as their energy needs are concerned.
11. It can also be used to power a drill, a woodworking lathe, a metal lathe and a circular saw.
12. The use of the dual-purpose bicycle will also help technologists provide employment to the unemployed and unskilled, and decrease their dependence on outside power sources.

If you find the text difficult, search for key words and phrases that refer to

- A a pedal power device (first)
- B another kind of pedal power device (second)
- C uses of the dual-purpose bicycle
- D conclusion

Reading

A bicycle-operated domestic pump

a

Skim through the passage and suggest suitable headings for the four paragraphs.

b

Read the text below and find out the meanings of the words underlined from the context.

A

The Centre for Water Resources, College of Engineering, took up an appropriate technology project in 1976 and completed it in 1978. This project is a practical project specially designed to suit rural conditions in India. Since the villages in India face acute power shortages, it was hoped that this project, when implemented, would prove a boon to the rural masses.

B

In this project the principles of using stationary pedal power to pump water for domestic and field uses are used. The pump used is an ordinary reciprocating type. This device consists of a permanent stand made of G.I. sheet (with pipes welded to its bottom) which is hammered into the earth close to the pump at a pre-calculated distance. The front wheel of the cycle is kept immovable by securing it to a stand or some other fixture. Thus the bicycle is held rigid.

C

To pump water, all that one has to do is to sit on the bicycle seat and pedal. The drive is transmitted from the front sprocket to the rear wheel which now acts as a flywheel and transmits the power through the second chain to the pump. As the pump is a positive displacement one, water can be pumped out even at low speeds. Also, no priming is necessary. After use, the clip is released and the chain is opened. Then the bicycle can be lifted from the permanent stand and used as a normal two-wheeler.

D

The cost involved is very low compared to the cost of a conventional motor for domestic use. The pumping test proved to be a success. An average person can easily pedal for two hours continuously without his or her experiencing much fatigue. This is thus good exercise and will also prove to be a boon to small farmers and domestic users.

i. List the tools and equipment needed to make a bicycle operate a domestic pump.

ii. Look at the diagram of a pedal-powered pump below. Label the parts.

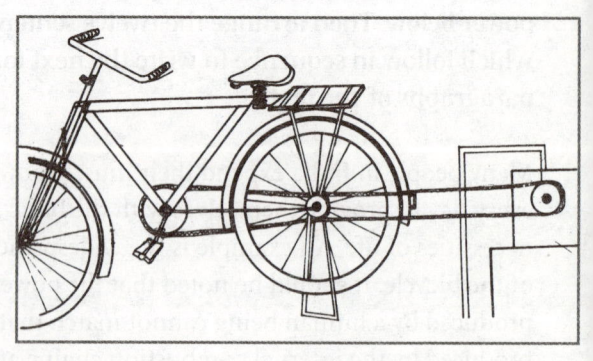

Discussion

Pedal power in Indian villages

Discuss in pairs how pedal power can help people in Indian villages. Be ready to report your views when the teacher asks you to.

Part 2

Language focus

Cement from rice husk

Complete the following text with suitable verbs in the passive form. Choose, if necessary, from this list of verbs.

| mix | produce | burn | obtain | use |

Rice husk .... from rice mills. It .... in such a large quantity that its disposal sometimes becomes a problem. Most of it .... as fuel and livestock litter. When it is difficult to store, it .... When rice husk .... in the open or under controlled temperature in a furnace, it leaves a residue in the form of a highly reactive ash. This ash when it .... with lime, acquires cement-like properties and has the potential to replace portland cement either fully or partially in certain construction works. Scientists at the G.B. Pant University of Agriculture and Technology have developed cement from rice husk. The cement produced from rice husk .... with sand to prepare mortar which can .... for plastering purposes, for laying bricks and stone masonry or for the construction of small houses in rural areas. The rice husk cement has a compressive strength of 30 kg/sq cm which is very low compared with that of portland cement. Rice husk cement cannot, therefore, ... for reinforced concrete constructions.

Writing

Cement from rice husk

The following flowchart presents the process of producing rice husk cement. Write a paragraph describing the various stages in the process of converting rice husk into cement. Use the flowchart and some of the words and phrases listed below for the description.

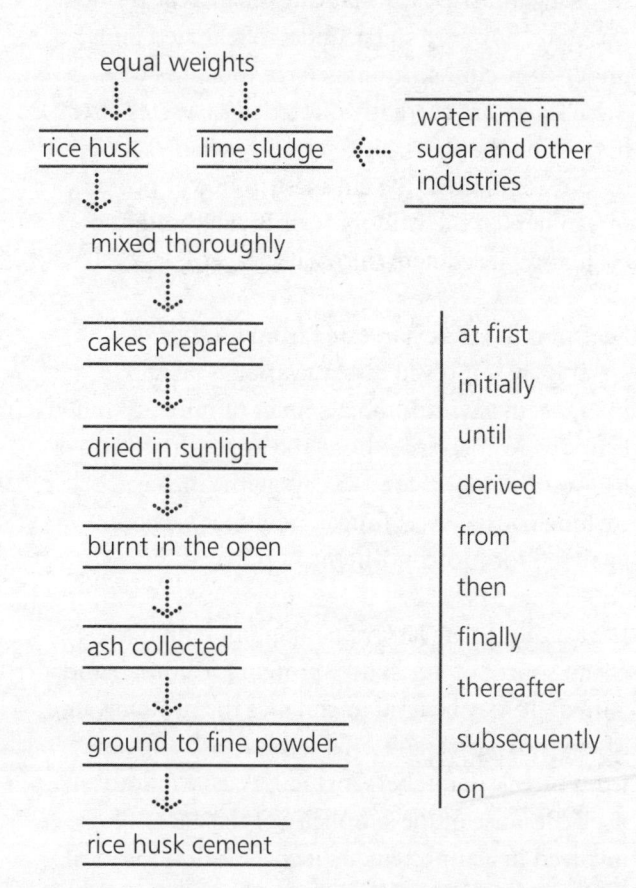

```
         equal weights
            ↓         ↓
                                    water lime in
     rice husk    lime sludge  ←---- sugar and other
            ↓                       industries
      mixed thoroughly
            ↓
      cakes prepared
            ↓
      dried in sunlight
            ↓
      burnt in the open
            ↓
      ash collected
            ↓
      ground to fine powder
            ↓
      rice husk cement
```

| at first |
| initially |
| until |
| derived |
| from |
| then |
| finally |
| thereafter |
| subsequently |
| on |

Reading

Find your feet

a

Go through the text below quickly and suggest headings for the paragraphs in the passage.

b

Read the passage in detail and answer the questions that follow it.

Technology: Appropriate Technology

Cassava leaves as a source of protein

Nagib Nassar

Cassava is a major staple food in Brazil and tropical countries. Its leaves are an all-year product. They are, however, so far under-researched and under-utilised. Accordingly large tonnages of these leaves are currently discarded as wastes after harvesting the roots. Since green vegetables have been recognised as the cheapest source of protein, researchers in the University of Brazil thought of evaluating its content in cassava leaves.

Leaf samples were harvested from local or genetically improved cassava varieties and interspecific hybrids too. Samples of fully expanded leaves were analysed. About 100 gm each of cassava leaf were sundried for 2–3 days with constant turning over to avert fungal growth. It was then analysed for protein content.

It was found that cassava has high potential as cheap source of alternative protein for human and animal. It may be used to enhance the protein value of low-nitrogen traditional staples such as flours from cereals and tubers including cassava flour itself. Because of the simplicity of this technology involved in leaf protein, its incorporation for local food production will be the most practical for a highly sustainable strategy.

The high protein content and nutritive value of cassava leaves are well documented by analysis. If cassava cultivars with low HCN content and high protein were selected it could offer a valuable source in the less developed regions of Brazil and other countries. The leaves contain high protein, as much as 32%. So they are excellent candidates to use in enriching root flour or in being consumed directly.

To increase the potentiality of cassava leaf as a protein source, a strategy for the cultivation of cassava aims towards leaf production in generous quantities. The plant density could be increased and harvested more frequently. With adequate irrigation and fertilisation, cassava plants can withstand defoliation for several years. Considering that the minimum of protein content in cassava is 21%, from one hectare of cassava, it is possible to obtain 140 kg of protein.

In view of the predicted world shortage of cereal grains, cassava leaves are a potential source of protein for livestock raising in the tropics. Because of competing needs for the expanding human population and the diminishing food producing capacity of the earth's surface, it is argued that the major priority is to develop livestock feeding systems which do not depend on cereal grains.
Cassava leaves are considered as a good source of supplementary protein too. They can be used for preparing dishes of cassava leaves adding variety to the diet as well as nutrients.

Therefore it has been concluded that the leaves of cassava are a considerable source of protein. They may alleviate nutrition deficiency in developing countries of the tropics and sub tropics. Cassava cultivars which are used for cooking purposes are good candidates to have their leaves enriched. For these reasons, using cassava leaves as a source of protein serves well for a highly sustainable strategy.

(Source:
Nagib M. A. Nassar and Antonio O. Marques
Departamento de Genética e Morfologia and
 Departamento de Nutrição respectively
Universidade de Brasília, Brasília, Brazil)

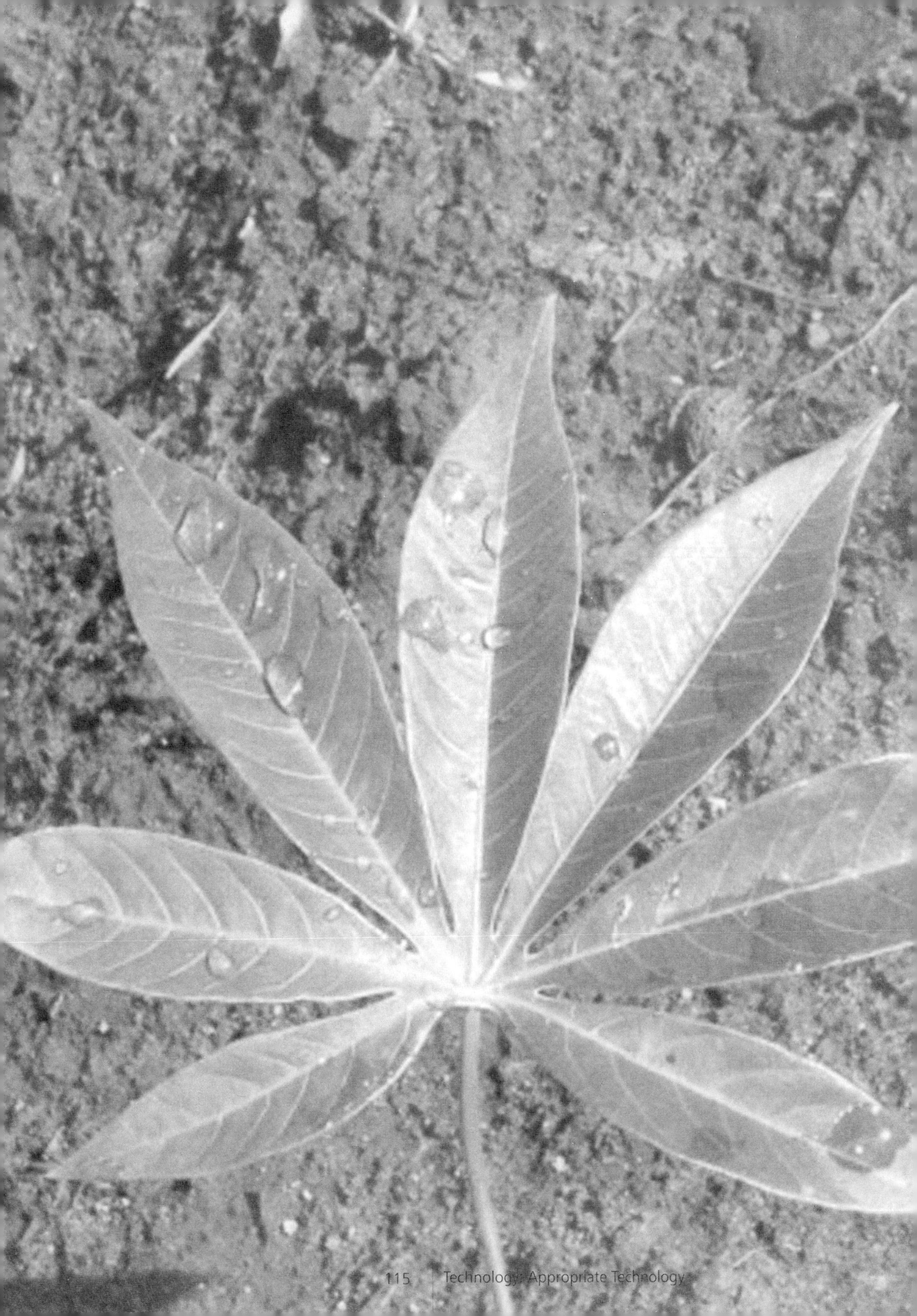

c

Why does cassava have high potential as protein sources? What is the evidence for the same?

d

Make notes from the text using the following outline:
- Plan/Aim
- Material and method
- Findings
- Conclusion

Follow-up

Language check

Complete the following text, with suitable words.

Appropriate technology is a kind of .... cost technology. It has relevance to the .... background of people. It arises from local .... and uses local ...., both human and material. Its benefits go to the .... community. Rice-threshers operated by .... power and gobar .... plants are two good examples of appropriate technology.

Comprehension check

a

Arrange in order the following steps of the process of working the bicycle-operated domestic pump.

- The rear wheel now acts as a flywheel.
- Water is pumped out even at low speeds.
- The drive is transmitted from the front sprocket to the rear wheel.
- After use the clip is released and the chain is opened.
- A person sits on the bicycle seat and pedals.
- The rear wheel transmits the power through the second chain to the pump.

Now look at the third paragraph of the text on page 112 and check the correctness of your answer.

b

Read the text 'A bicycle-operated domestic pump' on page 112 again and answer the following questions.

i. Guess the meanings of the words underlined in the text.
ii. List the advantages of the pump.
iii. What do you understand by the expression 'stationary pedal power'?

Writing skills development

Develop the following hints into a paragraph to describe a paddy-husk-combustor-cum-heat-exchanger.

paddy husk – considered waste – storage problem – disposal problem – its commercial use now for drying paddy in rice mills possible – a paddy-husk-combustor-cum-heat-exchanger developed for this purpose – device – vertical cylindrical combustor – heat exchanger mounted over it – main principle of its working – husk fed into the exchanger – delivered to dryer through ducts – parboiled paddy in the dryer – dried by this means

2

Printing

Preparation

Language development

When we describe a number of actions occurring one after another, we use words that indicate the sequence (sequence words). Here are some examples.

first	second (or secondly)	then
next	after that	finally

a

Rewrite the sentences in the following paragraph in the correct order. Use appropriate sequence words.

i. .... , the roller on the machine is inked, and .... , the roller is rotated either by hand or by means of an automatic device.

ii. .... corrections are carried out on the stencil paper.

iii. .... the stencil paper is placed in position on the duplicating machine.

iv. If you want to make many copies of a document or a letter, you can make use of a duplicating machine.

v. .... , the stencil paper is removed from the machine and stored for future use.

117 | Technology: Printing

vi. This is done by painting the correcting fluid on the mistakes, allowing the fluid to dry, and .... typing the correct words over the paint.

vii. .... , the letter should be typed on stencil paper, setting the typewriter to the stencil-cutting position.

b

i. Learn the meanings of these words. You will find them later in the text on page 120.

A	B
▸ type	reading-matter, as distinct from illustrations
▸ offset	a process of printing from a flat surface in which the impression is first received by a rubber-surfaced cylinder, from which it is transferred to the paper
▸ intaglio	engraving an incised figure or design in stone and similar substances
▸ letterpress	a rectangular block usually of metal or wood, having its face so shaped as to produce, in printing, a letter, figure or other character
▸ lithography	the art or process of putting writing or designs on stone with a greasy substance, and of producing printed impressions from this
▸ layout	the make-up of a page, a book, newspaper, etc.
▸ inventory	an itemised list of goods in one place
▸ enterprise	the ability to attempt something new, difficult or important
▸ obsolescence	a state of being out of date and no longer useful
▸ translucent	allowing light to pass through

ii. Complete the following text with appropriate words from column A.

Although there is evidence to show that some form of printing was known in ancient times, it was printing by movable .... that constituted a turning point in the development of printing. The invention of printing as we know it today is ascribed to the .... of Johann Gutenberg (1400–1468) of Strasbourg. Another invention made in the early years of the nineteenth century was .... This method makes use of the principle of repulsion between grease and water. A further advance in litho printing was made with the introduction of .... litho printing. In this method the impression on the litho plate is transferred to a rubber roller and then printed on paper. Whereas in lithography the printing plate is flat and in .... the type stands cut in relief, in .... printing the image to be printed appears as hollows recessed beneath the surface.

Oral practice

Work with your partner and fill in the first column of the chart below with as many examples of printed matter as you can think of. Then fill in the second and third columns against each example in the first.

examples of printed matter	purpose served	whether of permanent semi-permanent or temporary value
a. handbill	to make an announcement	temporary
b.		
c.		
d.		
e.		
f.		
g.		

Reading skills development

Given below are the title and the first paragraph of a piece of text. Look at the title first and try to predict what the text could be about. Then read the text.

PRINTING ON ITS WAY OUT?

For those of us who harbour the rankling fear that the printed word is on its way out and that the electronic age is about to take over the world of books, a visit to the children's section of a public library is a great source of satisfaction.

Part 1

Reading

Traditional printing methods

a

In pairs discuss
  i. what you know about the history of printing.
  ii. what you know about printing processes, old and new.

b

Look at the following flowchart which describes the process of lithography in the nineteenth century.

| image drawn on a metal plate using a greasy substance | ⇢ | non-printing areas of the plate wetted | ⇢ | application of greasy printing ink to the plate, where it sticks to the greasy image | ⇢ | image printed on paper |

Now read the text on the next page, **Traditional Printing Methods**, and check whether the information in the text about lithography in the nineteenth century is adequately represented by the flowchart given.

Traditional Printing Methods

Although there is evidence to show that some form of printing was known in ancient times, it was printing by movable type that constituted a turning point in the development of printing. The invention of printing as we know it today is ascribed to Johann Gutenberg (1440–1468) of Strasbourg. In 1456 the Gutenberg Bible, the first major printed book, appeared; it had more than 600 leaves, with two columns of 42 lines each.

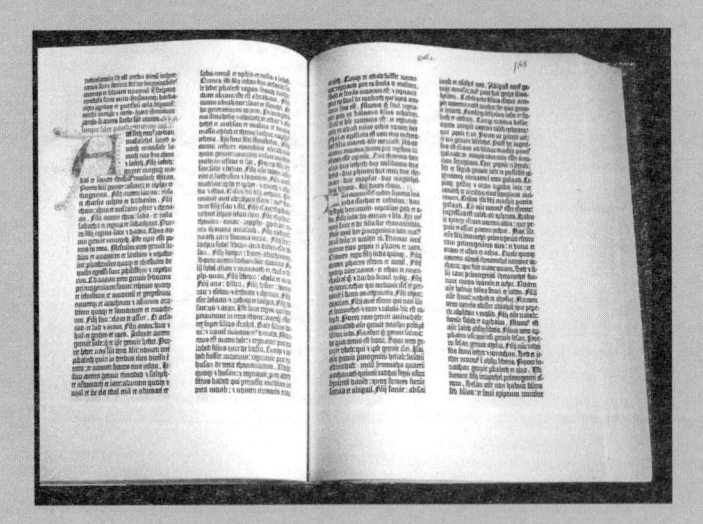

Typefoundry too developed side by side. The type was made by pouring molten type metal, generally an alloy of tin and lead, into a mould. Typesetting was done by hand and the types were wedged together in a tray. Ink was spread on the type and then the paper was pressed against the types. This continued to be the basic method of printing till the present day. Mechanisation began in the early years of the nineteenth century, when Friedrich Konig built a printing machine. In the early machines, the types moved first under a roller which inked them and then under a cylinder which carried the paper to be printed on.

Another invention made in the early years of the nineteenth century was lithography. This method makes use of the principle of repulsion between grease and water. In simple terms, the process consists of drawing the image to be printed on a metal plate using a greasy substance. Then the plate is wetted. The grease on the plate repels the water and consequently only the non-printing areas become wet. When greasy printing ink is applied to the plate, it sticks to the greasy image but not to the non-printing areas. From this plate, the image can be printed on paper. In photolithography the printing stone is coated with a light-sensitive substance and then exposed to light through a paper negative of the matter to be printed. By washing with turpentine or with acid, an image, either flat or etched, can be produced on the plate for normal printing.

A further advance in litho printing was made with the introduction of offset lithoprinting—in this method, the impression on the litho plate is offset or transferred to a rubber roller and then printed on paper. For this reason, the image on the offset litho plate is the right way round, and not a mirror image as in letterpress printing.

Whereas in lithography the printing plate is flat and in letterpress the type stands cut in relief, in gravure or intaglio printing the image to be printed appears as hollows recessed beneath the surface. The lower part of the cylinder carrying the image rolls is a reservoir of ink and as it comes out, a steel blade (the doctor blade) wipes the cylinder leaving ink only in the hollows. The printing is then done on paper. If you look at the printed matter produced by gravure through a magnifying glass, you will find that the image is made up of a large number of dots. The dots will vary in size and density to produce darker or lighter areas on paper.

C

Based on the information provided by the text, draw similar flow charts showing the following processes:

  i. printing by movable type

  ii. photolithography or gravure printing.

Listening

Paper for printing

You will now listen to a talk on paper used for printing in different contexts. Listen carefully and make notes using the following chart.

type of paper	property	use

Using the notes you have made write a paragraph comparing the different types of printing

....
....
....
....
....
....
....

Note: Use expressions of comparison such as 'whereas', 'while', 'but', 'on the contrary', 'in contrast to' etc.

Technology: Printing

ALTERNATIVE THINKING ABOUT PRINTING:

TO CHANGE THE WAY YOU WORK, CHANGE THE WAY YOU PRINT & COPY.

Gone are the days when printers printed, copiers photocopied and fax machines faxed. Today, office machines must manage. And that's what HP Multifunction printers have been built to do. Coupled with HP's legendary reliability and quality, the HP Multifunction printers come with enhanced network security features to protect your critical business information. And because it's also designed to pre-empt interruptions while delivering high-speed prints and copies, you are sure to increase the productivity of your office.

HP COLOR LASERJET CM6040 MFP
BW and Color A3 - size printing, copying & scanning

HP LASERJET M5025/M5035 MFP
BW A3 - size printing, copying & scanning

HP CM8060 COLOR MFP
BW and Color A3 - size HP revolutionary Edgeline technology

HP Dial-a-cartridge
3030 4499 (from mobile) or
1800 4254 999 (from MTNL/BSNL lines)

TO **WIN** AN HP PRINTER, LOG ON TO
www.hp.com/in/intelligentmfp

SMS **HMFP** TO **57575**
Call **1800 4254 999** or
3030 4499
(from mobile, prefix your STD code)
Visit www.hp.com/in/intelligentmfp

WHAT DO YOU HAVE TO SAY?

(hp)

*Conditions apply. © 2008 Hewlett-Packard Development Company, L.P.

For sales query contact: **North:** Siddharth Dass 98111 75469 • **Andhra Pradesh & Tamilnadu:** R Selvendran 98400 77604 • **Karnataka & Kerala:** Sumit Arora 98860 28862 • **Maharashtra & Gujarat:** Vishal Chauhan 98901 61989 • **Mumbai:** Rohit Shukla 99992 78788 • **East:** Dhrubha Saha 93305 51010

Writing

Inkjet or laser printer?

a

Talk to your partner and list a few of the advantages and disadvantages of an inkjet in comparison with a laser printer.

b

Imagine that your firm requires a printer for printing documents. You are responsible for choosing the appropriate printer. Write a paragraph explaining which kind of printer you would choose to buy—an inkjet or a laser printer. Use the list prepared, if necessary.

Part 2

Reading

Excellence in adversity

a

Discuss with your partner if the reading habit among children today is on the decline. Also discuss the factors supporting your conclusions.

b

Read the first paragraph of the following text and answer the question which follows it. Then read the second paragraph and similarly answer the question following it. Now read the rest of the text and then answer the questions at the end of it.

EXCELLENCE IN ADVERSITY
Ashok Mitra

A quiet, diminutive man, P.K. Ghosh, spelled a different universe. He was a literature buff[1]. Fairly late in life, he chose to set up a printing press, the money for which was provided by relatives. It was a printing press of the ordinary mould, and yet with a difference.

You have just read the first paragraph of the text. What do you expect the text to be about?

At the time he interested himself in the printing business, the letterpress was the staple[2] means of typesetting. Ghosh's Eastend Press catered, by choice, exclusively to printing in English. For Ghosh, printing was as much a mission as a profession. He would insist on advancing the cause of quality and quality alone. He revolutionised letterpress printing in the country. The relatives who had originally financed him had meanwhile suffered financial vicissitudes[3]. He, therefore, was not able to arrange the resources necessary for crossing over to either linotype or offset printing. What was a constraint[4] P.K. Ghosh turned into an advantage. He picked his types with meticulous care, visiting smithies and forgemen in remote Calcutta slums, spending hours with them, advising and exchanging information and suggestions. Beautiful type-sets were the result. That was his way out since funds were limited; moreover, imports were difficult because of foreign exchange restrictions.

But the search for quality types was only the beginning. He would economise on other raw materials too, he would improvise[5] on equipment, he would himself labour for long hours inside the dingy printing press arena, soiling his hands, encouraging his workers to do better and still better. That was however only one aspect of his missionary zeal. He would choose the manuscripts he would agree to print with great discrimination. Run-of-the-mill publishers he would politely turn away. He would also refuse to accept indifferent texts which established publishers would sometimes like to palm off on him...

P.K. Ghosh was no ordinary printer. He kept abreast of the latest developments in printing technology. He might have been bound by the bondage of the letterpress, but he knew everything about the nuances[6] of editing and production. He was, at the same time, an editor, an adviser and a scholar rolled into one. He would not flinch from admonishing the author of a manuscript if the style happened to be slipshod or verbose.

The Eastend Press was a small concern and Ghosh would agree to print only a limited number of works every year. The business was not money-spinning in any sense, but it satisfied his love for quality.

P.K. Ghosh did not make money; he still had a sense of fulfilment. As the years rolled, he watched the printing technology pass him by, even as the book fairs did. He knew the days of the Eastend Press were numbered. It did not however diminish his quota of satisfaction. At least in a little corner of this odd, haggard society of ours, he had established quality; quality was the only thing he dealt with. Not just the computer revolution in printing technology, but a family tragedy too wore him down in recent years. In early December, this man, Prabhat Kumar Ghosh, died in his Calcutta house quietly, as quietly as he had lived.

(Source: The Telegraph)

1 **buff**: a buff is someone who is very knowledgeable about a subject.
2 **staple**: main, the most used.
3 **vicissitudes**: misfortunes.
4 **constraint**: problem; a condition that prevents one from doing something.
5 **improvise**: change or modify as a way of being able to use something which could otherwise not be used.
6 **nuances**: finer aspects.

1. What was the one major cause for Ghosh staying with letterpress?
2. Why does the writer call his approach 'missionary zeal'?
3. In what ways was P.K. Ghosh 'no ordinary printer'?
4. If you were allowed only three words to describe P.K. Ghosh, what would they be?

Writing

Imagine that you are the President of the Association of Small Newspapers in India. Write a letter to the Government of India stating the problems faced by small newspapers in India and suggest ways in which the Government of India could help in the matter. If necessary, discuss the issue with your partner before writing.

> **Learner Awareness**
>
> You have learnt to practise the art of predicting the gist of a text as well as the organisation of its parts. This ability helps you read a text with confidence and ease.

Follow-up

Comprehension check

Guess the meaning of the words underlined in the following passage from their context.

Delhi is one of the few cities of the world that can boast of being both and ancient and modern.

A cultural <u>mosaic</u> and a <u>confluence</u> of different religions, it is also an ever-expanding modern city. There are many places of historical interest in and around Delhi. Apart from being the capital of India, the city is also the <u>nerve-centre</u> of Indian publishing.

It is in recognition of its expanding role in the field of publishing that UNESCO had declared Delhi as the World Book Capital for the year 2003–2004. The Government of India has designated the National Book Trust as the <u>nodal</u> agency for the implementation of the programmes envisaged under the declaration. These include a series of book fairs and exhibitions in India and overseas.

There cannot be a more befitting finale to the World Book Capital celebrations than the organisation of the New Delhi World Book Fair, a <u>mega</u> event in Indian publishing. The New Delhi World Book Fair is the largest book event in the Afro-Asian region organised <u>biennially</u> by the National Book Trust, India.

The publishing scenario in contemporary India is a conceptually exciting, linguistically rich and quantitatively diverse phenomenon. India is perhaps the only country in the world which publishes books in 24 languages. It ranks third in the publication of English books immediately after the USA and the UK. More than 70,000 new titles are published every year out of which 20,000 are in English.

Indian books have earned worldwide respect and commercial acceptability both for their content and quality of production. Their price, too, is reader friendly. Apart from offering a glimpse of the multilingual publishing industry in India, the New Delhi World Book Fair serves to establish fruitful communication between publishers, booksellers, book disributors and librarians on the one hand and professionals, intellectuals and academicians on the other.

Language check

Complete the following passage with appropriate words.

Newspaper printing and publishing in the United States had undergone a complete ……………….. in the past twenty years, first by the ………… of electronic and computer typesetting, and …………….. by the changeover from letterpress to offset lithography. More ………….. 80 per cent of all daily ……………………………. in America are now printed by offset.

Both electronic processes and computers have greatly advanced printing ……………..

Now check your answers with your partner's.

3
EVALUATING TECHNOLOGY

Preparation

✻ Language development

Work out the meanings of the words in italics in the following texts from their context. Consult a partner, if necessary.

A

The community-type hybrid solar cooker consists of a wooden box with a steel tray inside. The tray is painted black and covered with glass sheets which accounts for the quick heat trap. The black paint as well as the insulation prevent the heat from escaping. The *cumulative* heat built up inside the wooden box *accelerates* the cooking of food substances kept in the aluminium utensils.

B

This unit can be used for cooking a large quantity of food (e.g. for noon-meal schemes in schools). Conventional fuel is saved by 40 per cent. The disadvantage is that even though three or four items of food can be cooked *simultaneously*, depending upon the size of the box, the cooking has to be done in the open. This project proved to be economically *viable* after several experiments.

C

The import of technology at *prohibitive* cost has the disadvantage of widening the gap between the rich and the poor, imposing *alien* cultural trends and patterns of consumption on the local public, *perpetuating* technological dependence on others and *discarding* traditional technology.

❋ Reading skills development

Below are the first sentences of four paragraphs. Read them and then try to guess what the rest of each paragraph is likely to be about.

  i. Most people imagine that technology can only bring happiness and prosperity to the people.

  ii. What has been said about technology in general so far is also true of Indian technology.

  iii. Modern technology has become very much an integral part of our existence.

  iv. There was once a town in the heart of America where all life seemed to be in harmony with its surroundings.

Check your answers with your partner's.

❋ Oral practice

Technology has conferred a number of benefits on humankind. At the same time, it has created some problems, too. Discuss these with your partner and make two lists, one of benefits and another of problems resulting from technology.

❋ Writing skills development

Use your lists to write a paragraph either on the benefits of technology or on the problems created by it.

Part 1

Discussion

Solar energy

Today solar energy is seriously considered as an alternative to energy from oil. Discuss this issue with a partner. Note down the points you discuss. Now compare the features of solar energy with those of energy from oil. The following questions will help you to make the comparison.

  a. Will this form of energy run out? That is, will it be used up, and not be available in the future?

  b. Is a regular supply of this form of energy possible? (Hint: Think of winter, and of cloudy days.)

  c. Are transport and distribution costs high?

  d. Can the energy be stored and used when required?

Now here are some more facts about solar energy. Discuss them with your partner and decide whether they are advantages or drawbacks.

The photovoltaic cell can directly convert solar energy into electricity.

Photovoltaic technology is expensive.

Some large international corporations are turning solar energy into a high-tech industry.

Solar energy can be used to supplement fossil fuels and thus save them for peak periods of demand.

Reading

Solar cookers

a

By looking at the title of the text, try to guess what the text is likely to deal with.

b

Read the text and check whether your guess is correct.

c

Answer the questions that follow the text.

SOLAR COOKERS

Residential and commercial cooking and hot water in rural areas of developing countries are supplied primarily by direct combustion of biomass – in the form of wood, crop wastes, dung and charcoal. In recent decades, the decline in forest resources in many countries called attention to more efficient household use of biomass, as well as solar cookers. Driven by public programmes, household demand and declining resources, markets for more efficient biomass stoves and solar cookers are found in Asia and Africa. Markets for more efficient biomass stoves and solar cookers in Asia and Africa are driven by public programmes, household demand and declining resources.

Since 1980, many public programmes have disseminated close to 220 million new, efficient biomass cooking stoves. However, surveys suggest that only one third of the stoves in the Indian programme are still being used, and reveal that many stoves did not save energy, broke down and were poorly constructed.

This adoption of technology has proved easier for reducing charcoal consumption (as opposed to wood), and for urban markets to save purchased fuel (as opposed to saving collected fuel).

Solar hot water for residential and commercial uses is cost-effective in many regions. China's solar hot water industry mushroomed in the 1990s, with up to 10 million households served. Other major markets include Egypt, India and Turkey.

There are social benefits from lighting, TV and radio powered by solar home systems, minigrids and biogas, and even some economic benefits from reduced kerosene and candle use. Use of biogas for cooking and improved biomass stoves may also reduce expenditure on fuel and wood, in terms of either time or money. Solar home systems, minigrids and biogas do offer a number of solar and economic benefits for rural areas in developing countries.

Applications of renewable energy that provide income generation and social benefits, such as clean drinking water, cottage industry, and improved agricultural productivity, will appeal to increasing segments of rural populations.

The affordability of rural household systems such as solar home systems and biogas digesters has received much attention. Many argue that households can afford to substitute solar home systems for candles and kerosene lighting if the monthly costs for each are comparable.

(Source: From the paper 'Renewable energy markets in developing countries' by Eric Martinot, Akanksha Chaurey, Debra Lew, José Roberto Moreira and Njeri Wamukonya, in Annual Review of Energy and the Environment, Vol. 27 [2002], pp. 309–48.)

1. What is the usual source of energy for cooking and heating in rural areas of developing countries?
2. How does the adoption of solar cooking save on expenses?
3. What do you think is meant by 'direct consumption of biomass'?
4. Why do you think applications of renewable energy will appeal to rural populations?
5. Does consumption of biomass affect forest resources? How?

Part 2

Reading

A fable for tomorrow

SILENT SPRING

There was once a town in the heart of America where all life seemed to live in harmony with its surroundings. The town lay in the midst of a checkerboard of prosperous farms, with fields of grain and hillsides of orchards where, in spring, white clouds of bloom drifted above the green fields. In autumn, oak and maple and birch set up a blaze of colour that flamed and flickered across a backdrop of pines. Then foxes barked in the hills and deer silently crossed the fields, half-hidden in the mists of the fall mornings.

Along the roads, laurel, laburnum and alder, great ferns and wildflowers delighted the traveller's eye through much of the year. Even in winter the roadsides were places of beauty, where countless birds came to feed on the berries and on the seed heads of dried weeds rising above the snow. The countryside was, in fact, famous for the abundance and variety of its bird life, and when the flood of migrants was pouring in through spring and fall, people travelled from great distances to observe them. Others came to fish in the streams which flowed clear and cold out of the hills and contained shady pools where trout lay. So it had been from the days many years ago when the first settlers raised their houses, sank their wells and built their barns.

Then a strange blight crept over the area and everything began to change. Some evil spell had settled on the community: mysterious maladies swept the flocks of chickens; the cattle and sheep sickened and died. Everywhere there was a shadow of death. The farmers spoke of much illness among their families. In the town the doctors had become more and more puzzled by new kinds of sickness appearing among their patients. There had been several sudden and unexplained deaths, not only among adults but even among children, who would be stricken suddenly while at play and die within a few hours.

There was a strange stillness. The birds, for example—where had they gone? Many people spoke of them, puzzled and disturbed. The feeding stations in the backyards were deserted. The few birds seen anywhere were moribund; they trembled violently and could not fly. It was a spring without voices. The mornings that once throbbed with the dawn chorus of robins, catbirds, doves, jays, wrens, and scores of other bird voices, was now without sound; only silence lay over the fields and woods and marsh.

On the farms the hens brooded, but no chicks hatched. The farmers complained that they were unable to raise any pigs—the litters were small and the young survived only a few days. The apple trees were coming into bloom but no bees droned among the blossoms, so there was no pollination and there would be no fruit.

The roadsides, once so attractive, were now lined with browned and withered vegetation as though swept by fire. These, too, were silent, deserted by all living things. Even the streams were now lifeless. Anglers no longer visited them, for all the fish had died.

In the gutters under the eaves and between the shingles of the roofs, a white granular powder still showed a few patches; some weeks before it had fallen like snow upon the roofs and the lawns, the

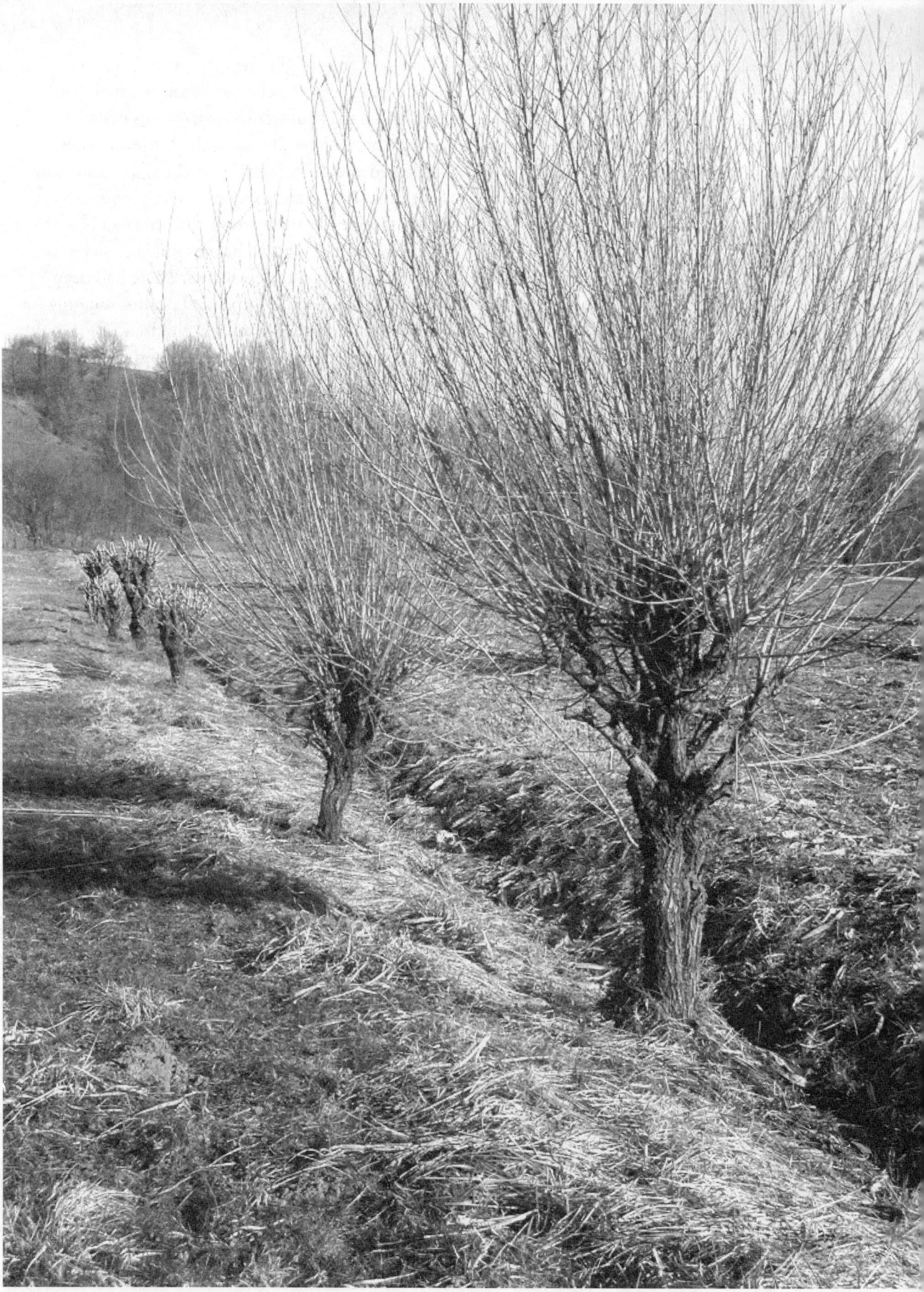

fields and streams. No witchcraft, no enemy action had silenced the rebirth of new life in this stricken world. The people had done it themselves.

This town does not actually exist, but it might easily have a thousand counterparts in America or elsewhere in the world. I know of no community that has experienced all the misfortunes I describe. Yet every one of these disasters has actually happened somewhere, and many real communities have already suffered a substantial number of them.

A grim spectre has crept upon us almost unnoticed, and this imagined tragedy may easily become a stark reality we shall all know.

(Source: Rachel Carson, Silent Spring, 1962)

After reading the essay, *Silent Spring,* answer the following questions.

a

The author's main purpose in writing this fable is
- to entertain readers,
- to present important information,
- to warn us about something.

b

Look at the way the fable is organised. Can you divide the text into three parts? Identify the places where the author moves from one part to the next.

c

Which paragraph describes the colours of spring? Which paragraph describes the sounds of spring?

d

Guess the meanings of the following phrases. Take the help of another student, if necessary.
- checkerboard of farms
- white clouds of bloom
- backdrop of pines
- mists of the fall morning

e

What happened to
- the birds?
- the farmer's relatives?
- the town's children?
- the apple blossom?

f

The words 'science' and 'technology' are not used in the fable. Find a place in the fable where the author seems to refer indirectly to science and technology.

g

Find the phrases used by the author (in paragraphs 3, 8 and 9) to describe the 'tragedy'.

h

How does the author argue that these are not imaginary sufferings?

i

Read the first sentence of the fable again. How does it describe life in the early days in America? Rewrite the sentence, using some of the same words with necessary modifications, to describe life in the same town after the tragedy.

❋ Language focus

Policy on technology

The Government of India has issued a technology policy statement in which the aims of India's technology policy have been spelt out. Some of these aims are listed below. Make seven sentences beginning with 'India's technology policy tries to. . . , and putting together three appropriate items, one from each of the three columns on the next page.

India's technology policy tries to …

A	B	C
provide gainful and satisfying employment to all strata of society		improve the quality of the habitat.
ensure maximum development	particularly	those with export potential.
develop technologies which are internationally competitive		in order to make full utilisation of by-products.
ensure the correct mix between mass production technologies	with	emphasis on the employment of those who find it difficult to get jobs.
reduce demands on energy	and	production by the masses.
ensure harmony with the environment		minimum capital outlay.
recycle waste material		energy from non-renewable sources.

Reading

Goodbye pictures, hello pixels

Read the following passage and answer the questions that follow:

GOODBYE PICTURES, HELLO PIXELS

Three weeks ago, the world's largest office products company, Staples, launched a new 'Copy and Print Online' service in the United States. Customers can now use the Web-based facility to create a document, brochure, business card, invitation or whatever, save it as a PDF file and email it to Staples.

Here, designers will redo the job in a professional manner and send proof copies back to the customer by return mail. If the design is approved of, the material is printed and shipped by courier, to reach the customer the next morning. This job is fuelled by a digital print management server called 'Fiery' and a software tool called 'Digital StoreFront'—both offered by EFI, a California-based global leader in the emerging niche of commercial print management print solutions.

INDIGENOUS EFFORTS

Large parts of the Fiery server and almost the whole of the StoreFront software, were crafted by Indian engineers at EFI's Bangalore-based development centre.

In a change almost as significant as the transition from manual to automated typesetting and from flat bed to offset, the commercial printing industry is today in the throes of a profound and fundamental change from an analogue to a digital domain.

The IPEX 2006, the global showcase of the printing business, which concluded in Birmingham, U.K., on 11th April, was an interesting barometer of change within industry. Jostling with the big names of offset printing were dozens of new players who till recently were better known for their computer-related consumer products, of which printers were but a small part.

Now they were jostling for attention with a new premise: it is time to go digital all the way! Hardcore analogue-era printer players too, were at pains to highlight offerings which allowed corporate customers to continue profitably operating legacy offset machinery, even while harnessing the undeniable advantages in adapting to a digital work flow regime.

The market today sees a clear segmentation. For large print runs—like newspapers and multi-million copy paper-backed books—offset still makes the best sense.

For smaller print runs, even high quality colour work, digital printers have to be seriously considered. And this was across the full spectrum of applications: books and magazine format publications are now served by high speed machines which scan, print, cut and bind all at one go. It is called VDP or Variable Data Printing.

SMALL MAGAZINES

It allows a small or medium-run magazine to print advertisements localized to the mailing address of every subscriber —and thanks to the speed of digital systems this can be done at near-offset printing speeds. Digital print process management can be leveraged even when the actual printer is not a digital machine: work flow tools like Fiery are available from third party vendors like EFI, who offer server-based solutions that promise to computerise the entire process from pre-press and have the added advantage of being Web-enabled.

EMBEDDED FEATURES

Fiery is also licensed by many new generation digital printer makers who embed the work flow monitoring features into their hardware. How will the printing industry in India, react to these digital options? Major centres of job printing like Jammu and Sivakasi are seeing a slow but perceptible lurch towards a digital work regime. Emerging pre-press centres like Mumbai and Bangalore are leading the way—out of sheer market compulsions.

If Indian players are to compete in the global arena, leverage their lower human resource and production cost structures, they have to adapt to international document exchange practices and standards—which means going digital at every stage of the process.

REINVENTING THEMSELVES

Tomorrow's printers cannot be just providers; they will have to reinvent themselves as digital graphics partners of their customers, interacting at every stage of the process from the routine to the creative collaborating everywhere in the work flow and jointly creating the end product.

There is no amber sign along this route: go digital—or die.

(Source: Anand Parthasarathy, The Hindu, *13 April 2006)*

a. What is the advantage of the new 'Print and copy online' service?

b. How is IPEX 2006, the global showcase of the printing business, which concluded in Birmingham, U.K., on 11th April 2006, an indication of the new changes in the industry?

c. How do you think Indian players can compete in the global arena? What are the criteria required for this?

Resources: Water

Follow-up

Writing

An Indian village a hundred years from now

It is sometime towards the end of the 21st century. Imagine you are living in an Indian village. Write a paragraph describing what the village looks like under the impact of technology over the years.

Reading

Mass production or production by the masses?

a

Look at the title of the text and try to guess what the text is likely to deal with.

b

Read the paragraph below and answer the question that follows.

As Gandhi said, the poor of the world cannot be helped by mass production, only by production by the masses. The system of mass production, based on sophisticated, highly capital-intensive, high energy-input dependent, and human labour-saving technology, presupposes that you are already rich, for a great deal of capital investment is needed to establish one single workplace. The system of production by the masses mobilises the priceless resources which are possessed by all human beings, their clever brains and skilful hands, and supports them with first-class tools. The technology of mass production is inherently violent, ecologically damaging, and self-defeating in terms of non-renewable resources, and stultifying for the human person. The technology of production by the masses, making use of the best of modern knowledge and experience, is conducive to decentralisation, compatible with the laws of ecology, gentle in its use of scarce resources, and designed to serve the human person instead of making him or her the servant of human machines. I have named it intermediate technology to signify that it is vastly superior to the primitive technology of bygone ages but at the same time much simpler, cheaper and freer than the super-technology of the rich. One can also call it self-help technology, or democratic or people's technology—a technology to which everybody can gain admittance and which is not reserved to those already rich and powerful.

(E.R. Schumacher, *Small is Beautiful,* 1973)

Using the information contained in the text, complete the following sentences to bring out the differences between the two types of technologies.

a. Mass production requires a heavy investment of capital, *but* ....

b. .... production by the masses, *on the other hand,* mass production uses sophisticated machines and instruments.

c. *Whereas* mass production makes use of labour-saving technology, ...

d. *While* production by the masses .... upsets the ecological balance.

e. .... the servant of machines, ... *in contrast,* ....

f. In mass production technology, non-renewable resources .... In Gandhian technology, ...

g. Intermediate technology is .... primitive technology. *At the same time,* it is .... mass production technology.

h. *Whereas* mass production technology is reserved .... , people's technology ....

Comprehension check

Read the text 'Mass production or production by the masses?' again and say which of the following statements are true and which are false. Correct the false statements.

1. Production by the masses is production of goods on a large scale, employing sophisticated technology.
2. Mass production is highly capital-intensive.
3. Production by the masses makes use of human resources, employing intermediate technology.
4. Mass production is the technology of the poor.
5. Production by the masses is not reserved only for the rich and the powerful.
6. The technology of production by the masses is harmful to ecology.

Language check

Complete the following passage with appropriate words.

Technology is a mixed package; it has its benefits and its .... Technology is the .... derived from the application of knowledge. This power has been sought to be utilised to improve the .... of living of people all over the world. It cannot be denied that advances in technology have had a tremendously beneficial .... on food production, health care, housing, education, transport, communication and other important .... of life. Technology has made human life more comfortable. Turning to the other side of the picture, we find that technology has led to the .... of the environment.
The concentration of human and material resources at a few centres has resulted in large-scale .... of rural population to urban areas and the consequent .... of urbanisation and slums.

Check your answers with your partner's.

THEME
communication

1
LANGUAGE

Preparation

❋ Language development

a

Look at the pictures below and name the objects. Check your answers with your partner's.

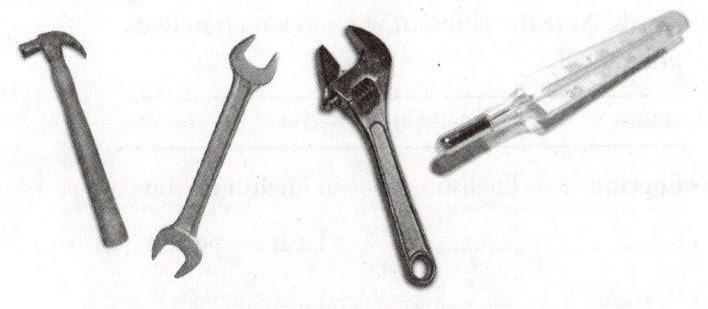

What purpose do the objects serve? Write your answers in sentences like this.

A barometer is used to measure atmospheric pressure.

Another way of expressing purpose is shown in the following sentences.

- The purpose of painting iron parts is to protect them from rust.
- The purpose of a thermostat is to maintain temperature at a constant level.
- The aim of the test is to predict the rise in pressure.

139 | Communication: Language

b

Use the hints below to make sentences expressing purpose. Use any of the patterns illustrated above.

i. **an aerial:** receives broadcast signals

ii. **a feasibility report:** makes recommendations on the practicality of a project

iii. **sending telegrams:** ensures that the message reaches the address quickly

iv. **an experiment:** demonstrates a principle

v. **constructing a bypass road:** reduces traffic congestion in a city

vi. **a sheet of carbon paper:** makes copies while one types

vii. **a litmus test:** identifies acids and alkalies

viii. **a flowchart:** represents a process as a series of steps

Oral practice

Study the following table, and write the missing words. Note the different ways in which natives are named.

country	language(s)	native of the country
England	English	an English person
…………	…………	a Japanese person
Pakistan	…………	…………
Australia	…………	an Australian
…………	Swedish	…………
Switzerland	…………	…………
Israel	…………	…………
Holland	…………	a Dutch person
Poland	…………	…………
India	…………	an Indian

Now read this brief description of the English language.

English is a member of the Indo-European family of languages, which includes many of the major languages of Europe and Asia. It is spoken by about 350 million people as their mother tongue. It is spoken in Great Britain, the USA, Australia, New Zealand and most of Canada as a native language. It has very rich vocabulary which includes words borrowed from every major language of the world. The English alphabet has 26 letters.

Use the above description as a model to present a brief spoken description of the following languages.

GERMAN

official language of Germany, Austria, Switzerland – 100 million native speakers – fourth most widely used after English, Russian, Spanish – Germanic branch of Indo-European family – Roman alphabet – spelling, pronunciation regular

SWAHILI

Bantu group of Africa — Zanzibar on east coast across central Africa to the Congo – communication between local people and Europeans – lingua franca in Tanzania, Kenya, Uganda

HEBREW

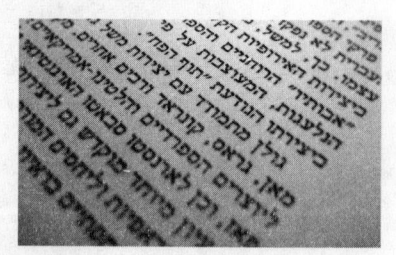

oldest living language – used in Biblical times – Semitic family – official language of Israel – also used by Jewish nationalities in other countries – 4 million speakers – words formed from roots by adding prefixes or suffixes, or by vowel change

MALAYALAM

Dravidian family – ancient language – Kerala, Tamil Nadu, UAE and Gulf countries – 30 million speakers – rich literature – its own alphabet – Telugu, Kannada, Tamil also Dravidian – many words borrowed from Sanskrit

Reading

The English Language

a

The text below takes a humorous look at the English language. Read it, then work in pairs to do the tasks which follow.

THE ENGLISH LANGUAGE

It is true that English is a peculiar language. Look at the following examples of its inconsistency. There is no egg in eggplant nor ham in hamburger; neither apple nor pine in pineapple. English muffins weren't invented in England or French fries in France. We take English for granted. But if we explore its paradoxes, we find that quicksand can work slowly, boxing rings are square and a guinea pig is neither from Guinea nor is it a pig.

Writers write but fingers don't fing, grocers don't groce and hammers don't ham. If the plural of tooth is teeth, why isn't the plural of both beeth? One goose, 2 geese. So one moose, 2 meese?

Does it not seem crazy that you can make amends but not one amend, that you comb through annals of history but not a single annal? If you have a bunch of odds and ends and get rid of all but one of them, what do you call it?

If teachers taught, why didn't preacher praught? If a vegetarian eats vegetables, what does a humanitarian eat? If you wrote a letter, perhaps you bote your tongue?

In what language do people recite at a play and play at a recital? Ship by truck and send cargo by ship? Have noses that run and feet that smell? Park on driveways and drive on parkways?

Have you noticed that we talk about certain things only when they are absent? Have you ever seen a horseful carriage or a strapful gown? Met a sung hero or experienced requited love?

You have to marvel at the unique lunacy of a language in which your house can burn up as it burns down, in which you fill in a form by filling it out and in which an alarm clock goes off by going on.

English was invented by people, not computers, and it reflects the creativity of the human race (which, of course, isn't race at all). That is why, when the stars are out, they are visible, but when the lights are out, they are invisible. And why, when I wind up my watch, I start it, but when I wind up this essay, I end it.

(Source: www.funehumor.com)

Work in pairs to do tasks b and c

b

Make a list of five words in which the letters 'a' or 'o' are pronounced differently.

c

How is the phrase 'put up' used in these three situations:
  i. put up a play
  ii. put up a poster
  iii. put up a brave front.

Listening skills development

You will now listen to a talk on 'Human language and animal language'. Make notes on the important points as you hear them. After completing the tasks look at your notes again, and ask the speaker questions about points you have not understood or points you have missed.

Writing skills development

Use the notes made in the earlier exercise to write a paragraph of five or six sentences comparing human language and animal language.

Part 1

❋ Discussion

What is communication?

a

The word 'communication' stands for different things in different contexts. Read the following sentences and work out the different meanings of the word 'communication'. Work in pairs.

   i. Among the hearing impaired, communication may be by using the finger alphabet.
   ii. Yesterday I received some confidential communication from the Delhi office.
   iii. Today India has an excellent communications network.

Read the third sentence again. Name the things that can be included in the term communications.

b

Here are some words and phrases which contain some form of the verb 'communicate'. Discuss these words in class and find their meanings.

mass communication	communications satellite
intercom	a communicable disease
communication cord	a breakdown in communication

c

In its simplest form the process of communication can be represented by the following sequence:

sender → message → receiver

Look at the following messages. Can you identify the sender and the receiver in each case?

LOCAL FORECAST

Sunday
Intermittent rains; surface winds will be strong and gusty at times, with wind speeds reaching 65 to 85 kmph. Gradual improvement of weather likely by Sunday evening

---

NOTICE

THE COLLEGE WILL REOPEN AFTER THE WINTER HOLIDAYS ON WEDNESDAY, 11 DECEMBER 2008

❋ Language focus:

The language of science

Complete the following passage with appropriate words:

People use language for various .... such as self-expression, transmission of information, persuasion, iden ……………….. with a group, and sheer delight in the sound of words. To the scientist, language is first and ……………….., perhaps solely, a tool for …………….. of information. The language of science has to be looked ……………… as a 'language apart', making statements that are free from any kind of amb ……………….., and aiming at the precision and clarity of ………………… equations. Emotion and humour have no ………………. in the language of science. The language of science must be ……………… from associations that come in the way of clear communication.

Look at this description of human beings by Shakespeare:

What a piece of work is man! How noble in reason! How infinite in faculty! in form and moving how express and admirable! in action how like an angel! in apprehension how like a god! the beauty of the world! the paragon of animals!

142 | Communication: Language

The scientist leaves both the god and the .... out of his or her de ...., which might read:

A woman or man is a metazoan, triploblastic, chordate, vertebrate, pentadactyle, mammalian, eutherian primate.

The language of the scientist is businesslike, unornamented, and s .... For the immediate **u** ....-ing for whom it is addressed. The layperson must not **com** .... that the words are 'difficult'.

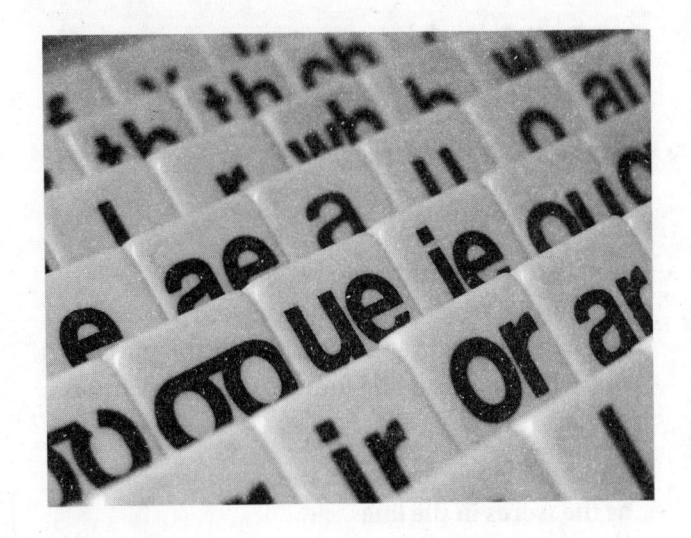

Listening

Increase your word power

You will now hear a talk titled 'Increasing your word power'. As you listen, note down in your notebook the important points in the order in which they are presented. Look at Table 1 and Table 2 below. Listen for the numbers that have to be written in the boxes, and complete the two tables.

Then write down in three or four sentences of your own, the main points of the talk you have just heard.

TABLE 1

number of words	percentage of text covered

TABLE 2

percentage of words understood	extent of understanding of text

Part 2

Language focus

Find the words

In Part 1 of this unit, you read about the vocabulary of science. Here is a word puzzle for you to complete. All the words in the puzzle end in -ity, which is an ending found in many scientific words.

The clues below are not in the same order as the words in the lines.

Words read across only, not down!

a a source of energy
b (in mathematics) one
c HCl and HNO3 have this property
d a thing that has real existence
e rubber has this property
f this is a vector quantity, while speed is a scalar quantity
g being sticky or semi-fluid
h large town
i clay has this property
j friendship
k the .... of 22-carat gold is 100 per cent
l the .... of a tank can be expressed in litres
m lack; being small in number or quantity (p........)
n a metal having this property can be drawn into a wire

144 | Communication: Language

Reading

Symbols—Towards universal understanding

a

In consultation with your partner, list at least five reasons why a universal language may be required.

b

Now read the following text which offers reasons and compare your list of reasons with what is found in the text. Does your list include any reason not covered in the text? Add to your list reasons in the text you had not thought of.

SYMBOLS
TOWARDS UNIVERSAL UNDERSTANDING

There are some 5,000 languages and dialects in use throughout the world, of which perhaps a hundred may be considered of major importance. In most instances, intercommunication among them ranges from difficult to impossible. One solution, of course would be to establish an international language, and hundreds of attempts have in fact been made in the last two centuries to develop an official second language that in time could be adopted in all major countries.

If a system of symbols could be compiled that would be equally recognisable in Lagos and Lapland, perhaps the dream of a universal basic means of communication could be realised. I believe this is possible.

In no way do I propose that this system be yet another language, for it is not really a language at all. Rather it is a supplement to all languages to help create a better and faster understanding in specific areas. Symbols have evolved to the point of universal acceptance in such areas as music, mathematics and many branches of science.

A Beethoven symphony sounds the same in Japanese as it does in the original German; a column of digits adds up identically in Polish and Spanish; and a Russian scientist easily deciphers equations discussed in an English scientific journal. Semiology or semiotics, is the scholarly term for the science of signs indicating ideas or symbols, and the *Oxford English Dictionary* defines symbols in two ways:

'Something that stands for, represents, or denotes something else.'

'A written character or mark used to represent something; a letter, figure, or sign conventionally standing for some object, process etc.'

These are functional, instructive graphic symbols. They are older than words; they are found in every culture however primitive; and in modern times they seem to be increasing almost as fast as the population itself.

In the beginning, we created the symbol—and pictures on cave walls were sufficient for a time to express our ideas about the relatively simple processes of procuring food and shelter. It was when people began to feel a need to express abstractions—differences in degree, nuances in definition, philosophical concepts—that symbols proved inflexible and inadequate.

Then languages began to proliferate. Symbols have multiplied to an alarming degree along much the same lines of divergence as languages. As the world grows steadily smaller, the need for easy communication becomes increasingly acute, and human beings have come full circle—from prehistoric symbols, to verbal communication, and now back to symbols, to help us all live together in today's Tower of Babel.

Years ago, as an industrial designer, I tried to persuade some of our clients to substitute symbols for written captions on their products. My first success was in the field of farm machinery, where we developed an entire vocabulary of symbols

Communication: Language

for vehicle and equipment operation. Our primary concern was safety. A simple, quickly comprehended form of colour, or combination of both, is translated to the brain far faster and more directly than a written word. In emergency or panic, the milliseconds saved in reaction time could save a man's fingers, his arm, even his life.

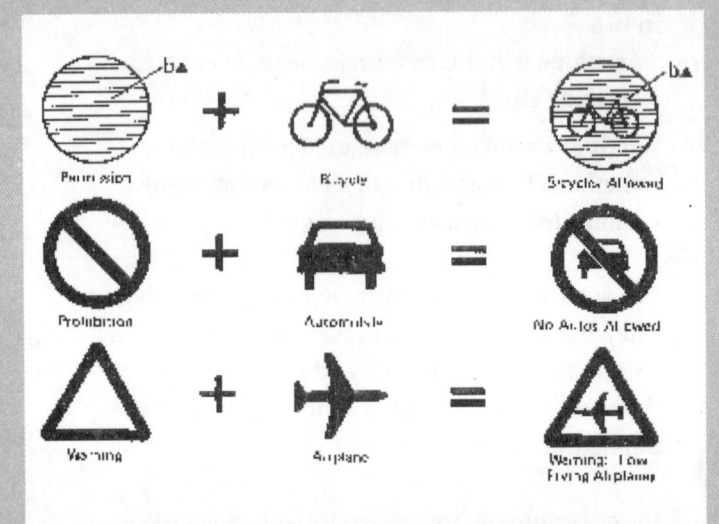

In addition to this primary human concern, there were other gains as well. Symbols fit on small control buttons and knobs, where written instructions would be too small to be legible.

Then too, manufacturers ship products all over the world, and translating various instrument identifications and instructions into the language of import countries is both expensive and time consuming. Imagine a German dealer, under the pressure of a harvest, urgently ordering 500 tractors and finding the nearest one is Paris—with French instructions! Imagine further that in Germany, once the tractors were converted, they might occasionally have to be operated by a Swedish or Hungarian worker! Happily, symbols can cut across such language barriers.

Experts—in the manner of experts—do not agree on precise distinctions between different types of graphic symbols. But to me, it seems logical to consider them as being either representational, abstract, or arbitrary.

Representational symbols present fairly accurate, if simplified, pictures of objects (a silhouette of a locomotive to denote a railroad crossing), or action (a man bicycling to direct one to a path reserved for cyclists).

Abstract symbols reduce essential elements of a message to graphic terms. These may once have been representational but have become simplified by design or degrees over many years, to the point where they now exist only as *symbolic indications*. For example, the signs of the zodiac were once realistic representations of gods or animals, yet today they bear faint resemblance to their original concept.

Arbitrary symbols are those that are invented, and accordingly must also be learned. The three triangle "pinwheel" directing one to a fallout shelter is a good example; also the familiar treble clef in music; and the mathematical plus and minus signs.

Humans on the moon looking back at this earth from which they came have an awesome view of our *opalescent* spinning sphere. They are among the few to see our world in its entirety.

Communication—people to people, nation to nation—is a vital ingredient to understanding. It would be *presumptuous to imply* that standardized graphic symbols will result in perfect intercommunication; but perhaps this is the first faltering step to convince us that it is imperative for human beings to be able to communicate with any other human being no matter where he or she may live.

(Source: Henry Dreyfuss from the Symbol Sourcebook)
(edited for difficulty level)

C

Answer the following questions.

i. What do you understand by 'human beings have come full circle'?
ii. How does the writer classify symbols?
iii. Do you think symbols have communicated effective messages to you in the past? Discuss with your partner five instances where symbols have helped you.

Writing

English will do

Imagine that you find the following letter to the editor in your newspaper. Write a letter in reply to it, arguing that there is no need for an artificial language like Esperanto, since English itself can be an international language. Write about its use in science and technology, in international commerce and in literature.

A Uniting Language

Dear Editor,
We are all agreed that the world needs an international language. There is no need to look any further for such a language, since there is a readymade language, Esperanto, which is now more than a hundred years old. Esperanto is an artificial language created by Zamenhof to serve as a language bridge, to further international understanding. Anyone can learn and speak it without much effort. Even at the first major Esperantist Congress held in 1905, the 700 participants could understand each other by using Esperanto. Esperanto is free from the irregularities and pronunciation problems of English. There are speakers of Esperanto in every part of the world. The language is very flexible and is, therefore, very creative. A British professor has said that Esperanto unites the power of English, the depth of German, the elegance of French and the melody of Italian. Instead of trying to spread English and facing all kinds of political and social problems, let us accept Esperanto as the lingua internacia.

Ajit Chowdhary, Lucknow

Language focus

Non-verbal communication

Complete the text with suitable prepositions.

We think .... communication generally in terms .... words and sentences, but this is not the only way .... which human beings communicate. There are other ways of communication which do not use language. Some .... these replace speech, and some supplement speech. The most obvious .... the latter are gestures .... various kinds, which we make while speaking. These gestures are so naturally a concomitant .... speaking that we make use .... them even when we are speaking .... the telephone. The word 'gesture' refers .... some significant movement .... the arms, hands or head. Other physiological means .... supplementing speech are the use .... facial expressions and positions .... the body. Gesture is, ... course, a feature of face-to-face interaction and is therefore associated .... spoken words. It has its analogue, however, ... written communication. Generally, ... written materials .... a technical kind, communicative devices like graphs, flowcharts and diagrams take the place .... gestures.

Now match the gestures and their meanings in the columns below.

thumbs down	helplessness or indifference
nodding the head	victory
shaking the head	rejection
the V sign	refusal
shrugging one's shoulders	agreement

Follow-up

Language development

a

The eight sentences below express the idea of purpose. Each sentence is followed by hints for a second sentence. Use the hints to construct another sentence in the same pattern.

i. We generally consult an almanac for the purpose of getting astronomical data.
   ... dictionary ... meaning of words.

ii. The aim of this study is to estimate the drop-out rate in the local secondary schools.
   ... book ... present the historical development of English.

iii. The purpose of a safety valve is to release excess pressure.
   ... catalyst ... speed up a chemical process.

iv. He migrated to Australia with a view to improving his career prospects.
   ... (took up) a part-time job ... (supplement) his income.

v. We use a camera for taking photographs.
   ... shorthand ... (write) rapidly while listening to a speaker.

vi. The words are printed in bold letters with a view to making them prominent.
   ... message written in code ...(ensure) secrecy.

vii. A writer makes use of graphs and charts with a view to making numerical data interesting and easy to understand.
   ... speaker ... slide projector ... (present) visual material with speech.

viii. The purpose of tempering steel is to make it harder and less brittle.
   ... proof-reading ... correct mistakes in the matter to be printed.

b

Many adjectives are formed with the ending -able or -ible. In the following sentences you will find adjectives of this kind. Find the correct ending and complete the word:

i. To create and propagate an artificial language that is accept…….. to all countries may not be feas…… .

ii. Language is not fixed; it is flex………. .

iii. Your handwriting is not leg……… .

iv. Some people believe that poetry is not teach…………. .

v. Because of the noise of the cars outside, the speaker's words were not aud…… .

vi. American English and British English are mutually comprehens… .

vii. To keep abreast of modern developments in science, a knowledge of English is indispens… .

viii. It is desir……. that every student learns at least one foreign language.

ix. Politicians are respons….. for many of the disputes over language.

x. It is prob….. that the Aryans borrowed many words from the Dravidian languages.

Oral practice

One aspect of the spread of English in India which has not been touched upon yet in this unit is the opposition to English by some groups in India. Work in groups and discuss the various attitudes to English found in India. Here are some arguments we often hear.

- English is the language of the imperialists.
- English is not an Indian language.
- English poses a threat to the Indian languages.
- People who know English consider themselves superior to others. English is more widely used in urban areas than in rural areas, and this leads to a division.
- People who know English tend to imitate the West and ignore Indian values and traditions.

Writing

Think of other points relevant to the discussion and write a paragraph on it.

2
The Media

Preparation

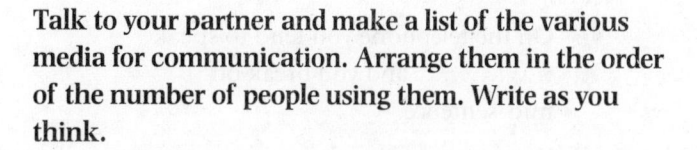

Oral practice

Talk to your partner and make a list of the various media for communication. Arrange them in the order of the number of people using them. Write as you think.

Language development

a

Match the words in column A with their meanings in column B.

A	B
indispensable	a piece of business done between people
anticipate	immediately
transaction	necessary
casually	response
enclosure	relaxed and friendly
informal	consider beforehand
instantly	something included with a letter in the same package
feedback	in an unplanned, careless manner

Learn to pronounce the words in column A correctly.

b

Use the words in column A to complete the following sentences.

i. A business letter can be very important when an agreement over a .... is involved.

ii. Newspapers are .... in a democracy as they provide information that enables the public to make informed decisions.

iii. When you speak on the telephone, you are likely to get an immediate ....

iv. When an important event takes place in any part of the world, it is .... broadcast over the radio.

v. When you speak on the telephone, you tend to become ....

vi. On the telephone you tend to speak .... and you break off mid-sentence.

vii. You can write your letter after careful planning and .... what the reader might want to ask.

viii. One advantage of a letter is that you can send an .... along with it.

Reading skills development

Read the following incomplete sentences. Try to guess what more they are likely to say. Add suitable words and complete the sentences.

1 Desktop computers are now able to play natural human speech together with full screen interactive video, an impossibility just a few years ago. Users can now ....

2 Advertising is a powerful communication force and a vital marketing tool. It helps to ....

3 Newspapers will survive not because editors and designers are clever but because they are ....

4 Tele-education or tele-courses have been in the United States since the early 1950s. The early programmes telecast the teacher at a blackboard, or used the simplest of visual aids. Today ... .

Writing skills development

Write a paragraph comparing the newspaper and television as communication media, using the following criteria for the purpose.

   cost
   number of people using the medium
   depth of reporting
   effort needed by the user of the medium

Part 1

Reading

Will newspapers survive?

The following text comprises excerpts from statements made by editors, publishers, designers and media watchers about newspapers.

a

First, skim through the article below and make a list of the issues it deals with (ignore the underlined words).

b

Now read the texts which together make up the article. Make notes under the headings of issues listed in answer to a.

WILL NEWSPAPERS SURVIVE?

Readers have been attracted to the electronic media, in some cases to the exclusion of newspapers. In general, however, the two media are supplementary and complementary. Newspapers are indispensable, performing functions that television cannot perform. In fact, in America, videotext companies have been failures because it is very boring to sit in front of a TV set and look at text being scrolled past you. There is a great deal of serendipity in how people read newspapers. People like to <u>leaf through</u> and discover things. In addition, the printed word leaves an impression that you don't get with something that is purely visual. People tend to depend less on newspapers and more on electronic media for international and foreign news and to look at newspapers more for local coverage. It is impossible, however, for the public to be well informed on a complex foreign issue by simply getting <u>capsule bits</u> of information from the electronic media.

1
People are spending less and less time with newspapers. We need to recognise that in the way we package newspapers. We need to write tighter and organise better so that people feel satisfied that the paper has been useful.

2
There was a time when television was supposed to run newspapers out of business. Television is important, but there are certain things a newspaper can do that television cannot. We want to continue to look for ways to adapt and adjust. We want to give the news context, meaning, and analysis.

3
Newspapers can report in greater depth than television. We can show things that television cameras, standing in one spot, aren't going to show.

4
The audience is fundamentally lazy, and that is why television is so popular. To read requires physical and mental effort. We have to be good to get the reader to accept that discipline.

5
We must provide information that you can't receive instantly over the air. The world has changed, and newspapers no longer bring society the first words. We must now write knowing that the people who read our stories already know the news from broadcasts. That means more explanation and analysis.

6
Newspapers will survive. Can you see yourself taking a television to the bathroom?

7
I am enormously bullish on the future of newspapers. I think they have never been better and have never realised as much as they do today the importance of still further improvement. There is an absolute need for an honest mass medium. People do not gather in the office and discuss what they saw on television last night any more. Everyone is doing or watching something different.
This segmentation of the marketplace offers an opportunity for newspapers.

8

Six or seven years ago, newspaper publishers were terrified that the electronic newspaper world put them out of business. That was not a realistic fear. Newspapers have their own sort of random access—you can take the paper anywhere. In addition, newspapers are cheaper.

9

Newspapers must be the eyes and ears of society. They must present a picture of reality in a complex world. A democracy depends on newspapers to provide a lifeblood stream of information that enables the public to make good decisions. But lately newspapers have missed the slow things happening in the world. Life has changed and newspapers must respond.

11

Newspapers will survive not because editors and designers are clever but because they are a cost-efficient way of providing information.

10

Most people think that when they read a newspaper, they are getting information, but that is not so. That is not the primary function of a newspaper. The newspaper is what gives order to your day after the chaos of your dreams. The newspaper turns light on to the world. It is almost like a drug, like your morning coffee. Newspapers are verbal caffeine.

(Source: Parade)

c

What do you think of the style of the texts? Is it
   i. descriptive?
   ii. narrative?
   iii. argumentative?

d

Do you find any contradictions, apparent or real, in the various statements? If you find any, what do you think of them?

e

Do you disagree with any of the statements made in the text? Say why or why not?

❊ Listening

Two types of tape-recorder

You will now listen to a talk comparing two types of tape-recorders. Listen carefully and write down the points of comparison. Prepare a table for the purpose.

❊ Writing

Television is popular

a

Talk to your partner and list the factors that are likely to make television more popular than other communication media.

b

Using the list, write a paragraph claiming television to be the most effective medium of communication.

Part 2

✻ Language development

Look at these three different ways of expressing purpose and means.

A

Cultural exchanges between countries are held <u>in order to communicate</u>, to exchange information and help towards better understanding.

B

Cultural exchanges between countries are held <u>in order that people may</u> learn about each other's way of life.

C

People of different nations learn about each other's ways of life <u>through</u> cultural exchanges.

Make similar sentences from the list below:

Your teacher will ask you to read out what you have written.

purpose	means
fostering ties of friendship	cultural festivals
promotion of goodwill	international exhibitions
understanding	art

✻ Language focus

Preserving Traditions

Complete the following text with suitable prepositions.

Industrialisation and urbanisation have inevitably put a damper ..... traditional and folk forms of art worldwide, but they are certainly not on the verge of extinction. Indeed .... several countries, including the US and UK these forms of art have a significant presence. The story is no different in India, either. Despite the growing penetration ... cinema and television and the general indifference .... the elite sections of society .... the folk medium, a substantial number .... India's folk art forms have managed not only to survive, but also to flourish ..... continued community support.

Proof .... this was available when over 250 folk artists ..... different parts of the country performed 23 art forms, each distinct .... the other ... Chennai ... July. The performances were part of a fortnight-long seminar-cum-cultural festival sponsored ... the Indira Gandhi Rashtriya Manav Sangrahalaya (IGRMS) an organisation established ..... the Union Ministry of Human Resources Development. The IGRMS is engaged .... identifying areas in the sociocultural lives ... people in different states. . . documentation and conservation in 'live' forms.

(Source: Frontline: 23 October 1998)

✻ Reading

Building an Internet culture

This is an extract from 'Building an Internet culture' by Phil Agre. As you read it make brief notes on the lines suggested below.

a

In your opinion what will happen to the way the Internet is used in the future?

b

What do the two examples (paragraphs 1 and 3) tell us about the Internet?

153 | Communication: The Media

Building an Internet Culture

In thinking about culturally appropriate ways of using technologies like the Internet, the best starting-point is with people—communities of people and the ways they think together. Let us consider an example. A photocopier company asked an anthropologist named Julian Orr to study its repair technicians and recommend the best ways to use technology in supporting their work. Orr took a broad view of the technicians' lives, learning some of their skills and following them around. Each morning the technicians would come to work, pick up their company vehicles, and drive to customers' premises where photocopiers needed fixing; each evening they would return to the company, then go out together. Although the company had provided the technicians with formal training, Orr discovered that they actually acquired much of their expertise informally while going out together. Having spent the day contending with difficult repair problems, they would entertain one another with "war stories", and these stories often helped them with future repairs.

He suggested, therefore, that the technicians be given radio equipment so that they could remain in contact all day, telling stories and helping each other with their repair tasks. As Orr's story suggests, people think together best when they have something important in common, think together in their own ways. This is perhaps the most common use of the Internet: discussion groups organised by people who wish to pool their information and ideas about a topic of shared interest. At the same time, we should not consider the Internet in isolation. Regardless of whether they are located in the same geographic region or distributed around the world, a community's members will typically think together using several media, such as the telephone, electronic mail, printed publications, and face-to-face meetings, and the Internet is best conceived as simply one component.

Social networks also influence the adoption of new technologies: if the members of a community already have social connections to one another then they are more likely to benefit from technological connections. Every culture has its own distinctive practices for creating and maintaining social networks, and a society will be healthier in political and economic terms when these practices are functioning well. For example, it has long been a mystery why the people of Sarajevo have maintained their tolerant culture as terrible wars rage around them.

A visit to the city, however, makes one reason entirely obvious: Sarajevo is organised around a pedestrian mall about two kilometers long, and the people entertain themselves by walking the length of this mall, meeting their acquaintances, and stopping for coffee. Social connections are thus continually renewed, and people are led naturally to introduce their friends to one another.

As these examples illustrate, the practices of social networking vary considerably and broad implementation of the Internet is one way to promote social networking.

Now compare your notes with your partner's.

Group discussion

Group discussion is an important and popular technique being used in a number of selection tests. The GD is an exchange of ideas among the members of small groups (5–8 people) on specific topics. Your teacher will explain the modalities and will monitor the discussion. Read the texts in this unit and make notes for your presentation.

TOPIC
Will the new media affect our culture and arts?

4 He can ask .... Rajendran—that's my name.

5 This movement has its origins .... national politics.

6 The first is a 15-minute episode of a continuing dramatic story dealing .... the adventures of a group of young people.

Now look back to the texts in Parts 1 and 2 and check your answers.

Writing skills development

a

Look at the following words describing actions connected with a tape.

| loading | threading | twisting |
| tearing | recording | erasing |

Use all these words in other contexts in sentences of your own.

b

Write a paragraph about one or the other type of tape-recorder.

Follow-up

Language check

Complete the following sentences with the appropriate preposition or adverb.

1 The message on the phone can be forgotten or lost if it is not put .... in writing.

2 On the telephone you tend to speak casually and you break .... mid-sentence.

3 To me the time saved seems to make .... for all the disadvantages you're talking about.

Learner Awareness

In spite of the negative influences of the Internet, there are many positive aspects that can be attributed to the Internet. One of them is communication through electronic mail (e-mail).

The following are tips for effective use of email:

▸ Because of speed and convenience, email messages are increasingly being used for personal and business communication.

One should remember the following when sending email:

▸ email messages should be brief and to the point.

155   Communication: The Media

the tone you use should be appropriate to the relationship you have with the recipient of the message

◀ In formal email messages, do not skip the subject line. Provide the essential content of the message in your subject line. If the recipient has too many messages in his or her inbox, only the subject line will help him locate your message when necessary.

◀ Avoid typing messages in capital letters. (This is considered rather rude.)

◀ Though email affords considerable privacy to users, remember that anything can be retrieved by hackers. So be careful not to provide confidential information. Also avoid writing anything which may be considered illegal or unethical.

◀ Be careful about who you copy a mail to. When necessary, use the bcc facility: that is, if the recipient of a copy would not like to be identified.

◀ In formal replies to business companies or institutions, do provide your address and telephone number and other details at the top or bottom of your mail so that if the recipient would like to contact you in any way other than by email, he or she could do so.

◀ If there are many points in your message, say so at the beginning of the mail and number the points where necessary. This helps the recipient gather all the information contained clearly.

◀ Use the reply mode when you are replying so that it helps you reply to all the points raised in the mail you are replying to. It also helps in keeping the address right and keeps the correspondence together for the recipient to make the connections between one mail and another.

THEME
environment

1

POLLUTION

Preparation

✱ Language development

When a word has more than one syllable, one of the syllables is uttered with greater force than the others. This is called stress. Here are some examples:
(Note: The stressed syllables are italicised.)

in*cre*dible	*de*luge	*poa*chers	explo*ra*tion
*at*mosphere	de*scend*	e*co*logy	me*tal*lic
*gar*bage	*da*mage	vege*ta*tion	de*duce*
dis*po*sal	pol*lu*tion	affores*ta*tion	natio*na*lity
wire	pro*duc*tion	expe*di*tions	*sanc*tuary

a

Learn to pronounce the words correctly. Find out how stress is marked in your dictionary.

b

Some words are stressed differently according to the various ways in which they are used.

Read the following sentences aloud:

A

i. The Object is placed at a distance of 10 cm from the lens.

ii. I obJECT to the member's remarks.

B
  i. The SUBject of my talk is 'Pollution'.
  ii. As a test the metal was subJECTed to great heat.

C
  i. The PROject was implemented last year.
  ii. We can proJECT the picture on a screen.

D
  i. That is the PERfect solution.
  ii. The design was perFECTed after years of effort.

Notice the difference in stress of the words when used as a noun and as a verb.

Some other words of this type are conduct, contract, contrast, export, rebel, produce, record.

Work in pairs to form pairs of sentences for these words. Read them aloud to each other.

C
  i. Exhaust gases poison the air we breathe and people who are exposed to such gases can suffer from lung diseases.
  ii. Electric cars, however, do not produce carbon monoxide.

D
  i. Exhaust fumes can also produce smog, which sometimes makes visibility poor on roads and on runways in airports.
  ii. Exhaust fumes are very hot since they come out of hot engines.

✸ Writing skills development

The sentences below form a paragraph. Read the first sentence (A). To select the sentences that follow choose one out of each pair after (A). Look for clues in vocabulary or meaning. Then write the sentences in the correct order. Work in pairs.

A
  Automobiles constitute one of the major sources of pollution in cities.

B
  i. Cars, lorries, motorbikes speed along the roads and often cause accidents.
  ii. The gases coming out of the exhaust pipes of automobiles contain carbon monoxide and other harmful products.

E
  i. Another kind of pollution caused by automobiles is noise pollution.
  ii. Smog comes from the words smoke and fog; another example is motel which is from 'motorist's hotel'.

F
  i. This is caused mainly by the horns of buses and lorries, the loud noise of engines and the high-pitched sound of motorbikes.
  ii. Loudspeakers are responsible for the noise pollution in our cities.

G
  i. Thus air pollution and noise pollution are serious problems in our cities.
  ii. Loudspeakers are found everywhere in our cities.

Listening skills development

You will now listen to a talk on detergents and pollution. As you listen take notes using the outline given below.

a

Disadvantages of soaps ....
....
of detergents ....
....

b

Problems caused by detergents
i. .... of surfactants ....
....
....
ii. .... of ....
....
....
In the USA: ....
....
....
iii. ....
....
....

c.

....
....
....
....
....
....
....
....
....

Part 1

Reading

Cleaning the heights

a

Look at the title and guess what the text is likely to deal with. Discuss this with your partner and make a list of two or three ideas that are likely to figure in the text.

b

Now read the text and compare your list with your partner's.

c

Make brief notes using the following framework:
i. description of the present state of the Himalayan heights
ii. reasons for the present state of the Himalayas
iii. ways of solving the problem posed by littering the heights
iv. difficulties involved in the process of cleaning the heights

CLEANING THE HEIGHTS

A

When travel writer Bill Aitken first set foot in the Nanda Devi sanctuary in the Garhwal Himalayas in 1979, he saw incredible beauty, immense power — and sprawling litter. Recording his experiences in *The Nanda Devi Affair*, Aitken wrote in absolute disgust of how he could deduce the nationality of the visiting teams from their expedition junk. Yugoslavian biscuit wrappers, British sardine tins and Coca Cola cans from the US vied for attention with Indian Army medical supplies.

Environment: Pollution

B

When the Inner Line restrictions were lifted in Nanda Devi in 1974, a deluge of foreign mountaineers descended upon it. But with them came garbage and deforestation. They burnt juniper trees and dwarf rhododendrons for firewood. The ecological balance was disturbed in a way that had not happened before.

C

The Nanda Devi sanctuary was made out of bounds for outsiders in 1982, and when an Army expedition was sent to clean up this biosphere reserve in 1993, it came back with a tonne of non-biodegradable waste and technical equipment left behind by earlier teams after destroying the biodegradable garbage. And though conservationists feel the restrictions on visits to Nanda Devi, the nation's third highest Himalayan peak, has only left the field open to poachers, it has become the most abiding symbol of India's snowy sentinels.

D

After Mount Everest was first scaled in 1953, its peak attracted as many as 12 expeditions and a hundred adventure seekers in that year alone. Today, the number has gone up to 500 mountaineering expeditions and over 50,000 trekkers each year, prompting the fabled mountaineer Reinhold Messner to claim that 'package-tour Everest' had ruined the mighty mountain. The mountaineering community has even suggested that Everest be closed down for at least five years.

E

But with the rising junk has come growing awareness. And it was evident in the goal set by the International Everest Environmental Expedition 1998. The expedition decided to clean the South-East Ridge route and brought down about 325 kilos of burnable and 200 kilos of biodegradable waste, 110 kilos of tin, cans and plastic, 206 kilos of mineral water bottles, 216 gas canisters, 157 oxygen bottles and 520 batteries.

F

The IMF charges $400 from each foreign expedition by way of an environmental levy, a part of which goes to the state where the peak is located. Still, it is just a tenth of the $4000 levy for Mount Everest.
As a result, the mountaineers start believing that they have paid their environmental dues by paying the money, even as the IMF and the government leave it to each other to undertake the cleaning process. Either way, the Himalayas are the losers.

G

To help stop the littering, the Himalayan Environmental Trust was founded in 1989 under the stewardship of Captain MS Kohli, leader of the first successful Indian expedition that put nine men on the summit. The Gangotri Conservation Project, the Trust's pilot effort, was launched in 1994. Though the project has installed an incinerator at Gangotri and opened nurseries to grow saplings, a lot remains to be done. Dodital, near Uttarkashi, which till recently was a pristine trekking trail, also bears the brunt of having been walked upon once too often.

H

Har-ki-Dun, another emerging favourite valley for the trekkers, is paying the price of its new-found popularity. Juniper and rhododendrons are fast dwindling in the valley. And the Valley of Flowers is fast gaining a reputation of being the Valley of Weeds. Nestling close to the pilgrim route to Badrinath and Hemkunt Sahib, the valley has been affected by the spiralling tourist traffic. Certain plants that flower during the tourist season, in fact, have disappeared, thus reducing the overall pollination and seed production rate.

Also, trampling has driven some species to virtual extinction. This is the reason why the number of visitors to the valley has been restricted to 50 at a time.

I

Badrinath is the other place that proves that cleanliness hardly ever accompanies godliness. Other areas that have been badly affected include the Pindari Glacier trail and the vicinity of the Char Dhams of Garhwal. Town garbage and road-building have caused damage to the mountain slope and the vegetation that thrives on it.

J

Around Kullu-Manali, the Solang Nala is heavily frequented and thus quite badly affected. The Rohtang road also causes spillover damage to the vegetation. And the entire Kullu region is devoid of pheasant life and certain alpine flowering plants too have disappeared.

K

In Jammu and Kashmir, the Nun and Kun peaks (7,135 meters), often called the Japanese peaks because of the large number of Japanese tourists they attract, have become the garbage dumps to watch. Back in 1997, a cleaning-up expedition was led by Colonel Amit Roy (retd), ex-principal of the Himalayan Mountaineering Institute, Darjeeling, along with HCS Rawat as the technical adviser. The climb, which cost the Jammu and Kashmir Government and the IMF an affordable Rs. three lakh, resulted in ten quintals of non-biodegradable junk being brought to the ground; a lot of biodegradable junk, moreover, was given a decent burial.

L

Fortunately, the Eastern Himalayas, largely because of their inaccessibility to regular tourist traffic, stand tall and pristine in splendid isolation.

Nonetheless, with Arunachal Pradesh also opening up to tourists, the danger of it too becoming a littering ground appears to be imminent. That'll truly be the height of junk, for the north-eastern Himalayas are the last outposts of high-altitude cleanliness which our nation just cannot afford to lose.

Devyani Onial
(*Source:* Indian Express 1999)

d

Work with a partner. Suggest other ways of solving the problem.

Role play

Cleaning the heights

Work in groups of four to discuss the ways in which the Himalayan heights can be cleaned. By the end of your meeting, you should have a concrete proposal to offer.

Student A

You are a botanist from the Jawaharlal Nehru University. You are convinced that the appalling situation calls for a solution based on engineering and technology.

Student B

You are the President of the Mountaineering Foundation. You hope to get over the problem with cooperation from the mountaineers and the local community

Student C

You are a pollution control officer, playing the role of the representative of the State Government of Jammu and Kashmir. You feel that the Government has already been doing something to improve the situation. However, you are conscious of the limitations under which the Government is functioning.

Before you hold the meeting spend five minutes preparing what you will say. Make use of points from the text 'Cleaning the heights' if necessary.

Writing

Report on the meeting

Imagine that you were present at the meeting between the botanist, the pollution control officer and the President of the Mountaineering Foundation. Write a brief report on the meeting. You can begin like this.

> "A meeting was held to consider the measures to clean the littered heights of the Himalayas ....."

Note: Your report must include

1. the title
2. names of those present at the meeting
3. the venue of the meeting
4. the significant or important points that featured at the meeting
5. the solutions suggested at the meeting

Part 2

Reading

Climate change in short

a

Discuss the following questions in small groups.

 i. What is meant by the greenhouse effect?

 ii. What is the connection between rising temperatures and greenhouse gases?

 iii. What are the effects of global warming?

iv. What should be done to reduce the emission of greenhouse gases?

b

Now read the following text and compare your answers to a with it.

CLIMATE CHANGE IN SHORT
Leonie Haimson

In December 1997, negotiators from more than 150 countries gathered in Kyoto, Japan, to decide whether to impose mandatory measures to address the most difficult environmental problem of our time: humanity's experiment on the world's climate. An agreement was adopted to require industrialised countries to make significant reductions in their emissions of warming gases over the next 10 to 15 years. To achieve this, nations will have to reduce their use of fossil fuels, such as coal and oil, and begin a steady transition toward a new energy system, based on efficiency and renewable energy.

THE SCIENCE DRIVING THE POLITICS

The earth's atmosphere is transparent, allowing sunlight to enter and warm its surface. Some of the gases in the atmosphere, including water vapour, carbon dioxide, methane, and nitrous oxide, are called greenhouse gases because they trap some of the resulting heat. Without the natural greenhouse effect, much of the sun's warmth would be lost to space, and the surface of the world would be about 61 degrees Fahrenheit colder, too frigid for most forms of life.

Since industrialisation, however, the levels of these gases in the atmosphere have risen substantially, due to the increased combustion of fossil fuels (coal, oil, and natural gas) used to produce electricity, power cars, run factories, and heat and cool houses. Greenhouse gases have also been emitted as a result of deforestation and certain agricultural practices. The accumulation of these gases is changing the earth's climate by trapping more of the sun's energy. The globally averaged temperature of the air at the earth's surface has warmed between 0.5 and 1 degree Fahrenheit since the late nineteenth century. The sea level has also risen about four to 10 inches since the nineteenth century, due primarily to the melting of glaciers and the thermal expansion of the oceans, phenomena attributed to global warming.

In 1988, in recognition of the gravity of this problem, the nations of the world appointed the Intergovernmental Panel on Climate Change (IPCC), consisting of more than 2000 leading experts from around the world, to assess the science and economics of climate change. In a landmark 1995 report, the IPCC concluded that "the balance of evidence suggests a discernible human influence on global climate."

The evidence continues to accumulate. The planet's 12 warmest years on record have all occurred since 1980, and the 1990s as a whole have been the warmest decade in an estimated 1200 years. 1998 broke the previous record set in 1997 by a substantial amount, and surpassed the 30-year norm by a full degree, according to the World Meteorological Organization (WMO).

The IPCC has predicted several probable consequences of future warming, including sea level rises of an additional six to 37 inches by the year 2100, and increased frequency and duration of many extreme weather events, such as heat waves and droughts. Heavy rains and flooding are also predicted to occur more frequently in many parts of the world, since higher temperatures lead to more rapid rates of evaporation and precipitation. In the United States, where the best data are available, an increased number of extreme rainfall events has already been observed.

For the 50 percent to 70 percent of the human population living in coastal areas, rising sea levels and more frequent storm surges could have devastating effects, subjecting millions of people's homes to periodic flooding or permanent submergence.

Global warming also has the potential to transform many of the world's natural ecosystems over the next century, causing, for example, about one-third of the Earth's forested area to undergo major shifts in composition. Among ecosystems most likely to experience serious disruption are those at higher latitudes, such as the far northern forests and tundra, as well as coastal ecosystems, with dramatic consequences for fisheries and marine biodiversity.

(Source: www.thegrist.com)

C

Answer the following questions.

i. Which are the greenhouse gases, and why are they considered dangerous?

ii. Why was the IPCC set up?

iii. What, according to the text, are probable consequences of future warming?

Language focus

Our challenge

Complete the following passage with appropriate words. Compare your answers with your partner's.

Addressing the problem of climate change in an effective and timely manner is probably the most complex and difficult challenge the nations of the world have ever faced. Additional warming is already ………………… , given past emissions, since most ………………… once released remain in the atmosphere for a century or more. ………………… There are powerful ………………… fighting decisive action, including the fossil fuel corporations and their allied unions, OPEC countries, and the many ………………… that rely heavily on the use of fossil fuels, such as auto, chemical, and metal-producing companies. Nevertheless, several multinational oil corporations, including British Petroleum and Shell, have begun to invest more intensively in ………………… energy, and pledged to reduce their emissions of greenhouse gases.

Developing nations bring further uncertainties to the mix. Though the ………………… countries lead the world in per capita greenhouse gas emissions, the total ………………… of developing nations are growing at a faster rate and are expected to ………………… those of the industrialised world early in the next century. Whether these countries can be ………………… to enter into binding agreements to cap their emissions will depend upon whether they believe they will be able to develop fast enough by adopting ………………… , efficient energy systems. One positive step forward was an announcement from two members of the developing world bloc, Argentina and Kazakhstan, that they will voluntarily take ………………… to limit their emissions.

(Source: www.thegrist.com)

Listening

Noise pollution

You are going to listen to a talk on noise pollution. Listen carefully and write your notes in the chart on the next page.

study conducted in	findings

Language focus

Noise pollution

Complete the following text with appropriate words.

From a study made of the problem of noise pollution in metros, it was seen that the sources of noise that people considered most annoying were the following:

i. automobiles
ii. loudspeakers
iii. aeroplanes
iv. radios and stereo systems

According to the ………………………. collected, the number of automobiles in the city had doubled in the last six years. The increase was more pronounced in heavy vehicles like buses and lorries. The vehicles were …………. with air horns or other high-pitched horns which could cause great …………… to hearing. Even in the vicinity of schools and hospitals, the horns were used indiscriminately. Besides the horns, the engines of many heavy commercial …………… contributed to the noise pollution. Many motorbikes had no ………………….. and were seen tearing through the streets at high speeds.

The second source of …………………….. was the loudspeaker. Many places of worship used loudspeakers to ……………… religious music or religious chants. During certain months, the music was played every day from 4:00 a.m. onwards. Houseowners and many citizens ……………………… in the neighbourhood complained about this noise. Another occasion when loudspeakers were ………………… was in weddings. Film songs were played from dawn …………………. well past midnight, and the songs were repeated so often ………………….. people reached the end of their patience.

Loudspeakers were also used at political meetings, and here again the noise continued till midnight. Very powerful loudspeakers were used and they were directed at residential ………….. . The meeting itself was preceded by two or three hours of film songs.

The third source was aeroplanes. This complaint came mainly from residential areas near the …………………, though some headmasters and principals complained that the planes took ………….. in the direction of their institutions, and classes were ………………….. .

There were a few complaints from people living in flats that their neighbours played their ………… and stereo systems at high………………… even late in the ………… .

167 Environment: Pollution

Writing

Noise pollution

a

Discuss with your partner about some measures to check noise pollution in metropolitan areas.

b

Write a set of recommendations to check noise pollution.

Follow-up

Comprehension check

Look back at the text, 'Cleaning the heights' on pages 161–4 and answer the following questions.

a

Which of the following statements are true?

i. Garbage removal-drives have been stepped up at Gangothri where cleanliness does not co-exist with godliness.

ii. Juniper trees and dwarf rhododendrons found in the Himalayan mountains have been cut to lay roads.

iii. The environmental levy charged in Himachal Pradesh is exorbitant when compared to the levy for visiting Mount Everest.

iv. The year 1953 attracted as many as 100 adventure seekers to Mount Everest.

v. Package tours to the Himalayan Heights ruin them.

b

Link the events mentioned in Column A with the dates mentioned in Column B.

A	B
The travel writer Bill Aitken first set foot in the Nanda Devi Sanctuary	in 1993.
The Nanda Devi Sanctuary was marked out of bounds for outsiders	in 1994.
The Inner Line Restrictions were lifted in Nanda Devi	in 1979.
An Army expedition was sent to clean up the Nanda Devi biosphere reserve	in 1982.
The Gangothri Conservation Project was launched	in 1974.

Oral practice

Hold a conversation on the problem of noise pollution in cities.

Student A

You are a citizen affected by noise pollution from various sources. Express your feelings strongly and demand corrective measures.

Student B

You are a police official. You appreciate the feelings of citizens and would like to be helpful. But you have practical difficulties in enforcing regulations.

Student C

You are a bus driver. You do not like using the horn unnecesarily. But you cannot help it when people do not abide by rules.

Before you start the conversation, spend five minutes preparing what you will say. Make use of the text, 'Noise pollution', on page 167 if necessary.

Writing skills development

You happen to live in an area where political meetings are held frequently. There is no check on the use of loudspeakers at these meetings. Write a letter to the editor of a newspaper complaining about the noise.

2

ECOLOGY VERSUS DEVELOPMENT

Preparation

❋ Language development

❋ You are already familiar with some prefixes and suffixes. Here are a few more which will figure in the texts of this unit.

prefixes:
con- has the meaning of 'with' as in 'conjunction'.
amphi- has the meaning of 'both' as in 'amphibian'.
sub- has the meaning of 'under' as in 'submerge'.
ad- has the meaning of 'intensification' as in 'adduce'.

suffixes which make nouns from verbs:
-ence, -ment, and -ing

a

Suggest examples of words with each of the prefixes and suffixes mentioned above. Write sentences using them.

b

Match the words in Column A with their meanings in Column B. Make sure you can pronounce all the words in column A correctly.

A	B
i. conservation	organism able to live both on land and in water

ii.	genetics	biology dealing with mutual relations between organisms and their environment
iii.	amphibian	reservoir, a place where water is collected and stored
iv.	submergence	preservation
v.	ecology	a reciprocal action or effect
vi.	afforestation	the scientific study of the way qualities are passed on from one generation to the next
vii.	deforestation	expansion of forests
viii.	catchment	being placed under water
ix.	repercussion	cutting down
x.	felling	clearing of forests

c

Fill in the blank spaces in the box given below with the appropriate forms of the words.

noun	adjective	person concerned
environment	....	....
nature	....	....
....	ecological	....
....	....	conservationist
....	....	geneticist

d

Look at the following examples and fill in the chart below.

present	past	past participle
i. fall	fell	fallen
ii. fell	felled	felled
i. see	....	....
ii.	....	....

i. find ....
ii. ....

Write three sentences with the three words in (ii) in any form.

Oral practice

Discuss the following in small groups.

a

What do you understand by the expression 'environmental conservation'? Specify three ways in which the environment can be preserved.

b

Do you think that environmental conservation acts as a brake on economic development?

c

What is meant by environmental degradation? Name three ways in which the environment is degraded.

d

Do you agree that environmental degradation leads to social injustices?

✺ Writing skills development

Write a paragraph describing how the environment can be preserved.

....
....
....
....
....

Part 1

✺ Reading

Bamboo forests

a

i. Look at the title of the following text. Write down 10–15 words which you expect to find in the passage. Compare your list with your partner's.

ii. Talk to another student and list three or four things the passage is likely to include.

iii. Now read the passage and check whether the words you chose in (i) appeared or not. Which words might have appeared but did not?

iv. Did the passage deal with any of the points you listed? Do you think that the passage missed something it ought to have dealt with?

BAMBOO FORESTS

Bamboo grows mostly in the Orient and in warm places such as Central America and parts of South America. Bamboo is the giant of all grasses. There are many varieties that grow as tall as trees. One type grows up to 120 feet in height, with a stem of three feet in circumference. It is one of the fastest growing of all plants. One kind has been known to grow three feet in 24 hours.

Tiny bamboo shoots are used as food. When the fruit starts to come, there is always an abundance of food for humans, birds and rodents alike. In some parts of India, the fruit is cooked and eaten as rotis etc. When bamboo fruits, the rodent population increases manifold and then when the seeds disappear, the rodents start destroying other crops and soon there is a possibility of famine.

The fruiting of the bamboo forests in turn leads to the drying up of the bamboo groves and therefore subsequent death. Also, dry bamboo is easily susceptible to forest fires and therefore need to be chopped off. As a result of this, there is all the leaf litter on the forest floor, increasing the risk from fires. Actually the seeds need to be renewed at this stage but tribals and cattle finish off whatever is left of the bamboo shoots. Therefore while the bamboo fruiting season is food in plenty, soon after that there is deprivation.

But the most important use for bamboo is in making furniture and building houses. It is used as roofing material on which the thatch or tiles are placed. It is also used to make fence posts, bridges, fishing poles, water pipes and parts of musical instruments. Bamboo is used in the making of mats which are in turn used to construct the sides and roofs of bullock carts, mud and wattle constructions and so on. Hollow bamboo poles are even used to store grain and water. The grass is used to make baskets, weave mats and to make decorations for houses. All constructions are carried out with bamboo scaffolding. Thus we see the immense use of this remarkable plant which grows in such large numbers in forests.

If there were successful operations to collect fallen bamboo seeds and use them as soil binders and conservators of soil moisture in order to regenerate teak, sal and other trees, it would be highly beneficial. But the extent of manpower and funds required for this operation is so much that we are not able to do it.

Bamboo was probably the wood used by the Chinese when they first made paper from wood pulp about 2000 years ago. Today bamboo is used in India and Myanmar to make paper. Some plant scientists think more bamboo forests should be grown as a source for wood pulp.

The earliest Chinese books were written on the backs of palm leaves and on flattened pieces of wood and bamboo. The palm leaf and bamboo books of the Chinese were strips fastened at one end much like a fan and then spread like a fan to be read. The Chinese did not use pens or styluses. Bamboo continues to be used in the making of paper. Thus we see the immense power of bamboo in sustaining human growth and the environment.

b

Answer the following questions:

i. What evidence is there in the text for assuming the following?
   Bamboo fruiting has mixed advantages.
   Nutrition is not the only value of bamboo.
   The destruction of bamboo is creating a problem for forests.
   The flowering of bamboo can be a boon to forest conservators.

ii. Note down all the words and phrases in the passage which refer to destruction in bamboo forests.

Language focus

Dams

Some of the words in the box belong in the text which follows. Read the text carefully once, then try to fill in the gaps with the most appropriate word.

distribute	proliferate	exploitation	depend
catchment	economic	aquatic	urban
problem	conviction	defend	among
triggering	ecological	eviction	disturb

DAMS AND THEIR ADVERSE ENVIRONMENTAL EFFECTS

Big dams have had several adverse effects on the environment and the people. Some of them are—the .... of thousands of families and their resettlement at some other site, making them refugees in their own land; the increase in the incidence of some diseases; .... of earthquakes and dam bursts; and the destruction of ecosystems. The last mentioned consequence has been a cause for great concern .... people. The design and constructions of dams in India have been achieved mainly as civil engineering tasks neglecting their harmful .... impact. Engineers seem to be concerned with instant solutions to problems rather than the long-term effects and consequences of the solutions proposed. Thus, the provision of the intended benefits to down-stream areas causes the neglect or wanton .... of the environment of the catchment regions upstream in most cases. Its immediate victims are the tribals, the peasants in the river valleys and the hillfolk whose lives .... on the resources provided by their immediate environment. This is, of course, a pitiable situation. But more so is the ecological ruin with its grave long-range .... consequences for the nation.

The decimation of vital forests in the .... areas is one of the most serious problems effected by the engineering approach. Large tracts of forests have been lost as a result, particularly in the Himalayan hills and the western Ghats. Submerging forest lands have aggravated the ....

Large scale deforestation for dams can lead to subtle imbalances in the ecosystem. Following the construction of dams, ... life is often grievously harmed. Changes in water velocity, water chemistry, temperature and turbidity .... the free passage of fish to and from their spawning grounds. Weeds often .... in irrigation reservoirs. The spread of diseases among human beings and cattle is often due to many of these weeds.

(Source: The State of India's Environment, 1982)

Check your answers with your partner's.

Writing

The importance of forest resources

Write a paragraph on the measures you would recommend to preserve forest resources.

Part 2

Reading

Bags of Rubbish

a

Discuss the following in groups.

i. What do you think of the debate on banning plastics in every day life?

ii. How will it affect the common tradesperson?

iii. What can we plan to use in the place of plastics?

iv. What solutions would you suggest for the disposal of rubbish?

b

Now read the following passage on 'Bags of Rubbish'. As you read it make brief notes on the lines suggested below.

1. the incident which brought plastic litter into prominence ....
....

2. the increase in plastic use ....
....

3. Indian tradition of recycling ....
....

4. recycling plastic litter ....
....

5. the terms of the Biodegradable Waste Act
....

6. the solution proposed
....

7. the encouragement this gave to the plastic industry ....
....

BAGS OF RUBBISH

Robert Edwards

In April this year the Lucknow *Times of India* reported that local cows were dying as a result of eating discarded plastic bags. The number of cows was estimated to be 100 a day. 'The affected animal has a skeletal body but an abnormally bloated stomach. It eagerly goes to the trough but only sniffs at the fodder apparently unable to eat anything. It gradually becomes weak due to starvation and then finally becomes immobile.'

Plastic litter has grown in proportion to the expansion of the plastics industry. In the mid-1980s the government of India sanctioned a huge increase in the national production of plastic so that India would become self-sufficient in petrochemical products and be able to compete in the global plastics market. Over 50 per cent of all plastic produced in India is used for packaging.

This problem of plastic litter is perhaps surprising in India with its well-known tradition of recycling. All over the country, material objects like bottles are cleaned out and reused many times in many different ways and if they break, they will be mended. And when the material is threadbare, and completely beyond repair, it is often picked up by human scavengers known as ragpickers – 60 per cent of whom are children, 30 per cent women and only 10 per cent men (mainly old and disabled) – who pick and sort waste with their bare hands and then sell it on for whatever they can get.

The Indian government and the plastics industry claim that India has the highest rate of plastic recovery in the world – between 40 per cent and 80 per cent of all plastics produced. But be this as it may, the waste problem remains; and mainly for the simple reason that the ragpickers don't collect plastic bags, for simple reasons of economics. Although plastic fetches about 12 rupees per kilo in the waste market, it takes between 450 and 800 flimsy polythene bags to make up a kilo – and if they are soiled the price drops. This makes them an extremely unattractive economic proposition for even the most destitute ragpicker.

The first Non-Biodegradable Waste Act passed in 1996 didn't ban the use of plastic bags in Himachal Pradesh, it merely banned the 'haphazard discarding' of non-biodegradable waste. Further legislation was passed which taxed local production of plastic bags, to discourage their use in favour of paper or jute bags. But the lack of nationwide action meant that, to avoid the tax, plastic bags were simply manufactured in Delhi or elsewhere and then transported to Himachal. The people of Simla are now much more aware of the plastics problem – but the problem is still with them.

It was in this context, that the government of India proposed its first 'nationwide solution' to the plastic bag problem which was that plastic bag waste was too thin for the ragpicker to collect and recycle.

Therefore the solution was simple: plastic bags should be made thicker. The government promptly passed a 'notification', to be implemented in all states. Only bags at least 20 microns thick could now be manufactured.

For the plastics industry, this 'solution' is perfect. The ragpickers, in theory, will now collect the bags for recycling, so the public eyesore will be removed. This in turn will remove the plastics industry's image problem. And, crucially, more plastics will be needed – so more will be produced, to the industry's great pleasure. As a result, there will also be more resource use, more pollution – and probably more waste.

(Source: www.theecologist.co.uk)

✱ Writing

Development at the cost of environment?

Do you agree that development should not be at the cost of the environment? Write a paragraph expressing your views on the question.

✱ Listening

The environmental movement in India

You are going to listen to a talk about the environmental movement in India. Listen carefully for the details and take notes of as many of them as you can on the lines indicated below.

a government measures
   and schemes   ....
                      ....
                      ....

b voluntary efforts ....
                      ....
                      ....

c aim of the environmental
   movement   ....
                      ....
                      ....

Role play

The Chipko movement

Make use of the notes taken on the environmental movement in India to frame the questions as well as to answer them. Start when you are both ready.

Student A

You are a journalist. You want to write an article about the Chipko movement. You are going to interview Mr Sunderlal Bahuguna, one of the leaders of the movement. Prepare a list of questions to ask him.

Student B

You are Mr Sundarlal Bahuguna, one of the leaders of the Chipko movement. You are going to be interviewed by a journalist who will ask you questions about the movement. Prepare yourself to answer them.

Follow-up

Comprehension check

Look back at the passage, 'Bags of Rubbish' and say whether the following statements are true or false. Correct the false ones.

i. The plastics industry has grown far quicker than the plastic litter created.

ii. India is well-known for its tradition of recycling.

iii. Ragpickers don't collect plastic bags because it isn't worth it financially.

iv. As thicker bags are produced industry will be pleased but pollution may be greater.

Writing skills development

Using the notes taken by you in the listening exercise on page 176, write a paragraph on the measures taken by the government towards environmental conservation.

Oral practice

Work in pairs. Using the notes made by you on plastics on page 175, ask and answer questions about plastic production and disposal in India. Use question words such as where, what, why, how, etc. Try to answer the questions as quickly and as clearly as you can.

Language development

The terms *cause* and *effect* refer to the relation between events, occurrences, etc. The cause of an event is the reason for it. The event is itself the effect or the result of the cause.

> For example: Scarcity is the *cause* of the rise in the price of articles.

The verb forms of 'cause' and 'result' can also be used to express the same relation.

> For example: The rise in the prices of articles is *caused* by scarcity.

Now look for at least ten words or phrases in the texts of this unit expressing causal relations. Check with your partner. If you have time look for five more. Now your teacher will ask you to read out some of these.

3

OUR LIVING ENVIRONMENT

Preparation

❋ Language development

Read the following newspaper report.

Chennai, March 23:
Two black bucks have died in the IIT campus recently. While a pregnant black buck died after it was hit by a vehicle a couple of months ago, another was found dead today near the Electrical Sciences Block in the campus, wildlife enthusiasts say.

About 15 black bucks including four stags were recorded in the premises. Their population had come down to 13 with the death of two—a female and a male.

The problem with the safety of deer has prompted the authorities to address letters to various organisations including the IIT, Anna University, Air Force Station, Tambaram, requesting them to provide care to the local spotted deer and black buck population. But no institutional mechanism has evolved yet for this.
IIT sources said the institution was taking several steps for the safety of the animals. Chief among them was the creation of ponds within the campus to provide them water. Carcasses of animals killed in rare accidents and due to natural causes like snake bite were handed over to Blue Cross.

Stray dog menace, increased garbage dumping, appearance of chain-link fences and speeding of vehicles were some of the reasons for the death of deer, according to wildlife officials.

Fencing of buildings inside the IIT premises was a recent phenomenon, and this may not be conducive to the free movement of the animals, say naturalists. A decade ago, there was a huge canopy of trees. But this also started disappearing with the arrival of several new blocks. 'There is a need to safeguard various flora and fauna found inside the IIT premises', say naturalists.

(Source: The Hindu)

Use the information in the report to match the cause with the effect in the two sets of sentences below.

Cause
 a vehicle accident in IIT
 stray dogs on campuses
 creation of ponds to provide water
 fencing of buildings inside the IIT campus

Effect
 to ensure safety of the animals
 a couple of black buck died
 death of deer
 hampers free movement of animals

Now link the cause and effect using connecting words like because, since and as. After you have written the sentences, rewrite them using therefore, consequently and as a result. Note that with these three connectives, you get two separate sentences, or two main clauses connected by and.

Writing skills development

Write brief descriptions of an animal and a bird familiar to you. Here are some hints to describe a cat.

mammal – quadruped (having four legs) – furry skin – soft paws – eyes can adapt to darkness – carnivorous – kills and eats rats and other little animals – good as pet

After you write your descriptions, compare them with your partner's.

Role play

Animals as pets

Student A

You and Student B live next door to each other. B is fond of dogs and has an Alsatian as a pet. You want to tell B that it is not good to have pets in the house. Think of the points you can make.

Student B

You are fond of animals and have a pet dog in your house. When Student A tells you that it is not good to have pets around, you want to convince him that there are many advantages in keeping a pet dog at home. Prepare yourself for the role.

Begin when both of you are ready.

Part 1

Language focus

The compensation

Read the following story carefully, and note what happens in it.
Paterson was a businessman. He once bought a new car. He was fond of driving and spent a lot of time driving the car along the streets of his town. Later he drove into the countryside.

One day he was driving along a road on the edge

of a forest. On one side was a beautiful river, and on the other side was the forest. In the distance he could see a small village.

The scenery was so beautiful that Paterson could not take his eyes off it. 'I should spend my next vacation in that village. I should bring my wife and children with me,' he said to himself.

All on a sudden he saw a man in front of his car. The man was leading a dog by a leash.

He tried to stop the car, but it was too late. The man jumped aside; but the car ran over the dog, which died on the spot.

Paterson got out of the car and said to the man, 'I'm very sorry. It was my mistake. I didn't see you, as I was lost in the beauty of the place…. And the dog? Is it yours?'

The man said, 'Yes, it's mine'.

'I am sorry that I have killed your dog. I don't know how I can make amends.'
Paterson took his briefcase and gave the man some money. 'I hope you will accept it. The dog is dead and there's nothing we can do about it. Please accept it.'

The man took the money and put it in his pocket. Paterson turned to get into his car. It was then that he noticed the gun which the man was carrying.

'I see you were going hunting,' said Paterson. 'I am so sorry I spoiled your fun.'

'Oh, no,' said the man. 'I was not going hunting. This dog has been very ill for three weeks now, and has been suffering terrible pain. I could not bear to see his suffering, and wanted to put an end to his pain. So I was taking him to the forest to shoot him. But now that won't be necessary, since he is dead. Anyway, thank you for the money.'

Imagine that you meet the man who got the money from Paterson. He tells you his story. Given below is the story as told by the man. Write the appropriate forms of the verbs in the brackets.

'One day I was (walk) with my dog along the road leading to the village when all on a sudden a car (appear) before me. The man at the wheel (drive) the car very fast. I (see) the car just in time and (jump) to a side. But the dog (run over) by the car and died.

The man (stop) the car and (come) to me. He (say) that he (not see) me because he had been lost in admiration of the scenery.

He (take) out his briefcase and (give) me some money. He (say) that the dog was dead and there (be) nothing we (can) do about it. I (take) the money.

Then the man (see) the gun I (carry). He (say) that he (be) sorry to have spoiled my hunting. Obviously, he (think) that I was going hunting because I (have) the dog and the gun with me. I (tell) him that I (not go) hunting. I (explain) that the dog (be) ill for three weeks. It (suffer) great pain. So I (want) to end his suffering and (take) him to the forest to shoot him. But now this (be) not necessary because the dog (be) dead. I (thank) the man for the money and (bid) him goodbye.

Reading skills development

Read the following text and answer the questions.

A

Salim Ali, the pioneer Indian ornithologist and environmentalist, made a sterling contribution to the field of conservation. His life was avidly dedicated to the study of birds and his work of over fifty years has been instrumental in the protection of bird life, and the setting up of national parks and reserves. His contribution to wildlife conservation was so immense that weaver birds probably weave his initials in their nests and swifts perform parabolas in the sky in his honour!

B

In his autobiography, *Fall of a Sparrow*, he recaptures instances when he and his nephew as little children used to buy partridges and quails from markets with the intention of setting them free. His interest in the scientific study of birds was kindled when as a young boy, he found the carcass of a bird. He took the bird to the Bombay Natural History Society where a member identified the bird to be a yellow throated sparrow. The young Ali was impressed with the man's knowledge and decided then to apply himself to the study of birds—a field in which he so excelled that he later became known as the 'Birdman of India'.

C

Salim Ali was not only a great naturalist but an explorer. He knew every square inch of India and travelled extensively. The very volume of his field work and its precision earned him a place among the great naturalists of the world.

D

Even though he passionately considered birds his friends, as an ornithologist his love for them was never of the sentimental type. For a scientific approach to bird study, it was often necessary for him to collect specimens, and while mentioning this killing of birds in his autobiography, he affirms, 'I do not enjoy the killing, and sometimes even suffer a prick of the conscience .... alas ...... it would have been impossible to advance our taxonomical knowledge of Indian birds but for the methodical collection of specimens'.

E

Meticulous observation and verification of data, journeying through forest and desert unmindful of hazards—such was his work for a lifetime. India shelters more than 2000 species of birds. Salim Ali studied a large number of these and then classified and described them. The monumental ten-volume *Handbook of the Birds of India and Pakistan* (written by Ali in collaboration with Dillon Ripley) stands testimony to this. His autobiography is a very lively work, notable for its wit and humour.

F

While living in Dehra Dun in 1934 he researched economic ornithology, which includes detailed studies on the food and feeding habits of birds. In his opinion, birds can be highly destructive to cereal crops and orchard fruits: 'but also highly beneficial in controlling the ravages of insects and vermin such as rodents'. They also effect cross pollination and 'are thus of great usefulness in the propagation of plants'. Another area which fascinated him is the camouflaging colouration of desert animals and birds. After a thorough study, he stated that greater exposure to ultraviolet radiation results in greater paleness of colour and attributed this cause to the sandy colour of desert birds and animals.

G

He was totally, relentlessly immersed in his work. And he often said that his work was its own reward. It is this 'scientific temper' of Salim Ali that people wishing to pursue research must try to understand. This scientific temper is a method, a discipline and goes hand in hand with sustained, unruffled, silent work.

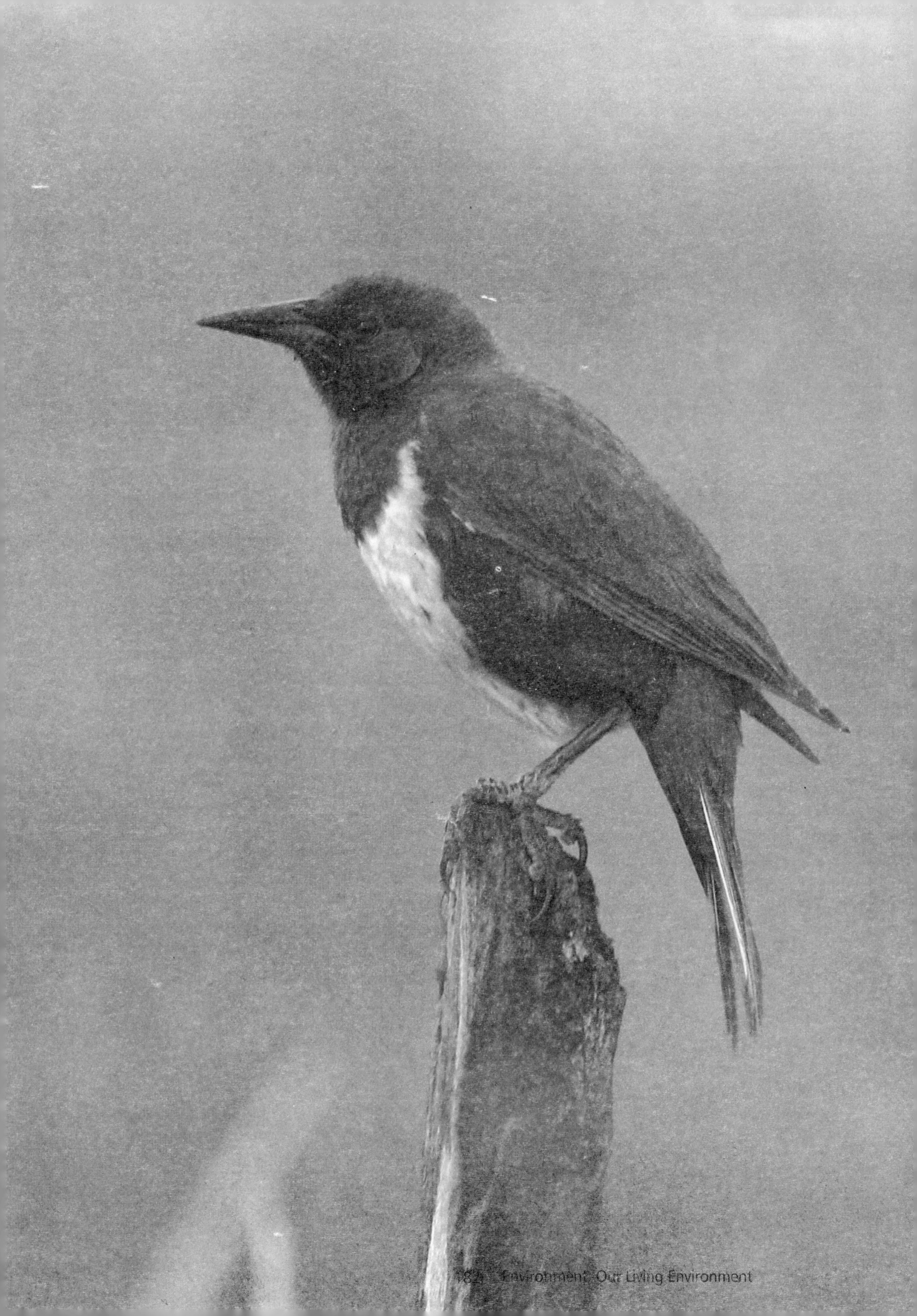

H

Recognition came to Salim Ali late, but abundantly. He received numerous awards, the Paul Ghetty International award, the Golden Ark of the IUCN, and the Gold medal of the British Ornithology Union—something that is rarely awarded to non-British people. The Indian Government awarded him the Padmashree and Padma Vibushan. He was nominated to the Rajya Sabha in 1985. He also initiated the creation of the Keoladeo Ghana and Silent Valley National Park.

I

He also rediscovered some rare species (for instance Jerdon's doublebanded courser in the scrub forests of Andhra Pradesh). He authored several books, like the *Book of Indian Birds*, bird books of Kutch, Kerala, Sikkim, Indian hill birds and the 10 volumes of *Birds of India—Pakistan*. These books now form the bible of all birdwatchers in India. In 1987, at the age of 91, Dr Salim Ali passed away from prostate cancer. The legendary Birdman is no more, but his legacy lives on.

a

Read paragraph A again. What does the author say about weaver birds and swifts? Are these statements true?

b

Compare what is said in paragraph B and paragraph D. How do you explain the difference in Salim Ali's treatment of birds on these two occasions?

c

Why is it necessary to collect data on birds and describe birds?

d

In what ways are birds useful to humans? In what ways are they harmful?

e

What do you know about camouflage among animals and among birds? Can you give an example from your everyday experience?

f

Is camouflage always a conscious attempt on the part of animals to escape from enemies? Discuss Salim Ali's findings about desert animals.

g

Can you say what the scientific temper is, and what it is not?

❋ Oral practice

People hold different opinions about the following subjects. After discussing in groups, speak in support of either side of the argument. One student from each side of the argument can speak. Others can ask questions.

  i. The use of animals for scientific experiments
  ii. Ill treatment of animals being reared for slaughter
  iii. Wild animals forced to perform in circuses.

Part 2

❋ Reading

Vanishing animals

The following text is from the writings of Gerald Durrell – the proprietor of the Jersey Zoo – who loved animals, and strove to save animals which were in danger. Read the text and answer the questions.

Unfortunately, the Pere David deer and the white-tailed gnu are not the only creatures in the world that are nearly extinct...

From this sentence, can you guess what the author has said in the preceding paragraphs? What do you expect the author to say in the remaining part of the text?

The list of creatures that have vanished altogether, and others that have almost vanished, is a long and melancholy one. As man has spread across the earth he has wrought the most terrible havoc among the wildlife by shooting, trapping, cutting and burning the forest, and by the callous and stupid introduction of enemies where there were no enemies before.

Take the dodo, for example, the great ponderous wedding pigeon, the size of a goose, that inhabited the island of Mauritius. Secure in its island home, this bird had lost the power of flight since there were no enemies to fly from, and, since there were no enemies, it nested on the ground in complete safety. But, as well as losing the power of flight, it seems to have lost the power of recognising an enemy when it saw one, for apparently it was an extremely tame and confiding creature. Then. . . **Before you read on, look at the word, 'Then ………' What do you expect the author to say next?**

Then man discovered the dodos' paradise in about 1507, and with him came his familiars: dogs, cats, pigs, rats and goats. The dodo surveyed these new arrivals with an air of innocent interest. Then the slaughter began. The goats ate the undergrowth which provided the dodo with cover; dogs and cats hunted and harried the old birds; while pigs grunted their way round the island, eating the eggs and young and rats followed behind to finish the feast. By 1681 the fat ungainly and harmless pigeon was extinct—as dead as the dodo.

All over the world the wild fauna has been whittled down steadily and remorselessly, and many lovely and interesting animals have been so reduced in numbers that, without protection and help, they can never re-establish themselves. If they cannot find sanctuary where they can live and breed undisturbed, their numbers will dwindle until they join the dodo, the quagga and the great auk on the long list of extinct creatures.

Of course, in the last decade or so, much has been done for the protection of wildlife: sanctuaries and reserves have been started, and the reintroduction of a species into areas where it had become extinct is taking place. In Canada, for instance, beavers are now reintroduced into certain areas by means of aeroplane. The animals are put in a special box attached to a parachute, and when the plane flies over the area it drops the cage and its beaver passenger out. The cage floats down on the end of the parachute and when it hits the ground it opens automatically and the beaver then makes its way to the nearest stream or lake.

But although much is being done, there is still a great deal to do. Unfortunately, the majority of useful work in animal preservation has been done mainly for animals which are of some economic importance to man and there are many obscure species of no economic importance which, although they are protected on paper, as it were, are in actual fact being allowed to die out because nobody, except a few interested zoologists, considers them important enough to spend money on.

a
Humans are responsible for the destruction of animal species, both directly and indirectly. What does the text say about their direct responsibility? In some cases humans have not destroyed animals intentionally, they have introduced certain factors that have led to the destruction of animals. What are these factors?

b
What evidence is there in the text to show that an animal may lose a faculty it does not make use of?

c
Pick out the adjectives in the text that show the sadness, cruelty and foolishness involved in the destruction of animals.

d
What are the efforts being made at present to preserve wildlife?

> **Learner Awareness**
>
> The text you have just read contains a large number of new words. Still, you were able to understand the points the author wanted to make. To understand a text, it is not necessary to know all the words in it. The meanings of many words can be guessed from the context. Don't be put off by unfamiliar words that you may come across while reading.

e
After reading the last paragraph, decide which of the following sentences sums up the author's attitude.

 i. Animals must be preserved because they are useful to humans.
 ii. Animals must be preserved because animal life is precious.
 iii. Animals must be preserved because they are weak and affectionate.
 iv. Animals must be preserved because they are dumb creatures.
 v. None of the above.

Follow-up

Reading skills development

Read this passage and complete the notes in the outline which follows it.

ANIMALS AT NIGHT

The animal kingdom can be divided into four categories. The first category comprises the diurnal animals, which are active during the day. In the second category, we have the nocturnal animals, which move about at night. Then we have two less well-known varieties, the crepuscular animals, which are active during twilight hours, and the arrhythmic animals, which go about during both day and night. Probably such a division began when simple and weak animals began to come out in the dark to escape from diurnal predators. Today, although we associate the night with peace and silence, two-thirds of the mammals of the world move about at night, such mammals as mice, bats, foxes, flying squirrels and leopards.

How do the nocturnal animals find their way in the dark? Domestic cats, as we know, have eyes that can adapt to darkness. But in the wild, the mechanisms are more sophisticated. The eyes of an owl, for example, contain a large number of rods and nerve cells. These cells respond to dim light and to changes in light intensity. Would you believe it if you are told that an owl can detect a moving mouse in one millionth of a candle power of light? Snakes make use of the sense of smell at night. Their tongue picks up small particles from objects around them and sensors at the roof of the mouth smell the particles. Another sense that helps animals to find their way is the sense of heat.

The snake, again, can record the heat emitted by objects around it and move in on the objects with deadly precision. Some animals have a sort of kinesthetic sense which helps them to move about at night in familiar territory. It is a sense of the movements of the body involved in a particular action. Many of us walk down the stairs in the dark, open a cupboard and pick an object from inside with precision. It is this kind of sense that an owl uses to cover familiar territory. What do you know about a bat's ability to fly at night?

Most of us imagine that the main activities of animals at night consist of chasing and capturing their prey. To a certain extent this is true. Many animals seek and find their food at night. Owls pick up mice; tigers go out to feed upon animals which they have caught and stowed away earlier. But there are other activities at night. Animals play at night: raccoons, for example, play and gambol, as our pet dogs do in our garden. Male animals can be observed courting the females of their species. Spiders and toads court and mate at night: such behaviour has been observed by animal watchers.

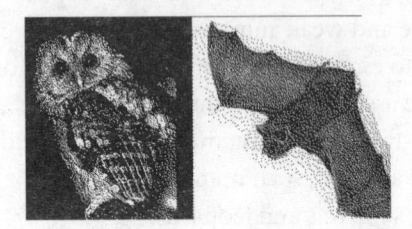

But how does one watch animals in darkness? What are the techniques used for observing and taking pictures of animals at night? Any bright light will scare away the animals. Here scientists take advantage of the fact that most animals are blind to red light. They therefore, use a torch with a red mask. Infrared telescopes have also been used to observe animals at night. Today, with very sophisticated cameras and lighting devices, it is possible to photograph and make recordings of the cries of animals in their dark and inaccessible forest haunts.

Animals at night

A ....
  i. diurnal animals = ...
  ii. .... = ...
  iii. .... = out in twilight
  iv. .... = ...

B ....
  i. eyesight = ...
  ii. ....
  iii. ....
  iv. ....
  v. sound : ....
  ....

C
  Activities at night ....
  i. ....
  ii. ....
  iii. ....

D ....
  i. ....
  ii. ....
  iii. ....

Writing skills development

Using the notes given below, write a paragraph about king cobras.

king cobras – largest venomous snakes in the world – found in tropical rain forests – Western Ghats, Sunderbans and Andamans – also in Southeast Asia – largest specimen caught 18 feet – average 12-15 feet – usually dark brownish black with thin yellow stripes – reclusive, rarely attacks – only snake known to build nest for young – baby king cobras brown with enough venom to kill a person – endangered due to cutting of rain forests – also killed on sight due to bad reputation

Oral practice

Here are statements about snakes. Work in pairs and discuss whether the statements are true. Then tell the class whether you agree or disagree with each statement.

1 Snakes are slimy creatures.
2 The majority of snakes are very poisonous.
3 Snakes are very aggressive and will attack anyone who passes by.
4 Snakes use their tongue to smell objects.
5 Snakes dance to the sound of the snake-charmer's pipe.
6 Snakes can be tamed and kept as pets.
7 If a snake is cut into two, the two pieces will become two snakes.
8 Snakes reproduce by laying eggs.
9 A snake can swallow a prey that is many times its own size.
10 Cobras spit venom into the eyes of their enemies.

THEME

industry

1
Personnel and Production

Preparation

❋ Oral practice

In pairs, discuss the problems involved in getting a suitable job after becoming an engineering graduate. Suggest a few solutions to the problems you have specified. Be ready to report to the class when the teacher asks you.

❋ Writing skills development

Letters constitute an important type of communication between individuals, between individuals and companies, and between companies. Students completing their course of study will begin to look for employment, and at that time they will have to write letters applying for jobs.

Discuss this situation in small groups and decide on the details to be presented in a letter of application for jobs. Discuss the format of the letter.

In five minutes, be ready to report your decisions when the teacher asks you to. Here is a letter of application for a position in a plastics manufacturing company. Note the different parts of the letter and study the notes in the margin.

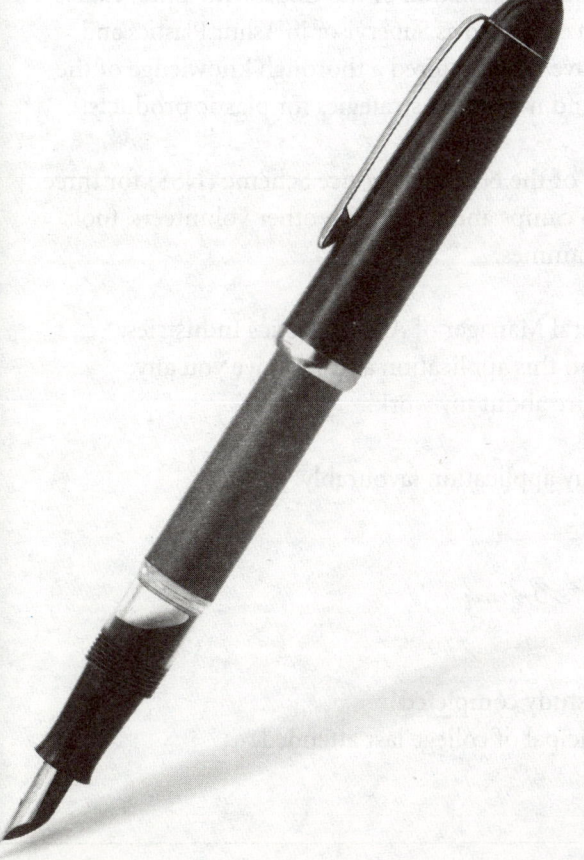

V. KRISHNA KANT BHADE

22, 10th street, Shivaji Nagar, Pune 227 948

18 June 2008

The General Manager
Care Plastics Ltd
Bhubaneshwar
ORISSA 2543490

Dear Sir/Madam,

I would like to be considered for the position of Sales Engineer which you advertised in *The Sentry* of 17 June 2008.

I passed the B.E. examination from BTM University in May 1999 with a first class and was first among the candidates of the year. Earlier in 1995, I passed the Higher Secondary School examination of the CBSE with a first class. Since June 2000, I have been employed as Supervisor in Ashur Plastics and Chemicals in Mumbai. I have now acquired a thorough knowledge of the manufacturing processes and marketing strategies for plastic products.

In college, I was a member of the National Service Scheme (NSS) for three years. I attended three NSS camps and along with other volunteers, took part in social service programmes.

Mr K Satyanarayana, General Manager of Ashur Plastics Industries, has agreed to be a referee on this application and will give you any information you may require about my work.

I request you to consider my application favourably.

Yours faithfully,
V. Krishna Kant Bhade

Encl.
(Transcripts for academic study completed)
(Testimonial from the Principal of college last attended)

Notes:

- Note that the letter is aligned to the left of the sheet.

- Do not assume that the general manager is a man, and do not use the plural 'sirs'. If you know the person's name you can say Dear Mr Adikari, Dear Ms Sharma, etc.

- Mention key points of your biodata briefly.

- Again left-aligned as is the whole letter. It is also correct to say 'Yours sincerely' in modern business correspondence. Do not forget the comma. Include signature.

- List enclosures so that they can be checked.

a

Now write a similar letter applying to any firm you are interested in, giving the firm information about yourself. Discuss your letter with your partner. Would you give your partner the job? Would your partner give you the job? Be ready to report this to the class.

b

You will notice that in the above letter the applicant has written about his education, experience and/or extracurricular activities. He has named a referee who can supply information about him to the company.

Today one is often expected to give details about oneself in an easy-to-read form. This statement goes under the name of biodata, curriculum vitae (cv for short) or personal data sheet. Here is a simple data sheet. Transfer the details from the letter to the appropriate places in the data sheet.

Curriculum Vitae

Name ....

Address ....
....

Age and Date of Birth ....

Email and Telephone No. ....

Academic Background

Institution	Year	Examination	Class/Division

Work Experience

Name of Organisation	Period	Position Held

Extra Curricular Activities

References

Some companies have printed forms for personal data. Details like marital status, state of health, hobbies, and memberships of clubs or professional bodies, are sometimes included in the biodata.

In the next lesson, you will complete a form of this kind.

Writing

A letter of application

Look at the advertisement below.

We have over 3000 employees and require

DESIGN ENGINEERS

for Special Purpose Machines

Candidates should be mechanical engineering graduates—preferably with a postgraduate qualification in machine design.

They should have a minimum of 5 years' experience in designing special-purpose machines pertaining to metal cutting/metal forming/assembly machines for light precision work.

They should be capable of independently designing SPMs from the concept stage.

They should have knowledge of low-cost automation.

Salary and service conditions will be attractive and not a restricting factor for the right candidate.

Please apply with complete biodata, salary last drawn and salary expected, and a brief description of the most interesting machine designed, within 15 days to

The Personnel Manager
Sharp–SRJ
39 Asaf Ali Road
Delhi 110002

SHARP-SRJ

a

When you send an application in reply to the advertisement, you should carefully consider the qualifications and experience the company has specified. If you are sure that you possess these, you should write a letter of application.

> The Personnel Manager
> Sharp SRJ
> 39 Asaf Ali Road
> Delhi 110 002
>
> Dear Sir/Madam,
>
> I should like to be considered for the position of Design Engineer advertised in ——— of 16 June 2008.
>
> I enclose my biodata sheet which shows that I have the qualifications prescribed by you. My specialisation in my undergraduate course was machine design, and my experience with Weller Machine Works has enabled me to acquire a sound knowledge of special purpose machines.
>
> I would be grateful if you could grant me an interview in the next few days.
>
> Yours faithfully,
> Sujit Gupta
>
>
> Sujit Gupta
> 94/2 Gandhi Nagar
> Delhi-110 001
> 25 August 2008
>
>
>
> Enclosures: biodata
>   description of a machine designed

b

Prepare the CV to be sent with the above letter. Use the form below.

Curriculum Vitae

Name

Address with Telephone

Email

Age and Date of Birth

Education

Institution	Dates	Diploma/Degree	Subjects	Scholastic Standing	Prizes Won

Experience

Name of Organisation	Period	Position Held	Responsibilities

Extra curricular Activities

Hobbies

References

Signature
Date

Learner Awareness

The résumé (pronounced re-zyu-may) is the name for curriculum vitae in American English. It is usually sent along with a short letter of application for a job or admission to a course of study. Unlike a bio-data, which is a detailed record of one's background including personal details, education and work experience, a résumé limits itself to the education, work experience and motivation relevant to the job/position applied for. Personal information such as marital status, family and hobbies need not be included. A résumé might also include a statement of career objective and expectations.

Part I

Language focus
Units of measurement

a

Look at the following expressions.

The pipe is three feet long.
a three-foot long pipe... .

The curing lasts 60 minutes.
a 60-minute curing cycle... .

Note that when the numerical expression is placed in the position of an adjective before the noun, the singular form is used; the plural forms feet and minutes are not used.

Now rewrite the following expressions as shown above.

- a flask with a capacity of 10 litres
- a journey of 20 miles
- a match lasting five days
- at intervals of 10 minutes
- a DC supply of 240 volts
- a lamp of a power of 60 watts
- an investment of Rs 3,50,000
- a research grant of Rs two lakh
- pipes having an id (internal diameter) of three inches

b

You are familiar with some of the abbreviations used for the names of units of measurement. Write out in full each of the expressions below.

3000 rev/min	6.28 m/s	1500 kg/m^3
150 rpm	40% v/v	273 K
300 ppm	530 kHz	500 Btu/ft^3

Reading
The dry cell battery

Read the following text to locate the main ideas discussed by the writer. Then divide the text into four paragraphs.

The dry cell battery has long been a familiar object in our homes. Its main use was to supply power to torch lights. The demand was stagnant for many years, and it was only with the introduction of portable radios and tape recorders that the manufacture of dry cell batteries became a profitable industry. Today dry cells of different sizes are used in transistor radios, calculators, portable tape recorders, quartz clocks and torches. International sports events like Wimbledon and the World Cup in cricket have increased the demand for dry cell batteries. Indian industrialists have been quick to foresee the increase in the demand for dry cell batteries and today the market for dry cell batteries in India has reached an astounding Rs 300 crore mark. The market leader is Eveready which commands nearly 50 per cent of the sales.

Nippo and Novino each command a little less than a quarter of the market. These three together with Toshiba and Geep constitute the major brands in the industry. Though the promise held by the dry cell industry seems to be bright, there are problems. The most serious of these is the fact that the installed capacity in the industry is far in excess of the demand. When the transistor was introduced in the 1960s, the increase in demand for dry cells was so sudden and so exciting that entrepreneurs enthusiastically set up units, small and big, for the manufacture of dry cells. Besides the five major manufacturers there are small industrialists. Some of the manufacturers have obtained the technology from advanced countries and invested heavy sums as capital. As against a demand for about 1200 million cells, the installed capacity is about 2000 million cells. This is the problem facing the industry. What are the prospects for the future? The major units are engaged in severe competition spending large sums of money in the promotion of their products through advertisements in the media. The smaller units find it hard to face up to such high-pressure promotional strategies. They may find it difficult to survive, unless there is some technological development that leads to a repetition of the boom witnessed in the 1960s.

a
Mark the places where the passage can be divided into paragraphs.

b
Make a statement of the topic of each paragraph in one sentence.

c
Pick out the main points of each paragraph and write them down in note form.

d
Say which paragraphs contain factual information and which contain opinions or suppositions, or statements of cause-and-effect.

Part 2

Reading

Virtual reality

Read the following passage on 'Virtual reality' and answer the questions at the end of it.

VIRTUAL REALITY

Virtual reality seeks visionaries to speed its change from novelty value to industrial worth. "The perception is that VR is great for games and toys, but the fact is, there are many things we'll be able to do with this technology," says Bob Voiers, virtual reality guru at EDS, the former General Motors subsidiary that developed the Cave.

Automotive engineers are using VR to check and approve new designs without having to create clay models; they are crash testing cars without building costly prototypes; and they are creating "factories in a box"—assembly line simulations that can identify bottlenecks and quality control problems.

But VR applications extend far beyond the world of the virtual automobile. The technology is also helping medical students improve their surgical skills. Architects can "walk through" their designs. And new pilots at Rotterdam Harbour, the world's busiest seaport, are being trained on simulators so realistic you can almost taste the salt air—and a new system at the EDS Virtual Reality center in Detroit will go so far as to add the salt air, and other scents, at appropriate moments. Indeed, the applications are almost endless.

But it takes time, effort and training to bring VR to its full potential. So EDS, which operates a VR "showroom" in Detroit, has opened North America's first VR university. The Virtual Reality Institute in Troy, Michigan, is a joint effort with Prosolvia Research and Technology. Swedish-based

Prosolvia is a world leader in VR software, training and technology. And it operates six other VR institutes in Europe.

Teachers at the school acknowledge that so far, virtual reality has delivered on more promises than reality. But they insist that it is the result of not having enough visionaries who know how to make the technology live up to its expectations. It takes more than just a 3D headset and sound effects to justify the investment. Through the Institute, they hope to create some well-trained disciples who can go forth and proselytise.

VRI runs two distinct courses. The first is a four-evening professional seminar. The programme costs $500 and is aimed at project managers, marketing executives and other middle managers with a need to understand and use virtual reality. "If you don't understand the process, it's difficult to implement it in your organisation," says Mats Johansson, president of Prosolvia's US training subsidiary and an instructor at the Virtual Reality Institute. With proper training, however, VR "can build bridges between departments, rather than walls, like some technologies have done in the past."

The second, and far more in-depth, course is the proficiency programme, costing up to $10,000. When you have been on this 20-week full-time seminar, you will be able to create your own virtual world. Students spend six weeks developing a theoretical base of understanding. That is followed by a 14-week project phase, during which each student will complete a VR programme for a real customer.

One of the first projects under development at the Troy centre is a driving simulator to help medical experts assess and understand the neurological damage a person suffers as the result of a stroke.

Another student will develop a virtual home, which can be used as a permanent extension to a Houston annual trade fair—the Builder's show. "We're building a house into which companies can instal their floors and appliances," Johansson says.

Each VR institute emphasises one or two core industries. Not surprisingly, the Michigan centre focuses on cars and manufacturing. And VR-related technology is finding a willing audience among the carmakers.

As Frank Ewasyshyn, Chrysler's vice-president of advanced manufacturing engineering, says, "we now have the ability to go from the development of a concept right through to the development of the manufacturing process in a virtual world."

a
What was the understanding of 'virtual reality' in the past?

b
What is the present view?

c
Name at least three leading industries in which 'virtual reality' has proven to be of great value.

d
What are the courses available on virtual reality? Who is the targeted audience? Who are the organisers and where are these courses conducted?

e
Sum up the advantages of the concept of 'virtual reality' and its future applications.

Listening

A process to make washing soap

You will listen to a description of a process by which washing soap can be made at home. Take notes of things required for making soap and write about the process in the form of a set of instructions.

a

things required for making soap

i. ....
ii. ....
....
....
....
....

b

process in the form of a set of instructions

i. ....
ii. ....
....
....

Follow-up

Language check

The prefixes **infra-** and **sub-** are added to words to mean 'below, lower down'; the prefixes **supra-**, **ultra-** and **hyper-** are intensifying prefixes, which mean 'above, higher up, beyond'.

Add one of the prefixes above to the following words to mean the words given against them:

.........**conductivity**: the property of having zero electrical resistance

.........**violet**: having a wavelength beyond the violet end of the spectrum

.........**zero**: less than zero

.........**red**: having a wavelength just below the red end of the spectrum

.........**sensitive**: abnormally or excessively sensitive

.........**heat**: heat above boiling point without causing vaporisation

.........**sonic**: (sound waves) just below the level of audibility

.........**saturate**: add to solution beyond saturation point

.........**continent**: large land mass, not large enough to be called a continent

.........**sonic**: having a speed greater than that of sound

.........**national**: going beyond or above national limits or national considerations

.........**standard**: not having the required or normal quality

.........**sonic**: (sound) having a pitch above the upper limit of human hearing

.........**tension**: abnormally high blood pressure

.........**structure**: subordinate underlying parts on which something is built

Reading skills development

In the following passage, you will read about an industrial process. After reading the passage, answer the questions.

Spread over five hectares, the joint Indo–US plant is located in one of the most industrially backward areas of Andhra Pradesh. But it is an area rich in high-quality clay—the main raw material in the manufacture of quality ceramic tiles.

The clay used by Spartek is really sediment deposits which collect at the bottom of irrigation tanks and village ponds. 'Most villages in this region,' says Tripuraneni, the Managing Director of Spartek Ceramics, 'have irrigation tanks that fill up during the rainy season. During the summer months the rainwater is used by the people, leaving behind fine red clay. In mining this clay, we also help desilt the tanks so that farmers can use them again.'

'The clay is just right for the making of tiles. It has the right strength, the right plasticity—in fact all the essential properties that Ceramic US insisted it must have to make first-rate tiles,' he said.

The mined clay is brought to the Tirupati plant and mixed with other ingredients in a ball mill and wet ground into a fine slip. The slip is then stored for a few days and spray dried to form a fine powder of uniform consistency so that, when it is compressed in a 680-tonne press, it maintains its homogeneity. The massive press gives the tiles the required strength, shape and thickness.

From the press the tiles are sent along a 90-metre long glazing line, where they acquire surface finish, and where the requisite designs are screen-printed.

From the glazing line the tiles are automatically fed into specially designed rail trolleys. The trolleys take the tiles to the head of an 84-metre long kiln.

The massive kiln is the heart of the tile-making operation. Inside it rages a ball of fire—at 1,200 degrees celsius! It bakes about 2,000 tiles a day, and each tile takes an hour to reach the other end of the kiln on a belt of 1,680 rollers. And throughout the 60-minute curing cycle, operators closely monitor the tiles on closed-circuit television to ensure that each one is fired to just the right degree. 'The kiln is crucial to the whole process,' Tripuraneni points out. 'Normally tiles in India are baked in a tunnel kiln in which the firing time is somewhere in the range of seventy-two hours. In our kiln, it is just an hour. Ceramic US, which has the same kiln, uses even less time—a 30-minute cycle for certain kinds of tiles.'

The Spartek kiln is by all accounts the most advanced of its kind. It uses liquefied petroleum gas (LPG), one of the cleanest fuels. 'Many tile plants in India run on furnace oil or coal, both of which affect the quality of tiles. Oil has sulphur in it and coal has tar and ash content which interfere with colour quality. Moreover, sulphur reacts with the chemicals used for glazing tiles, and this leaves a patchy effect and pinholes in the tiles. That is why most overseas manufacturers of tiles of international quality have switched over to gas-fired kilns.'

Another big advantage of an LPG kiln is its fuel efficiency. 'We save about seventy per cent in fuel expenditure, which is the single biggest cost component in tiles. In the manufacture of tiles roughly fifty per cent of the cost is accounted for by the fuel. This saving gives us a vital cost advantage.'

One leaves the Spartek plant, amazed at how modern technology transforms a waste product – the lowly earth – into tiles of exquisite beauty and a joy for the modern home or office.

(Source: Span)

a

Note the various steps in the process of tile making. Draw a flowchart representing these steps.

b

Why was this region in Andhra Pradesh selected for the location of the plant?

c

Complete the following sentences.

i. The function of the glazing line is to ………………………. .

ii. The function of the ball mill is to ……………………….. .

iii. The function of the kiln is to ……………………………… .

iv. The function of the press is to …………………………… .

In what order are these functions performed in the process of tile making?

d

Make a comparison of the Spartek kiln with the kilns normally used for tile making in India. Complete the following table:

feature	Spartek kiln	other kilns
i.		
ii.		
iii.		
iv.		

2

Safety and Training

Preparation

❋ Oral practice

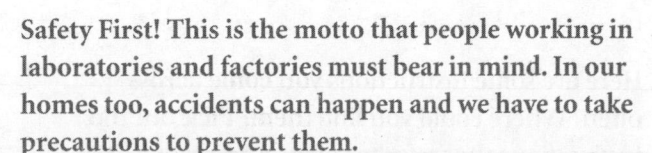

a

Safety First! This is the motto that people working in laboratories and factories must bear in mind. In our homes too, accidents can happen and we have to take precautions to prevent them.

In small groups, discuss the accidents that can happen in a chemistry laboratory. Note them down and think of the safety rules that must be observed. Tell the class about the danger and about the rules to be observed. Here is an example.

> There is a likelihood of pieces of glass being scattered on the floor. Acids too may be spilt on the floor.
>
> **Do not work in the laboratory barefoot.**
>
> **Wear shoes to protect your feet.**

Find as many other safety rules as you can. Here are some hints to set you thinking: clothes, gloves, labels on bottles, transferring liquids, mixing liquids, cuts, burns, suffocation, explosion, gas cylinders.

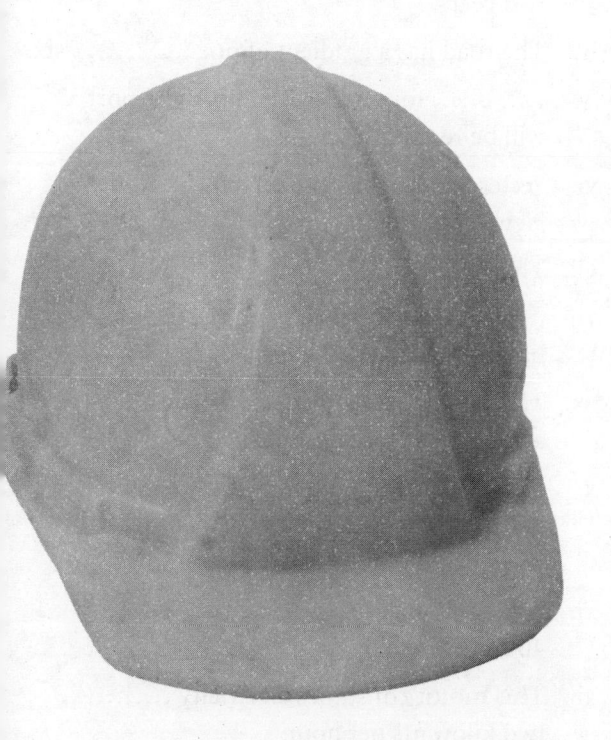

b

What are the following things used for? Why are they known by these names?

| safety pin | safety razor | safety lock |
| safety belt | safety lamp | safety valve |

Writing skills development

a

Here are some instructions you come across often. Where could you find them? Pick out the instructions that refer to safety, and write a brief note on each of them. Write about where you may find the instruction, what it means and why it is useful.

> Keep out of the reach of children.
> Keep off the grass.
> Do not distract the driver.
> Write your name in block letters.
> No smoking!
> In case of an emergency, break glass.
> Write nothing in the space below.
> For external use only.
> Do not pluck flowers.
> Shake well before using.

b.

Read the text 'Personal versus Professional Relationships' on page 203 and take notes under various heads such as

i. Qualities of personal relationships
ii. Qualities of professional relationships
iii. Difficulties that arise on combining the two
iv. Tips to remember in professional commitments

Language development

Use the appropriate prepositions and complete the following sentences.

i. She drove the car .... a speed of 80 miles an hour.
ii. He was not prepared to act .... his principles.
iii. The factory has been closed .... two years.
iv. The road has a gradient of one .... six.
v. .... tomorrow evening, the report will be ready.
vi. Yesterday the chairperson left .... New Delhi.
vii. The ball missed the goal .... inches.
viii. .... the last earthquake, the town has been facing many difficulties.
ix. The value was calculated .... an accuracy of three decimal places.
x. As the spaceship sailed .... Jupiter, it sent photographs of the planet to the earth station.
xi. The room measures 60 feet .... 40 feet.
xii. This motor consumes electricity .... two kilowatts per hour.

Part 1

✺ Reading skills development

Read the following text and make notes around the important points in it.

PERSONAL VERSUS PROFESSIONAL RELATIONSHIPS

Sanjeev Duggal

For most of us, the term 'relationship' usually stands for personal relationships. However, professional relationships are equally important. One needs to form and nurture these in a business environment.

A common confusion occurs between personal and professional relationships. In personal relationships, there are shared interests and often, mutual dependence, and a fairly high degree of openness and trust. These relationships grow out of basic psychological needs—to build bonds with other human beings. Professional relationships are more 'held back' and less open. What makes the two different is the degree of openness and trust.

We cannot apply the same yardstick to work relationships that we apply to personal ones. The nature of the two is different. In business, we may build a sound relationship with a customer, or with other departments in the organisation. Most people assume that since the relationship is built over a period of time, it is a personal relationship. Sometimes even those with a lot of experience say that they have a good personal rapport with their customer.

I say this relationship is still a professional one. Once we begin confusing the two, there are difficulties. I once had a colleague who said he was reluctant to remind the customer every day about outstanding payments because he had a good personal rapport with the customer. The customer had financial problems, he was not trying to avoid paying. It took me a while to explain to my colleague that it was his duty to remind the customer about payments, no matter how bad he felt about it.

It is important to do unto your professional partners what you would like them to do to you. Honour your commitments. Be punctual. Build the relationship. The list is endless.

(Source: A and M magazine, September 2001)

✺ Writing

Using the notes you have made, write a paragraph on maintaining a good relationship in the college with your peers, teachers and others during your college days.

✺ Listening

Safety measures in a chlorine plant

You are now going to listen to a talk on 'Precautions to be taken in a chlorine plant'. Before the teacher plays the tape, prepare by discussing with a partner the properties of chlorine that make it a dangerous gas.
As you listen, write down the relevant points in the outline provided.

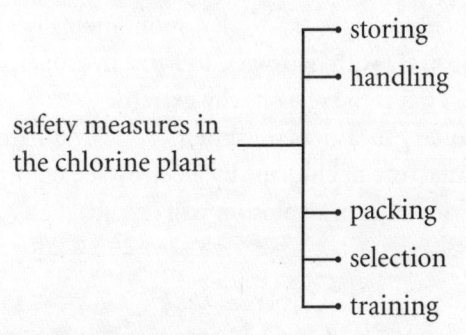

safety measures in the chlorine plant
- storing
- handling
- packing
- selection
- training

Writing

An accident in the factory

The works manager of Industrial Gases Limited has reported to the chairperson of the company that there has been an accident in the factory. Three employees in the gas filling section have been hospitalised after inhaling chlorine gas. The chairperson asks the chief engineer to conduct an inquiry into the accident and submit a set of precautions.
Imagine that you are the chief engineer of the company.and write a set of safety measures to be adopted to avert such industrial accidents.

Language check

Look at the list of words given below. Use these words to fill the blanks in the text that follows. Change the form of the words if necessary.

evaporate	contact	excessive	pulmonary
adopt	affect	occur	exposure
presence	copious	danger	build
attribute	react	increase	

Chlorine gas is primarily a respiratory irritant. Restlessness, throat irritation, sneezing and .... salivation are the results of prolonged .... to the gas. In extreme cases, lung tissues may be .... resulting in severe .... disease. If liquid chlorine is splashed on the eyes, skin, or clothing, it will cause irritation and chemical burns on the body.

Chlorine causes not only health hazards, but also explosion hazards. In the .... of sunlight, chlorine gas .... spontaneously and explosively with hydrogen to form hydrogen chloride. That is the reason why extreme precautionary measures must be .... during the manufacture of chlorine by electrolysis, failing which serious fire or explosion will ....

A similar risk of explosion is involved in the case of liquid chlorine because it .... in volume when it .... So there is always the .... of rupture of containers, pipelines and other equipment where chlorine is used, whenever .... pressure is .... up due to heat.

Fire is another hazard .... to chlorine, as it may react to cause fire or explosions upon .... with turpentine, ether, ammonia, sawdust and phosphorus.

Part 2

Discussion

Employee training

Answer the following questions. Work in pairs.

a

What are the objectives of training to employees? Arrange the following in order of importance.

  i. increasing productivity
  ii. ensuring safety in the place of work
  iii. increasing the employee's earning capacity
  iv. promoting good interpersonal relations in the organisation
  v. preparing for the future

Can you think of other objectives?

b

The following is a list of both conventional and unconventional methods of training. Which of them do you consider conventional?

  i. the audiovisual method
  ii. training through skits or songs
  iii. lectures

iv. apprenticeship
v. self-learning kits
vi. games
vii. case studies
viii. quiz programmes
ix. distance education

Speak to the class briefly about any one of the unconventional methods you are familiar with.

Reading

Training in industrial organisations

Read the following passage and then answer the questions that follow.

Training forms the axle of the industrial wheel. It is an inevitable and continuous process in an industrial setup, and no industrial organisation can function successfully without training its employees. C.R. Dooley, an American writer, while writing about training within industry, says,

'Training is not something that is done once to new employees—it is used continuously in every well-run establishment. Every time you get someone to do work the way you want it done, you are training. Every time you give directions or discuss a procedure, you are training.'

Training plays a vital role in industries for the following reasons.

- The newly appointed employees in any industry have to be trained to get themselves introduced to their new employer's work environment and to be taught to perform specific tasks.

- Second, if an employee is promoted or is given new assignments, new skills must be developed.

- Third, even if an employee continues in the same job, he or she needs to be given training in order to update his or her technical knowledge.

- Fourth, when the skill and ability of an employee is found to be inadequate for the particular area at the time of appraising his or her performance, he or she needs to be trained.

- Fifth, training is needed in order to make an employee cope with the changing goals of the organisation.

Any industrial organisation will definitely fail to achieve its ends if these training programmes are ineffectively conducted. The organisation, the trainer and the trainee are the three key factors which contribute in equal importance to the effectiveness of training.

Every organisation employs various techniques and methods to give training to its employees. Case method, role play, lectures, films, incident method, problem-oriented exercises and projects, and programmed instruction are some of the very common methods adopted by organisations. These methods vary according to the goals, structure and administrative practices of the organisation.

Apart from these, the learner's specific needs and his or her ability to understand and learn are the other factors which make the management think of other methods of training.

The primary aim of training in any industry is to educate and to help its personnel rise to certain standards to meet the workplace's requirements.

At the same time, some unplanned advantages by-products spring up through training. They are prevention of accidents, averting damage to machinery and equipment, reduction of scrap generation, high-quality production, increase in production, and better industrial relations.

a

Look at the above text as a whole. Do you think it is properly organised? Is it logically arranged and divided into appropriate paragraphs? Answer 'yes' or 'no'. Come back to this question after answering the remaining questions.

b

Which part of the text forms the introduction? What does the author do in the introduction?

c

Where does the second part of the text begin? Where does it end? Compare your answer with your partner's.

d

What does the author say in the second section?

e

Do you think the essay has a good conclusion? Can you write a different conclusion?

f

The text has twelve paragraphs. Do you think it could do with fewer paragraphs? How would you reorganise the paragraphs?

✻ Writing

A checklist on safety

A checklist is a list of items that people use to make sure that everything is in order before any important activity is taken up. Here is a simple checklist: can you say when it can be used?

	YES	NO
1 Is there water in the radiator?		
2 Is there petrol in the tank?		
3 Are the brakes in good condition?		
4 Are the tyres properly inflated?		
5 Is the oil level in the engine right?		

In the passage which follows, you will read some instructions about the construction of temporary structures such as shamianas and tents. These are often put up for public functions, cultural programmes, weddings and other events. The risk of fire in such structures is very high and, therefore, the Bureau of Indian Standards has suggested the following guidelines. Prepare a checklist for safety from these guidelines.

▶ All combustible material used in the structure should be treated with a fire-retardant solution of ammonium sulphate, ammonium carbonate, borax, boric acid, alum and water in such proportion as specified in the Standard.

▸ The main structure should be put up with at least 100 mm diameter wooden posts preferably of sal, casuarina or bamboo using light poles and trusses tied together with steel wire for the remaining structures.

▸ The minimum height of the ceiling should be three metres.

▸ All fabric, decorative material and coir ropes used in the construction and decoration of the temporary structure should be dipped in a fire-retardant solution before use.

▸ A clear space of three metres should be kept on all sides between the structure and adjacent buildings.

▸ No temporary structure should be erected beneath live electrical lines or near furnaces, railway lines, electrical substations or chimneys.

▸ All sides of the temporary structure should be kept open and, where it is not possible to do so, the lower portions of the side walls should preferably not be fixed.

▸ There should also be provision for at least two separate, remotely located exits with their width determined on the basis of at least one unit of 50 cm for every 50 persons but not less than 1.5 m.

▸ There should be a clear indication of the EXIT sign in plain legible letters and the exit light should be adequately illuminated with a reliable light source.

▸ Temporary lighting of the structure should be installed by a licensed electrical engineer, and the load per circuit, insulation and the installation should conform to IS 1646: 1982 Code of Practice for Fire Safety of Buildings (General): Electrical Installations.

▸ Portable incandescent gas lights should be placed on securely fixed separate stands instead of being hung from the ceiling of the pandal.

Write down other items to be added to the checklist.

Language focus

Word formation

Below is a list of verbs. Two nouns can be formed from each verb, the first one referring to an action or state, and the second to a substance or material. The first line is completed for you. Write the nouns for the remaining verbs.

verb	noun 1	noun 2
pollute	pollution	pollutant
explode	....	....
catalyse	....	....
disinfect	....	....
corrode	....	....
refrigerate	....	....
adhere	....	....
absorb	....	....
resist	....	....
react	reaction	reactor
detonate	....	....
stimulate	....	....
retard	....	....

Follow-up

Comprehension check

Go back to the text on pages 205–6. Answer the following questions.

a

How does C.R. Dooley's view of training differ from the view commonly held?

b

Look at the five reasons for training given in the text. Which of these apply to individual employees? Which of them refer to group training?

c

In India, industry has been asked to focus on rural areas. Which of the five reasons given by the author applies to this situation?

d

What is the need for training (i) a new employee, and (ii) an employee already in service?

e

What part can group discussion play in the training of employees?

f

Read the last paragraph again. How can training help in

- the prevention of accidents?
- the reduction of scrap generation?
- averting damage to machinery and equipment?

g

Outline a programme of training for a person who has just been selected as a management trainee. Discuss this with your partner and then write the outline.

✽ Reading skills development

The detection of toxic gases

Read the following description of an alarm system which detects the presence of dangerous gases such as nerve gas and sends out a warning signal. Then label the diagram with the names of the parts of the system found in the text.

The air to be tested is drawn into the system by a *pump*. After passing through a *coarse filter* and a *fine filter*, the air enters a *chamber* with a *window* on one side. A *beam of light* from an *infrared* source falls on the air in the chamber through the window. The light passes through a *rotating chopper*, with one half black. This turns the light into alternating bright and dim pulses. When any toxic gas is present in the chamber, it absorbs the infrared light and then the temperature in the chamber rises slightly. Consequently the pressure increases. But because the infrared light is in pulses, the pressure fluctuates with the same frequency.

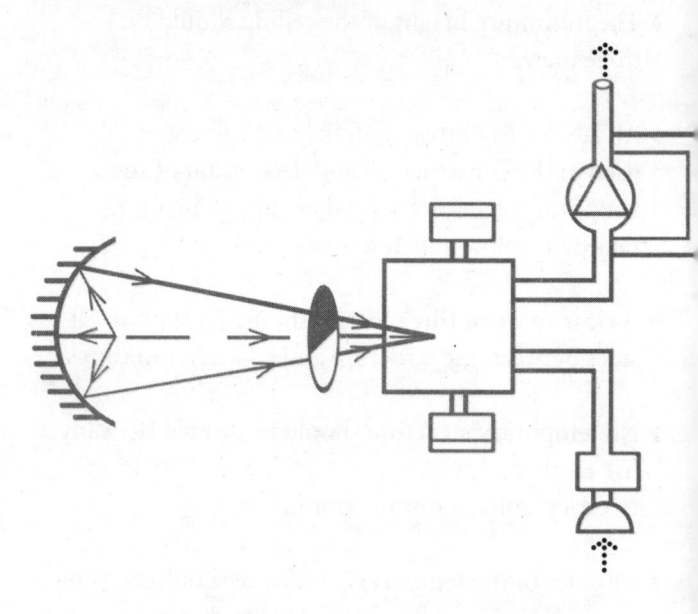

The fluctuation in pressure is turned into an acoustic wave. This acoustic is turned into a sound signal by the two *microphones* on the walls of the chamber.

The pump draws the air out of the chamber and releases it into the atmosphere through the *air outlet*.

✽ Writing skills development

Write a paragraph about the importance of computer training today. You can write about the use of computers in banks, travel agencies, railways, airlines, and business houses. Pay attention to the logical arrangement of the sentences in your paragraph.

3
SELLING PRODUCTS

Preparation

✽ Oral practice

Discuss the following questions in small groups. Be ready to report your ideas to the class when you are asked to.

a

What are the strategies of selling adopted by firms today to promote the sale of their products?

b

What do you think of the role of advertisements in the sale of products? What are the media involved for the purpose?

c

What do you think is the part played by exhibitions and fairs in promoting the sale of products?

d

Can you mention some Indian products for which there is a worldwide market?

Language development

Match the words in column A with their meanings in column B. Make sure you can pronounce all the words in column A correctly.

A	B
target	bind one(self) to a course of action
support price	system of services forming a basis
commitment	possible or probable customer
trade fair	objective, result aimed at
infrastructure	system of defending home industries
proposition	stipulated minimum amount of money to be paid for buying a commodity
statutory	a scheme suggested
prospect	periodical gathering for sale of goods at fixed place and time
protectionism	planning
projection	required by written law or legislation
constraint	seeing as a whole, and not in parts
impediment	limitation or restriction imposed forcibly
holistic	obstacle, hindrance

Reading skills development

a

Read these three short texts quickly and say what they are about.

> CUSTOMERS RARELY GIVE SECOND CHANCES.

> IN TODAY'S COMPETITIVE MARKETPLACE, THE CUSTOMER DECIDES WHO WINS AND WHO LOSES.

> I REALISE THAT PEOPLE NEVER BUY LOGICALLY, THEY BUY EMOTIONALLY AND THEY BASE THEIR DECISION ON 'DO I OR DON'T I LIKE THE SALESPERSON?'

b

Work with a partner and discuss your views about these statements. If you don't agree with these views, say what you think.

Writing skills development

An instruction tells you what you should or should not do. A warning informs you beforehand of a danger to come.

Write down as many instructions or warnings as you are likely to find on the following things. (a) is an example.

a. a packet of cigarettes: *Cigarette smoking is injurious to health.*

b. a container of chemicals:
....

c. a bottle of medicine:
....

d. a packet of fragile material such as glass:
....

e. a film roll:
   ....

f. a tube of ointment:
   ....

Part 1

Reading

The Deadly Sins of Customer Service

Read the following text and do the exercises that follow.

THE DEADLY SINS OF CUSTOMER SERVICE

The real sin in business comes in multiples of six. The customer is a nuisance to many, not an asset. Every service we offer, every product we sell, every idea we wish to market must have a customer, and most businesses need repeat customers. Let's take a look at the deadly sins, the quicksands that pull us down unless we are alert.

1
Disinterest or boredom
At a local office, someone leaned down and picked up a scarf off the floor. She looked around, didn't see anyone who appeared to be looking for it, headed to a nearby counter to ask for directions to the lost and found department. The woman at the counter looked up, bored and annoyed, and said, 'If you want information, go over to that line.' The person who found the scarf looked at the line, moved over to it and after ten minutes shrugged in disgust, tossed the scarf on a bench and left. It took the employee as long to redirect the woman as it would have taken to help, but her harsh tone, rude manner and glower turned off the customer.

2
'That's not my job.'
A service-driven company's employees realise that the customer is everyone's job—they run the company, they pay the bills.

3
Haughtiness
Have you ever wondered why the person you encounter first in many business establishments seems to have been selected to drive you away?

4
A missing person
The business world seems to have a large number of people who give customers a 'thank-you-have-a-good-day' with vacant eyes and glued smiles.

5
'It's our policy.'
Businesses use this line to put off customers who might have special requests.

6
Pass the buck
'I'm so sorry, I don't handle that.' 'Oh I wish I could help, but that is not my department, let me transfer you, or I'll tell him when he gets back from holiday next month.'

(Source: Customers run your company, they pay the bills!)

a

Think of two more 'sins' which put customers off, for example, knowingly selling a customer a defective product. Write two lines about each. Your teacher will ask some of you to read out your statements.

b

Work with a partner. Choose one of the 'deadly sins' from the text above. Imagine a real shopping situation and describe the sequence of events. Write these down in the form of a dialogue.

Part 2

Reading

Selling New Products

a

Below are two news items about products which are for special purposes. From the headings, try to predict what features the product might have, and write down these words/phrases. Then read the descriptions and check if any of the words/phrases you expected appear there.

COOKWARE FOR HEALTHY COOKING

Ever cooked pulao without a drop of oil? The thought of a healthy but not a real pulao would make you turn away. But with the AMC range of stainless steel cookware, cooking can be a pleasure. The AMC method paves the way to fat-free and waterless cooking. The food is cooked in its own moisture, ensuring retention of nutrients, natural flavour, colour and appearance.

SOUND THE ALARM!

Fear of burglars or intruders can prove to be a nightmare. But not if you take adequate precautions. The new Home Intruder Alarm Systam launched by SOS acts not only as an emergency alarm but is based on an infra-red scanning system attached to a 110-decibel siren. It can be attached to a sensor which detects opening of doors/windows, mounted on walls and activated by remote control, connected to a key-chain. Priced at Rs 6,475, the device is ideal for shops, offices, strong rooms and homes.

b

Underline the features which make each of these products unique, for example, waterless cooking. With a partner, sequence these in the likely order of their importance to the customer.

c

Discuss the answers to the following questions with a partner, then write your answers in one or two sentences.

i. Who are the persons most likely to be interested in the cookware?

ii. What questions might they want to ask the dealer who sells them the cookware?

iii. What fear is the second product based on?

iv. Why do you think the price of the burglar alarm is mentioned?

v. Is there any significance to the order in which potential customers are mentioned at the end of the news item?

Writing

Previous IITF Flashback

Write a paragraph connecting the hints given below:

PREVIOUS IITF FLASHBACK

India International Trade Fair 2005 —participation of 7500 Indian companies—overseas participation—33 countries—Turnover of 2,75,000 business visitors—91 delegations from 53 countries—693 delegates.

Seminars organised by Focus State—West Bengal and Uttaranchal— as well as NSIC—73.75% participantsfound IITF 2005 cost effective —93.86% showed interest in IITF 2006. IITF 2006 participation charges and early bird discount same as IITF 2005. Closing ceremony presided by Union Minister of State for Commerce & Industry. The award winners for IITF 2005: State Government Pavilion: Gold medal: Gujarat. Silver medal—Kerala and Chattisgarh. North Eastern State Pavilion: Gold medal: Meghalaya. Silver medal: Tripura, etc.

Discussion

Advertising style

These are some common characteristics of advertisements.

- conversational style
- play on words
- allusions to other contexts
- superlatives
- quoting facts and figures
- paradox

Look at the three advertisements in the following pages, which appeared in different publications. Choose one advertisement you like and study its characteristics. Discuss in groups what you like most about its style, and then write down your conclusions. Be ready to report your views to the class when the teacher asks you.

IF THIS IS HOW GOOD WE ARE AT BALANCING IMAGINE WHAT WE COULD DO TO YOUR CAR TYRES

Ceat Shoppe

OUR DIAPERS ARE DESIGNED TO OFFER MAXIMUM COMFORT. FOR DAD

We at Baby Soft understand that motherhood can be tough. Thats why our diapers come with a one-step refastable tapes that make them extremely easy to put on. So easy, even dad can do it! Because we know there will be times that you just wont be able to get out of bed.

And that's not all. Comfy dippers are made to ensure that your baby stays comfortable for long periods. Their unique super gel absorbent system draws the moisture deep inside to keep the baby completely dry. The pad is longer and wider for better fit and improved leakage protection. Specially combined fluff and super absorbents protect against rashes. Check out the Baby Soft range. And you will know that you have a friend. Who knows baby. Ands understands Mummy.

Wirpo Baby Soft Product Ad

build the blocks of future........

CRY - Child Relief and You

Follow-up

Role play

The questions and answers may be about the brand name of the refrigerator, its price, lifespan, guarantee period, features, advantages over other brands, etc. Start when you are both ready.

Student A

You are a customer interested in buying a refrigerator. A saleswoman has approached you offering the product of her company. Prepare a list of questions to ask her about the product.

Student B

You are a saleswoman promoting the sales of a refrigerator made by your company. You will be asked questions about your product by a prospective customer. Prepare yourself to answer them.

The questions and answers may be about the brand name of the refrigerator, its price, lifespan, guarantee period, features, advantages over other brands, etc. Start when you are both ready.

Language development

Read the list given below and match the advertisements to the companies.

Advertisements	Companies
Give with one hand Take with both	Hindustan Sugar Mills Ltd.
For 50 years we have been making your life a lot sweeter	Limca
Just 72 hours back this was an old, worn-out floor	Allwyn Trendy Quartz Coordinates
Thirst profession	Unit Trust of India
Discover 125 exciting ways to switch and match	Spartek Ceramics India Limited

Writing skills development

Write two paragraphs on different selling strategies. Make use of at least four phrasal verbs in your writing.

Learner Awareness

Phrasal verbs

A phrasal verb is a verb that consists of a verb followed by an adverb or a preposition and functions as an independent verb or as a complete unit of meaning. For example, 'bring up' and 'run away with'.

Dictionaries do list phrasal verbs and so you can look up a dictionary to find out the meaning of any phrasal verb. Some examples of phrasal verbs:

They could not **break down** the wall.

The burglars **broke into** the house.

The party was able to **bear down** its opponents and win the elections.

The Indian team **bore away** the trophy.

It was difficult to **put up with** his violent temper.